D1524758

WITHDRAWN

DE PROPRIETATIBUS LITTERARUM

Series Maior, 23

Hubert C. Heffner, Distinguished Service Professor of Speech, Theatre, and Dramatic Literature, Indiana University

STUDIES IN THEATRE AND DRAMA

ESSAYS IN HONOR OF

HUBERT C. HEFFNER

Edited by

OSCAR G. BROCKETT

1972

MOUTON

THE HAGUE · PARIS

LIBRARY OF CONGRESS CATALOG CARD NUMBER: 70-190149

Printed in The Netherlands by Mouton & Co., Printers, The Hague.

FOREWORD

Hubert Crouse Heffner has now completed almost fifty years of teaching and scholarship since taking up his first position in 1922. His has been a long and distinguished career, and those who have contributed to this volume wish in this way to pay tribute to him.

Honors are not new to Professor Heffner. In 1959 he received the Distinguished Service Award of the American Educational Theatre Association, which in 1965 also enrolled him in its select list of Fellows. In addition, he was honored in 1961 by Theta Alpha Phi, national honorary society of the theatre arts, for his contributions to the American theatre. Indiana University paid tribute to him in 1961 by naming him a Distinguished Service Professor, a rank reserved for those faculty members of the very highest distinction. He has also been awarded two honorary degrees: Doctor of Humane Letters by Illinois Wesleyan University in 1964; and Doctor of Letters by the University of North Carolina in 1969.

Such honors are inadequate indications of Professor Heffner's lifetime of service to his profession. He began his career at a time when Theatre and Drama were fighting for acceptance in American higher education and in that fight he was to be one of the principal warriors. He was one of Frederick Koch's first students at the University of North Carolina in 1919 and one of the founding members of the Carolina Playmakers. From 1926 to 1930 he was Associate Director of the Playmakers and manager of the tours for which it was famous. After teaching at Northwestern University, he went to Stanford University in 1939 to found and head the Department of Speech and Drama, which rapidly came to offer one of the most prestigious programs in the United States. Since 1954, he has taught at Indiana University, where he has concentrated especially on training graduate students in dramatic literature, theory, and criticism and on supervising doctoral dissertations.

In addition to these four universities, he has filled many short-term appointments in others: New York University, University of Colorado, University of Bristol (as a Fulbright Lecturer), Cornell University, University of California at Berkeley, University of Denver, University of Hawaii, University of Arizona, and University of Wyoming. A mere listing of the universities at which he has taught, however, does not suggest his enormous presence in the classroom and his power to instill in his students respect for learning and scholarship of a high order. These attributes (which he has in the highest degree), even if he had no other accomplishments, would make him worthy of honor, for it would be difficult to estimate the number of students whose lives he has profoundly touched. He did not transform all of them, but through many he has left an indelible mark on his profession.

His mark has also been made in other ways. He has been one of the principal formulators of a philosophy of theatre in American education, and his high ideals have led some to call him "the conscience" of his profession. He has served in other ways as well. In 1949 he was President of the American Educational Theatre Association, and from 1954 to 1956 Editor of the *Educational Theatre Journal*. He has been a member of the Administrative Council of the Speech Association of America, Chairman of the Research Committee of the Western College Association, a member of the screening committee for Fulbright Awards, and a member of the selection committee for Guggenheim Fellowships.

Professor Heffner has also set an example for others through his own scholarship and writing. Since 1935, *Modern Theatre Practice* has been a standard guide for theatre practitioners, while his *The Nature of Drama* (1959) has given many students their first real insight into dramatic literature. In addition, he is the author of articles too numerous to list here.

This brief summary of Professor Heffner's career and accomplishments can only hint at the extent and complexity of his work. In honoring him, we honor ourselves, for he is one of those who has done most to make our field worthy of esteem.

Bloomington, Indiana, August, 1970   O. G. B.

TABLE OF CONTENTS

HUBERT C. HEFFNER

THEATRE AND DRAMA IN LIBERAL EDUCATION[1]

In this all-too-brief discussion of theatre and drama as one legitimate means towards the liberal education of young Americans, I should like to begin with some generalizations which will, I hope, be acceptable without the documentation available for them. It is apparent that every society and every culture must evolve its own pattern of education, and every nation must develop its educational system in accordance with that pattern. No nation can therefore take over lock, stock, and barrel the educational pattern and system of another. American civilization has perforce had to evolve a pattern and system of education consonant with American culture. Our Founding Fathers were well aware — notably among them Thomas Jefferson — that the success of the American experiment rested upon an educated electorate; hence, general education was from the early days of the Republic considered an obligation of the state. It was this idea that developed into our notion of mass education, a conception that much later influenced the democratic societies of Europe. It was not until after the close of the last World War that the English conception of aristocratic education began to change into a pattern of general education for every young Englishman. Modern pressures have rapidly extended the idea of mass education in America to encompass advanced and higher education. In colonial times, when higher education was available in a few private colleges, it could be — indeed, it had to be — restricted to the elite few. With the establishment of the first state tax-supported university in North Carolina in 1792, the basis was laid for the extension of higher education to

---

[1] Throughout his career, Professor Heffner has been a spokesman for Theatre and Drama as an integral part of a liberal education. This article summarizes his views well. It was originally presented at the Convention of the American Educational Theatre Association in 1963 and was subsequently published by the Columbia University *Teachers College Record* and the *Educational Theatre Journal*. It is reprinted here by permission of the Editor of the *Teachers College Record*.

all capable of it. With the establishment a century ago of the land-grant colleges, that extension was widely enlarged.

The establishment of the land-grant colleges, devoted not merely to general higher education but also to the agricultural, engineering, and mechanical arts on advanced levels, focused a clear light upon an aspect of American education that has characterized it from the beginning. That aspect is the multiplicity of functions which the American college and university is expected to fill in our national life. For example, since the days of Roosevelt's Brain Trust, it has become evident that American universities must supply an increasingly important segment of trained intelligence for the operation of our ever more complicated federal government. At the State University of Iowa and elsewhere, the School of Law is expected to serve as an advisor and guide to the state legislature. The School of Business and the Departments of Politics and Economics at Indiana University and elsewhere supply expert advice to the state in its taxation policies and in its promotion of industrial and commercial expansion. Massachusetts Institute of Technology, California Institute of Technology, and scores of other engineering schools are required to supply expert information on all kinds of technical, scientific, and engineering problems with which state and federal governmental bodies must deal. Such contributions by academic institutions to American government, commerce, and industry have become matters of common expectation.

These and many other functions are required of American institutions of higher education *in addition to their primary business of educating the young.* A particular function which I specifically want to dwell upon for a moment is that of the college or university as the cultural center of a community, a state, or a region. The University of North Carolina has for many years partially supported and supervised a state symphony orchestra which has elevated the musical taste of the entire citizenry. Many American educational institutions maintain such orchestras, chamber music ensembles, and concert musicians, not solely for the musical education of students on their campuses, but also for the cultural benefit of the entire community and region. Princeton University has for some years been the hospitable host to an excellent company of theatre artists. If it were not for the college and university theatres now established in most of our institutions of higher education, Americans would be almost completely without access to the great masterpieces of drama from Aeschylus to Shaw outside the covers of a book. Young Frenchmen, by contrast, have readily available to them in excellent productions the great plays of their dramatic heritage; hence, they are provided opportunities for the development of taste and appreciation denied to us. Our professional commercial American theatre is no longer considered a cultural institution obligated to keep alive our inheritance from the past; therefore, the colleges and universities have rightly assumed that responsibility.

Another assumption which I must mention is that any educational system is changing constantly and must continue to change with the development of the national culture and learning. When I was a youngster in prep school and college, we thought we knew exactly what constituted a liberal education. It was that education obtained through a curriculum centered around eight years of Latin and six years of Greek. Prior to my college days, English language and literature had been accepted as a decent academic discipline, but American literature was only beginning to be admitted to the curriculum in a few rather advanced — and hence suspect — departments. While I was an undergraduate, psychology was a minor part of the curriculum in the department of philosophy, and I well remember in later years a famous and protracted debate within a university faculty over the admission of psychology as a department within the social sciences. Theatre and drama as academic disciplines are of even more recent vintage. You are all well aware of the long struggle which Professor George Pierce Baker had at Harvard to win grudging permission for the academic instruction which he wished to offer, ending in 1925 in his final defeat and removal to Yale. His academic opponents in Cambridge then said that Baker's hegira to New Haven proved the rightness of their firm opposition!

We have today respected colleagues of high probity and equally high academic attainments who frankly maintain that theatre and drama have no place as academic studies in an institution of high seriousness. Let me hasten to admit that I know certain programs in certain institutions which fully justify this adverse opinion. But I am also acquainted with similar programs in more ancient disciplines which, if this were the basis of judgment, would likewise justify the exclusion of traditional departments from great institutions. I know other colleagues who say that since America is committed to mass education on the higher levels, and since obviously many students are incapable of higher education, then programs in such fields as theatre and drama must be maintained in colleges and universities to keep the incompetent occupied, just as we must offer courses on women in the home and golf in the meadow.

Yet others hold that since we have admitted courses in cooking, beauty parlor operation, automobile repairing, and other similar trade trainings into some institutions, we might likewise allow in similar institutions training in professional theatre to a restricted few. Unfortunately, too many of the academic programs in theatre and drama are "trade oriented" and thus raise serious questions about the whole nature and purpose of undergraduate studies in this area. I am by no means casting aspersions on the justifiable pride which all of us take in the professional achievements of our former students; but we are all aware, I believe, that that limited number of students cannot possibly justify the large number of programs in theatre and drama found in most American colleges and universities today. Let me further point out that Princeton University, which has no department of theatre and drama, has over the years furnished an unusually large number of talented people to the professional American theatre.

What, then, is the justification for the large number of curricula and the vast number of courses in theatre and drama offered in our institutions?

My contention is that when such enterprises are properly taught and properly coordinated with other disciplines, studies in theatre and drama, in addition to professional training, offer an unusually effective kind of liberal education and are therefore justified for large numbers of students who will never become professional theatre people.

And now I must attempt a definition of liberal education. Obviously, I do *not* mean merely an education centered upon the study of Latin and Greek, nor, for that matter, an education exclusively oriented around any one recognized academic discipline. With Hoyt Hudson, I begin my definition by recalling the root word, *liber*, from which the term liberal is derived. The Latin word *liber* meant a free man. A liberal education is a freeing education; it frees a young person from something and for something. It frees him, or should free him, from ignorance, intolerance, and superstition, from narrowness and parochialism. It frees him for citizenship in the realm of the intellect.

What are the instruments for the accomplishment of this liberation? In stating these, I should like again to turn to another source for assistance, this time to the Harvard report on *General Education in a Free Society*, with some borrowings from the report of the Stanford Conference on Liberal Education, held in 1946 at Mills College. If, following these documents, I list as they give them the relevant aims or objectives, I think it will become readily apparent that there are numerous instruments and disciplines available to the liberal educator. The Harvard Report places first in its list of objectives training in the ability to communicate orally and in writing the results of thought. I suspect everyone would give immediate and facile assent to the assertion that the man who cannot correctly and adequately manipulate his own language is not liberally educated. Having served as an associate editor of the *Quarterly Journal of Speech*, editor of the *Educational Theatre Journal*, and advisory editor for two learned journals in the areas of languages and literature, I can say without equivocation that a considerable number of members of faculties in our colleges and universities are without this major accomplishment of liberal education. That condition by no means invalidates the objective. Theatre and drama, arts which in major ways are seriously concerned with words and inextricably allied with rhetoric, should be in an academic discipline an ideal adjunct to other studies in equipping students adequately in oral and written communication and in giving them a love of language and its effective use.

The second objective in liberal education is training in logical reasoning and the development of the ability to arrive at supportable conclusions. It is unnecessary here to demonstrate in detail how effective, well organized, and well taught courses in stagecraft, stage lighting, costuming, and other practical courses in theatre arts can be in pursuing this goal. On a somewhat more advanced level, courses in play analysis and in directing may admirably serve the same purpose. Moreover, such courses may be as rigorously organized and as systematically taught as are courses in mathematics or the sciences.

The third aim of a liberal education is training in the ability to make valid judgments. A value judgment may be as simple as a choice between two instruments of approximately equally effectiveness in the lighting of a stage area; it may be as complex as an evaluation of O'Neill's *Mourning Becomes Electra* as against the *Oresteia* of Aeschylus as tragedy. The making of a value judgment requires discrimination, knowledge, and taste. The liberally educated person realizes that evaluation is not a mere or momentary personal preference. Not until after we have come to know what constitutes excellence in any area, subject, or phenomenon can we make a defensible evaluation with respect to the subject; hence, a liberal education entails training in the knowledge and appreciation of excellence, and I would place at the apex of achievement a knowledge and appreciation of human excellence. What subject of study deals more profoundly with human excellence and the failures

of men to achieve excellence than does drama? Where can you find
man's ethical values and moral dilemmas more adequately and effectively presented than on the stage? At the same time, where can you
find that which degrades man or that which renders him ludicrous
more cogently and compellingly expressed?

These three minimum aims of liberal education are its basic tools.
To them I would add certain other requisites. First, a liberal education
must introduce the student to his heritage in order that he may better
know and more discriminatingly evaluate the present in which he must
live. What body of our heritage is more glorious and more adequately
representative than the drama from ancient to modern times? Almost
every great idea, the summation of human thought from classic Greece
to our own day, is incorporated in that vast corpus; and in that corpus
are some of the supreme achievements of human genius. A student can
literally gain a full introduction to the whole of Western civilization
through a study of the development of the Western theatre and drama.
It can be the focal center from which the student is motivated to reach
out for a knowledge of history, aesthetics, ethics, and social thought.

You will note that I have consistently used the phrase theatre *and*
drama, refusing to separate the two terms. While I hold that they are
separate arts, I also affirm that they are conjoint enterprises which
attain their supreme effectiveness when conjoined. Drama, of course,
can be and is legitimately taught as a literature in departments of literature. Every student of drama is grateful for what literary scholars have
contributed and for the light which they have shed upon the great
dramatic masterpieces. All of us would be impoverished without their
research and their critical insights. And yet drama differs from other
literary forms, and the student of theatre and drama must be primarily
concerned with drama as drama. For further clarification, I wish to
quote a paragraph from Elder Olson's recent excellent book, *Tragedy
and the Theory of Drama*, in which he says the following:

We find, thus, further confirmation of our view that drama is not essentially
a form of literature, but rather a distinct art which may or may not employ
language as an artistic medium. It is literary only through its employment
of dialog, though Shaw, for one, has made it literary through its stage directions and through dramatic prefaces as well; and while, beyond all doubt,
the highest forms of drama demand dialog, dialog itself cannot be regarded
as the most important element, though it is frequently thought of as precisely that. On the contrary, it is a subsidiary part. Without it, certainly, a
great number of subtle effects would be impossible; more than that, the
profundity of great drama would be impossible; but the very considerations

show that it is simply the medium through which these effects are achieved, under the governance of plot. The dialog exists to give the plot its quality and power; therefore it is subordinate to plot. Since the representation determines when dialog is proper and when it is not, and what the nature of the dialog shall be, the dialog is also subordinate to the representation. Indeed, in one respect, the dialog is simply an extension of the representation, detailing what words shall be said and in what order.

It is this concern with drama as drama, not as lyric poetry, not as epic, not strictly as literature, but drama as a composition for stage performance, which must be incorporated into curricula of theatre and drama. Valuable as they may be, courses in dramatic literature, taught in departments of literature by men who conceive drama to be merely another *genre* or type of literary writing to be acquired from the printed page, are not adequate to our purposes. It is therefore inescapable that a relevant curriculum include not merely the specific arts of the theatre, but also drama and theatre history.

There is yet another requisite of a liberal education which I must advance. Any education which does not aid, encourage, and stimulate the student to acquire a passion for knowledge cannot be truly called a liberating education. This passionate desire to learn more and more about some subject is the distinguishing characteristic of the educated man and the foundation of genuine scholarship. Students will never attain it unless they are required as students to work fairly consistently at the top level or near the top level of their capacities. It is this requisite that makes the study of science on our campuses today a stimulating challenge to our intellectually most gifted young men. Discipline in the sciences is rigorous, continuous, graduated, and systematic. The discipline in theatre and drama is only in part analogous; it must include the development of aesthetic discrimination and skill in the expression of human emotions. Such a discipline can nevertheless be as systematically organized and as thoroughly taught as can courses in mathematics or physics. I say "can be" but I admit with shame that they too seldom are. There is an old saying that confession is good for the soul; on the contrary, I think it is primarily humiliating. Nevertheless, I am about to confess. Academic curricula in theatre and drama, especially when not integrated (as they ought to be) with the actual stage production of plays, are, more often than not, haphazardly organized, unsystematically taught by individuals who have no genuine interest in worthy academic instruction and therefore substitute showmanship for the hard effort necessary to real teaching. It is not surprising, therefore, that we have

enrolled in our departments too many mere "theatre bums", academic
beatniks, who, whatever little narrow talent they may possess, are a
detriment to scholarship and the liberating purposes of education. If
these lazy loafers appear in other academic departments, they seem
especially attracted to the arts. Let me endure a further humiliation by
confessing that we have too many of these "theatre bums" on our
faculties. Clever as some of them may be as designers, technicians, or
directors, they will never become great teachers, much less great scholars. They degrade the academic dignity of our profession.

Thus far this discussion has been largely concerned with liberal
education as intellectual discipline and the place of a properly organized
and effectively taught program of theatre and drama in the training of
minds. The development of the ability to reason logically and to evaluate, the acquirement of the skills to communicate the results of reasoning, and a grasp of the facts and ideas essential to logical reasoning
are, as I see it, the criteria which differentiate education from mere
training. If these are missing from the instruction in theatre and drama,
the result may still be quite good "trade training" but hardly worthy to
be called academic education. There is, however, another element in
and inherent to liberal education. For want of a less suspect designation, let us call that other element the training of the creative imagination, a designation that has become questionable among many thoughtful people today. Creative imagination is difficult to define and its
cultivation is far more difficult. In describing the necessity for the poet's
intuitive imagining of a dramatic action before he could compose a
drama, Aristotle in Chapter 17 of the *Poetics* said: "Hence it is that
poetry demands a man with a special gift for it, or else one with a
touch of madness in him. . . ." Today with our cult of personality and
gospel of depth psychology the emphasis is almost entirely upon the
"touch of madness". The creative artist, be he musician, painter, actor,
or playwright, succeeds best it is assumed if he can dredge up the
materials of his art from his subconscious self and those who are a bit
"queer" are most apt to possess creative imaginations. Even teachers
in respectable colleges and universities express such points of view and
you are almost sure to hear these in the cult schools of acting. If this
point of view were wholly true, then it follows that our greatest works
of art should come from the insane and the demented.

Conceding a grain of truth in the "touch of madness" theory, let it
be noted that such an exercise of the creative imagination or, for that
matter, the exercise of similar faculties by one with a special aptitude

for it, gives merely the raw materials, so to speak, upon which the artist must work. After he is in possession of the materials of his imagination, the artist – poet, dramatist, painter, musician – must then set about the laborious and intellectual process of orderly composition if he is to produce a work of art. Composition, the proper arrangement of the parts into a form which will produce or elicit predetermined effects, requires knowledge, skill, judgment, evaluation – the intellectual disciplines which have been discussed. Without these disciplines the most brilliant creative imagination that ever existed would be unable to present its imaginings in a work of art. For these reasons it would seem that the creative imagination of the scholar or the scientist does not differ essentially from that of the artist. It is this disciplined and recreative imagination which distinguishes the writings of the great historians from the mere filers of facts. Without it, the questions that led to the discoveries of a Galileo, Newton, Darwin, or Einstein would never have been raised. Important as we know it is for the making of the great scholar in any field, we nevertheless do not know the methods of systematically developing this capacity in the individual student. Aristotle seems to have been right in saying that it takes one with a special gift for it. Every great teacher of history or of poetry, even of science and philosophy, stimulates the development of this gift in those fortunate enough to possess the capacity.

To pursue this subject with adequacy a foundation should first be laid in which intuitive imagination and creative imagination are differentiated, in which the imaginative faculty is related to the reasoning faculty, in which feelings and imagination are joined and also distinguished, and in which Samuel Taylor Coleridge's discrimination between fancy and imagination are established. Space permits the laying of no such foundation; that task must await later statement. These few statements must, however, be made. The Greeks did not separate reason and imagination, indeed, would not have believed such a separation possible. Though they did not possess the term creative imagination, they possessed the faculty in full measure. Plato and Aristotle, long before Immanuel Kant, well knew that the intuitive imagination frequently completed the work of intellectual reasoning in the making of discoveries in philosophy, science, the arts. European Romanticism, on the other hand, joined feeling and imagination and the later Romantics, with their excessive concern with individualism, even eccentric individualism, established the basis of much of our modern confusion apparent among the cultists of contemporary "creative-imagination"

schools. Coleridge, and to a considerable extent also William Words-
worth, escaped that confusion, refusing to separate reason and imagination. Coleridge in his *Biographia Literaria*, Chapter XIV, put the matter
in these words in attempting to answer the question, "What is poetry?":

... it is a distinction resulting from poetic genius itself, which sustains and
modifies images, thoughts, and emotions of the poet's own mind. The poet
describes in ideal perfection, brings the whole soul of man into activity, with
the subordination of its faculties to each other, according to their relative
worth and dignity. He diffuses a tone and spirit of unity, that blends, and
(as it were) *fuses*, each into each, by the synthetic and magical power,
to which we have exclusively appropriated the name of imagination. The
power, first put into action by the will and understanding, and retained
under their irremissive, though gentle and unnoticed, control (*laxis effertur
habenis*), reveals itself in the balance or reconciliation of opposite or dis-
cordant qualities: of sameness, with difference; of the general, with the
concrete; the idea, with the image; the individual, with the representative;
the sense of novelty and freshness, with old and familiar objects; a more
than usual state of emotion, with more than usual order; judgment ever
awake and steady self-possession with enthusiasm and feeling profound or
vehement; and while it blends and harmonizes the natural and the artificial,
still subordinates art to nature, the manner to the matter; and our admiration of the poet to our sympathy with the poetry. . . . .
Finally, good sense is the body of poetic genius, fancy its drapery, motion
its life, and imagination the soul that is everywhere, and in each, and forms
all into one graceful and intelligent whole.

All of the arts, and especially the art of theatre and drama, are potent
nourishers and discipliners of the imagination, for two equally important reasons: the basis of artistic creation is the imagination guided by
reason, and the resulting work of art is designed to appeal to the
imagination. Because they allied imagination with feeling, the Romantics usually held music to be the supreme art; because they allied
imagination with reason, the Greeks considered drama the supreme art.
No understanding or adequate interpretation of a play is possible without the exercise of the imagination. No translation of the text of a play
to the stage in any of its various details – characterization of roles by
actors, designs of settings and costumes, the design of the lighting, the
unifying of these and all other details into a complete production by a
director – is possible without the exercise of the imagination. Further
argument is unnecessary for this conclusion: Proper instruction in
theatre and drama (which must include stage presentation) is one of
the best instruments available to the liberal educator in the developing
and training of the imagination of a student, assuming he has a gift for

it. Without the gift for it, no student should be allowed to continue in a program of theatre and drama.

Over the portals of the most sacred shrine of antiquity, the Temple of Apollo at Delphi, the Greeks carved a terrible injunction: "Know Thyself". Self-knowledge is the last, best knowledge that the educated man attains, and it is the most difficult to come by. It will never be achieved by the mere introspective contemplation of the self as self. To attain it, one must know man; and drama is the supreme art devoted to the full revelation of the nature of man. More than that, drama is the central art which depicts the relation of human character to human destiny, the relation of character to action. In drama one may come to know all kinds and types of men, good men and evil men, noble men and ludicrous men, social men and individualistic men – the whole varied pattern of human nature in all of its multifarious changes from the Greeks to the present age. The dramatists, said O'Neill, were great psychologists long before the study of psychology was born. In drama you may come to know the whole man in ways and with a completeness not possible through even the most intimate associations with other living persons. Drama is not the only art that deals with the nature of man; indeed, all arts do. But drama of all the arts is the one most widely accessible to the largest number of persons. No other art so completely depicts the human condition; hence, I dare assert that of all the arts, it is the one that can be central to a liberal education.

I have necessarily left much that I would like to say on this subject unsaid. I should like, however, to stress one further aspect of academic training in theatre and drama, an aspect which I believe makes it a significantly important adjunct in a liberal education. Instruction in theatre and drama is both theoretical and practical. It combines knowledge and skill; it requires that theory be tested in practice and that skill be demonstrated in production. That is why we insist that it must combine both classroom and laboratory instruction with staged productions in college and university theatres. All too often, however, our theatres are operated largely in independence of course instruction. When this independence is complete, or the relationship merely tenuous, it is then that the "theatre bums" take over and propagate a new generation of their kind. I concede the difficulty of operating theatres as a laboratory and at the same time as a cultural institution for the campus and the community, but that is merely a difficulty which must be solved. Its proper solution will make those theatres powerful instruments in the actualizing of knowledge and will make curricula in theatre and drama even better means for the liberal education of young Americans. Since George Pierce Baker organized the first program in theatre and drama in the early years of this century, and since Thomas Wood Stevens opened the first Department of Drama at Carnegie Institute of Technology in 1914, programs and departments have so multiplied that today there are few colleges or universities without academic instruction in the field. What is the justification for the enrollment of all the hundreds upon hundreds of students in such programs? Obviously, training for a profession cannot be the answer. The only justification that I can see for this continued proliferation is that instruction in theatre and drama, in proper conjunction with other studies, contributes validly and significantly to general education on a large scale. I hope that, in keeping with the nature of the subject, that contribution will be humanizing and liberating.

H. D. F. KITTO

DAMN THE TRAGIC HERO!

We seem to take it for granted that Tragedy without a Tragic Hero is as impossible as a monarchy without a monarch. From a recent book I quote the following as a forthright expression of what is, I think, the prevailing view:

The "man against fate" conception of tragedy, we have found [sc. in Aeschylus and Sophocles], itself determines that the tragic hero ... must be the centre of the action and that his catastrophe must be the climax of the play, the "moment of truth" at which the whole meaning of the play becomes clear.

The tragic hero is "the only and indispensible focal point in the depiction of human suffering", but Euripides' conception of tragedy was such that it "actually leads to the loss of the tragic hero himself".

I suggest, on the contrary, that the question is not when was the tragic hero lost, but when was he invented; that, so far as extant Greek tragedy is concerned, he is an alien, an anachronism and a public nuisance.

It is clear that this conception of the tragic hero does not work with plays, like the *Agamemnon* or *Electra* (of Sophocles), in which the chief characters are not in conflict with fate, or the gods, but on the contrary, are doing just what the gods have designed or are favouring; nor with plays, like the *Electra* or *Euminides* or *Philoctetes*, in which the (presumed) hero does not meet with catastrophe; nor with those, like the *Agamemnon* (if the King is the tragic hero there) and the *Ajax*, in which he does meet with catastrophe, but too soon in the play to provide the climax and the "moment of truth"; nor with those, like the *Trachiniae* and *Hippolytus*, with respect to which we debate intermittently and pointlessly which of two characters really is the tragic hero. I suppose the outstanding Greek tragic hero is Oedipus in the *Tyrannus*, but (as I will argue) we make him "the only and indispensable focus" of the play only at the cost of failing to understand what Sophocles was

talking about and of making some parts of his dramatic design unintelligible.

Certainly, the tragic hero struggling vainly with his Fate is a popular
and impressive idea: popular, I suspect, because it offers an instant
answer that saves a lot of trouble; impressive because "Fate", especially
when it appears in its German form, *Schiksal*, like a Brockenberg
spectre, is so daunting that we hardly dare ask it what it really is. But
since lucidity is said to be a mark of the Greek mind and of Greek
art, it might be possible, by inspection, to discover what Fate really
meant to Aeschylus, Sophocles, and Euripides, and how their tragic
heroes contended with it.

Aristotle made what appears to be a sensible remark in saying that
the most important element in a play is what he calls the *mythos*, or
"plot", and immediately defines it as "the putting-together, the disposition, of the material". It is this, he says, that represents the action,
and the action takes precedence over the persons. Naturally, he may be
right or wrong, but at least it will do us no harm to look at the choice
and disposition of material exhibited in some few of the most highly
regarded Greek plays, beginning with the *Agamemnon*. Was Aeschylus
manifestly so designing this play that the focus is a tragic hero whose
catastrophe is the climax and moment of truth? We shall find, I think,
that if that was his idea, some parts of the structure make little sense.

If it is built around a tragic hero, that hero is presumably Agamemnon, though some might nominate Clytemnestra, and it would be interesting to see what sort of case could be made out for Cassandra, who
is on stage much longer than Agamemnon and is perhaps the most
purely tragic figure.

Since we are so often told that the subject of the whole trilogy is the
Curse of the House of Atreus, it is just worth noticing that the first
eleven hundred verses do not mention that Curse (though they do
mention quite a different one, invoked on Agamemnon by infuriated
Argive citizens), but are concerned exclusively with the Trojan War.
And who began that? It must be our hero, out of guilty ambition, as we
are sometimes assured, or because he was under the Curse that
Aeschylus refuses to mention until the play is nearly ended. But there
is not a word about ambition either, and it is not for us to add something to the play in order to bring it within the reach of our own
understanding. The first thing we are told about the war is that it was
designed by Zeus, to punish the crime committed by Paris: Zeus "sent"
the two sons of Atreus, like an Erinys – a Divine Avenger – to wage

war with its inevitable violence. Soon the two Kings appear, in symbol, as two eagles ripping the body of a pregnant hare – a savage destruction of life that arouses the anger of Artemis. She so loathes "the lawless feasting of the winged hounds of her Father" that she will not allow the expedition to proceed except on terms that will ensure that the destroying avenger shall be destroyed in his turn, by his wife.

To make this clear Aeschylus invents a new Iphigeneia-myth – a point worth noting in view of the lingering idea that the Greek dramatists were hamstrung by the necessity of sticking to their ancient myths, which explains why they sometimes wrote bad plays. In the standard myth (to which Sophocles returned in his *Electra*, for an intelligible reason), Artemis demanded the sacrifice of Iphegeneia in savage reprisal for an insult that Agamemnon had offered her in the past; Aeschylus makes her angry not at something he has done already, but at what he is proposing to do, as the avenging emissary of Zeus: namely, behave like the eagles, indiscriminately destroying life. If he must shed innocent blood, let him first shed innocent blood of his own – and take the consequences.

That, briefly, is the material that Aeschylus invented for the opening scenes of his play. It may be awkward; facts often are – but we are not to shuffle out of them.

Is it, then, that Agamemnon, far from being a tragic hero, is only a helpless puppet in the hands of gods, killing men like flies for sport? That will not do either. We now see Agamemnon, through the eyes of the chorus, face to face with Artemis' appalling demand: disband your expedition, or kill your daughter. Some have complained that he has no real choice, and that is true, but only because he has chosen already: he made his choice when he took it to be his natural course to avenge his brother in war and bloodshed. In fact, as the play continues, the impression we are given, always, is that it is Agamemnon's war. The two very moving stanzas that conclude the second ode (vv. 241-76) describe the bitter indignation that is mounting in Argos against the Kings, as funerary urns come back from Troy containing the ashes of the living men who had gone forth in this "war for another man's wife", and the chorus darkly forsees some desperate act of revenge on the part of some angry citizens. Indeed, so much is it Agamemnon's war that when he returns, victorious, the leader of the chorus is made to say to him, by way of protesting his own loyalty: "I tell you straight: when you began this war, leading men to their death for the sake of a wanton woman, I thought it a disastrous idea."

Facts can be awkward, but it cannot be denied that these are among the "facts" of the play: that Zeus "sent" Agamemnon, like an Erinys – like the Erinyes whom we see on the stage in the *Eumenides* – to fight the war; that Agamemnon, like a fool, decided that he must lead an army overseas to avenge his brother; that Zeus, having "sent" Agamemnon to do this, at the head of an army which we are told later *was* an Erinys, will in the natural course of things see him destroyed for having done it, and that the Erinys will cooperate.

Who captured, sacked, utterly ruined Troy? We should be on familiar ground if a daemonic Agamemnon – something like Macbeth – did this in defiance of the gods, and then had to pay for it. Obviously, it was Agamemnon that did it, and three times, in an increasingly ominous tone, the chorus calls him "sacker of a city". Unfortunately, the chorus begins its second ode with the clear statement: "Zeus has thrown around the city such a net that none within it could escape, young or old. . . . Zeus has struck down Paris." So too the Herald who says that Agamemnon has won a glorious victory; he has overthrown Troy with the crowbar of Zeus the Vindictive. But clearly, Agamemnon was no more conscious that he was wielding a divine and imperishable pickaxe than he was of being sent against Troy by Zeus.

If it is not clear, we will ask another simple question: who killed Cassandra?

Once more we are given two explanations. Clytemnestra, as she explains later, took exquisite pleasure in slaughtering her husband's mistress on top of him – and we have no difficulty in believing *that*; it is just what this formidable lady would do. But – as if to discourage us from taking her as a female Tamberlaine – Aeschylus gives a second and entirely different explanation. Cassandra is a Seer, and what she sees, and displays to us, is that she enraged Apollo by first accepting his gift, or bribe, and then denying him her body; for which reason Apollo is venting his rage by bringing her to this palace, haunt of the blood-drinking Erinyes, to be done to death by a murderess and adultress.

Nobody in his right mind will suggest that Clytemnestra is a mere puppet of Apollo when she gleefully murders Cassandra, or of Artemis when she savagely murders Agamemnon, or that Agamemnon was acting under divine compulsion when he took back with him to Argos Cassandra, "the finest flower of the Trojan spoil". Nor is Orestes, in the next play, a puppet when he kills his mother, on the direct command of Apollo: it has not been sufficiently noticed that when he has described that fearful command he goes on to say that he would have to do it in any case, for personal reasons that he explains.

They are not puppets, but neither can any of them be a dramatic "hero" in our sense of the term, and we had better be careful in describing them as "dramatic characters", however vivid they are. For evidently, since a *theos*[1] is performing the same action, to that extent our attention is being directed to what is being done rather than to the person doing it – which, to the modern mind, is deplorably undramatic. Yet it accords perfectly with Aristotle's dictum that the *praxis*, the action, takes precedence over the persons; also with Homer's practice. For example, one hears the complaint that the help given to Odysseus by Athena in his fight with the Suitors takes away something from his heroic stature. But, although it would be foolish to deny that the *Odyssey* is a poem of heroic adventure, and that Odysseus is that hero, it is frustrating not to notice that it is also a poem about the inevitable triumph of Order, moral and political, over Disorder; a fact that explains much in the structure of the poem.

So it is with the *Agamemnon*. That sharing of the action between *theoi* and entirely autonomous human agents is, in one form or another, standard in Greek tragedy; the term "double determination" has become current. Its effect, and purpose, is always to enlarge the significance of what is going on. Since (with perhaps one or two quite formal exceptions) the human agents are always autonomous, it does not diminish the solidity and vividness with which they are presented – though it does mean that collateral aspects are disregarded, both of their characters and of the action: for example, were Clytemnestra and Aegisthus "in love" with each other? When Aegisthus enters, towards the end of the play, where has he come from? from the palace? from somewhere else? – but it does mean that our attention passes from them outwards and not inwards to their inner motives and feelings. In the *Agamemnon* Aeschylus, with his double-determination, is creating a dramatic (not of course a historical) world – one might almost say an "abstract" world – in which punishment, or revenge, or redress, through blind and violent revenge, is universal. "God is a Spirit", and the Greek gods can be much the same: in this play, the spirit of violent retribution. The end is bankruptcy: moral, philosophical, and political. For example, his mother's Erinyes will destroy Orestes if he kills her, his

---

[1] Since the English word "god" has connotations which may be quite alien to Greek, and therefore may be seriously misleading, it seems better to use the Greek word instead. See below, pp. 34-36.

father's if he does not (*Choephori*, vv. 505-06). It would take us too far from the theme of this essay to examine how the rest of the trilogy deals with that bankruptcy. Instead, we will look at one or two features of the play which are made almost unintelligible by our own "cult of personality".

Surprise has often been published that when Agamemnon's death-cry is heard the chorus splits into twelve futile individuals who, instead of doing something sensible, debate whether to try to save the King, and then decide to do nothing. The explanation has been offered that, by established convention, the Greek chorus never took part in the action, so that Aeschylus' audience would not have expected it to do anything at this moment. That will hardly do, since in the *Eumenides* the chorus takes a rather important part in the action.

This bit of dramatic incompetence is connected with another. Young students, and sometimes older ones too, find the end of the play disappointingly feeble: the mean, skulking Aegisthus is such an anticlimax, coming as he does after the splendid Clytemnestra. Odd, that Aeschylus did not see it. A pupil of my own once cleverly explained why it is not a total anticlimax: the explanation had something to do with the contrast between the masculine streak in Clytemnestra's character and the feminine streak in Aegisthus. She had been looking fixedly in the wrong direction, inwards not outwards, and therefore could have had no idea what the trilogy is about. Those two passages are connected – naturally: Aeschylus was a competent craftsman.

It may seem self-evident that the design of the play is centered upon Agamemnon; that his death is the climax and moment of truth. At that moment, obviously, the minds of the chorus and audience too must be entirely taken up with Agamemnon's fate. Therefore we invent a canon to explain the futile behaviour of the chorus. It is more profitable to read the text. The twelve members of the chorus are not talking about saving the King; half of them doubt if the cry they have heard means anything much; the rest assume that the King is already dead, and that what is going on is a *coup d'état*, the setting up of a tyranny. They are debating whether to break in at once, if they can, to confront the would-be tyrants, or to rally the city against them. This is not futility. Besides, they have already expressed their fear that somebody might attempt something of the kind, in vengeance for Argives killed at Troy: it is in fact being done by Clytemnestra, in vengeance for Iphigeneia, killed by Artemis' design, in order that the slayer at Troy might be slain on his return.

This moment is not the climax of the play; that comes at its proper place – the end. The play flows past this point without stopping. The murderess appears, glorying in what she has done and justifying it. She appeals to Justice, Retribution, the Erinyes, Ate, the Evil Spirit of the House – and it is only at this point that the Curse in the House of Atreus really appears over the horizon. Aeschylus knew what he was doing.

Cassandra, in one of her visions, saw the blood-drinking Erinyes in possession of the palace of Atreus. Zeus had "sent" Agamemnon to Troy as an Erinys; the chorus had feared that the *theoi* and the black Erinys might strike down Agamemnon – as they have done. Accordingly, when Aegisthus enters it is first to hail this bright "vindictive" day – using the adjective that has appeared in the play only once before, of "vindictive" Zeus who lent Agamemnon his crowbar to overturn Troy – and then to greet the body of Agamemnon enmeshed in "the net woven by the Erinyes" – the visible copy of the metaphorical net of destruction thrown over Troy by Zeus. What is – or should be – frightening in Aegisthus' bald story of Atreus' revenge for the crime of Thyestes which Aegisthus naturally does not mention (though Cassandra has done) is that the abominable crimes in the house of Atreus, presided over by the Erinyes, are the same, in kind, as the War with which the play began, and the vengeance designed by Artemis and executed by Clytemnestra – and as Apollo's vengeance upon Cassandra.

Where then is the anticlimax? But the real climax is yet to come. This occurs when Aegisthus proclaims himself tyrant in Argos. Readers of Shakespeare might see the point. For him too the deposition of the lawful King, "God's deputy", was the crime of crimes, a symbol of moral and political chaos. Whether this medieval concept was in direct descent from Greek thought I do not know, but it certainly was Greek to regard the *polis* as the symbol and expression of ordered society – as the *Politeia*, or "Republic", of Plato will sufficiently testify – and to regard Tyranny as its negation. Agamemnon was King "by grace of Zeus"; now Argos is under the heel of a lawless tyrant; and the more despicable Aegisthus is, the more cogent is the climax. Somehow, that contrast between the feminine Aegisthus and the masculine Clytemnestra seems rather too small, but it is the kind of thing we arrive at by fixing our attention entirely on the tragic hero and the persons who surround him.

I mention one other scene in the play, partly for the sake of future reference.

A recent commentator finds the Herald scene rather a bore: "That garrulous Herald . . . we wish he would go away, that we might learn the worst at once." Exactly: we are all agog to know what is going to happen to Agamemnon. The last of the Herald's speeches describes in detail a fearful storm that has blasted the returning fleet; only Agamemnon's ship came through safely. Why did Aeschylus contrive this? In order, we are told, that Agamemnon may arrive without the support of Menelaus and the army, and so the more easily fall victim to Clytemnestra.

There is nothing like keeping your eye firmly on the tragic hero and what happens to him: it makes so much of the play negligible. But that storm has its antecedents. For some reason, and perhaps unexpectedly, Clytemnestra's second speech ends with a kind of warning to, or about, the victorious Achaeans in Troy: "Let them remember in their victory to spare the holy places, lest the conquerors become in their turn the conquered. They still need a safe return." And from what kindly or malign motive should she say this? We may guess, but to no purpose and with no evidence. But the Herald, in his second speech, happens to say that Troy has been blotted out, temples and all. Then, later, comes his report of the storm, caused by "a compact made by those inveterate enemies, Fire and Water". The army did not respect the holy places, and they have not had a safe return.

And what has this to do with Agamemnon and his coming destruction? Obviously, nothing at all. But it has a great deal to do with the play – and the play is not about Agamemnon in particular. It is about Dike, the fundamental law that offence incurs retribution, "the Doer will suffer"; the problem that runs through the whole trilogy is: in what way can that law be satisfied without landing us in everlasting chaos? The *Agamemnon* is built on the principle of aggregation, not of concentration upon one central person; or we might say instead of this, that it concentrates on the working of that law, which is always being satisfied, here, through violence. Paris offended: he has been struck down, by Agamemnon and Zeus. Agamemnon has offended, in shedding so much blood. (In passing, we may note that the first part of that speech of Clytemnestra's is as queer as the second part, the "warning"; for why should Aeschylus have chosen her, and not the Herald, to describe the tumult and carnage inside Troy? The Herald was in Troy to see it; Clytemnestra was not. The obvious answer is that Aeschylus wanted to place it between the Omen of the devouring eagles, of which it is the fulfillment, and what we are to hear immediately from the chorus: "Zeus has cast over Troy a net from which none could escape.") To resume: the army too offends, and the army is punished at once, swiftly and terribly. Agamemnon's turn must surely come.

In corroboration we notice another strange fact. The chorus that hears that desperate news from the Herald consists of older citizens of Argos. Aeschylus gives them an ode to sing as soon as the Herald has gone. Obviously they will sing about the overwhelming disaster that has befallen their city. But it was not at all obvious to Aeschylus: he makes them sing about Helen's offence; how the Trojans welcomed her with bridal songs, now turned into cries of lamentation. The storm is never mentioned again, not even by its survivor, Agamemnon. It has done its work − if we can see the point of it − and there Aeschylus leaves it. The ode adds yet another instance of offense that occurs retribution. The rhythm of the play flows past the storm without stopping, but it has received from it a powerful tributary. Aeschylus did not devise it in order to make things easier for Clytemnestra. Considerations like that belong to a kind of drama utterly different in scale, and in this one are only an obstructive nuisance.

If we took the time and space to consider the rest of Aeschylus' surviving work, we should find nothing to disturb the broad conclusions to which our survey of the *Agamemnon* has led us. The centre and focus of a play is not in the persons, not in a tragic hero. To see any of his plays in its true proportions, and thereby to understand what he is talking about we have to stand back, at such a distance that complexities of character and of personal relations are lost to view. For example, myself when young did lucidly explain what is wrong with the *Persae*: it lacks a strong central character, for Xerxes is not strong, nor particularly central. The explanation was rather less than intelligent − though worse ones have been offered.

In this play too "double determination" reigns throughout: the universal alongside the particular. Aeschylus boldly manipulates very recent history in order to make a picture of ambition and apparently overwhelming that end in utter disaster. (Thucydides' handling of the Sicilian expedition makes a bitter counterpiece.) On the one level, Aeschylus attributes the ruin of the Persian host to the better weapons, better political system, superior spirit, discipline and intelligence of the Greeks; to a sufficiency of money in Attica, to the valour that they displayed at Salamis, to the "Dorian spear" that is going to complete the work at Plataea, and to the inhospitable nature of the Greek countryside which destroys the retreating multitude by hunger, thirst, and exhaustion. On the "divine" level, there is the "deceiving" *theos,* Atê, or Infatuation, who smiles and lures a man to destruction, the *theoi* (or daimon, or Zeus – for Aeschylus does not mind which it is) who give the victory to the Greeks and desolation to Persia. And when the Greeks and the soil of Greece have done nearly all the hard work, Aeschylus brings the two levels together, as it were, by causing the *theos* first to freeze, then thaw, the broad river in order to drown the remnant whom battle and hunger have spared.

The character of Xerxes is of course important, but he is not the focus of the drama. The canvas is much bigger than that. And the best way of making nonsense of it is to call the "divine" activity "supernatural". It is the essence of what is natural.

But the case is surely very different with Sophocles, with whom the art of tragic drama, among the Greeks, reached its peak. With him the last trace of primitive stiffness (as we like to say) has disappeared: he was a master of plot-construction, and in character-drawing and range of dramatic diction he, and no one else, can stand alongside Shakespeare. Yet two of his plays, the *Ajax* and *Trachiniae*, have caused interminable trouble and produced untenable explanations, and it is odd that the two plays that most convincingly fit the doctrine of the tragic hero, the *Electra* and *Oedipus Tyrannus*, are the two which leave critics wondering if he had anything to say that was worth saying.

As for *Trachiniae*, it has been suggested that there was a period in Sophocles' artistic career when he built his plays on a double foundation; the *Antigone* would be another, and more successful, example: in the former, the tragedy of Deianeira *plus* the tragedy of Heracles; in the latter, Antigone's *plus* Creon's – with Antigone forgotten towards the end. But why should either a dramatist or an architect imagine that two foundations are better than one? The *Ajax* offers not this difficulty but a worse. Ajax is one of the most splendid tragic heroes that we shall find anywhere. His suicide would have made a terrific climax to the play, if only Sophocles had not made the mistake of putting it not at the end but in the middle, and followed it with what has often been called a long and rather tedious wrangle about the burial of the body. A recent translator of the play is only echoing many predecessors in saying that Sophocles has not found an entirely happy solution to the problem of concluding the play. But what kind of dramatist is it that gratuitously sets himself a problem which he cannot really answer? Why did not Sophocles tear up his unfinished manuscript and begin again? Most of the "solutions" that we have been given of this "problem" collapse under their own weight, small though that is. In any case, why should a popular and experienced dramatist offer his audience a "problem"? *We* are the problem: why do we insist that the play revolves around one person or should, when all the evidence shows that it does not?

We turn Deianeira into a tragic heroine, and certainly for the first part of the play she discharges the function excellently well, especially if we shut our eyes and ears at the proper places. She has her *hamartia*: she is too simple. She does something without proper consideration, and it destroys her. But then Sophocles makes her son do exactly the same sort of thing: Hyllus hastily denounces her as a murderess; then, when she has killed herself and he learns that she was innocent, he bitterly reproaches himself. Her tragedy being consummated, we have the tragedy of Heracles, with the minimum of connection. It was a Professor of English (for a change) who explained that Sophocles had run out of material. The last verse of the play is: "Nothing of this except through Zeus." Is this only the piously intoned formula with which the priest concludes the service? Well, Zeus is mentioned over twenty times in the play. We may not be sure what he meant to Sophocles, but perhaps the play gives us the chance of finding out.

The first ode is a particularly fine one, too often dismissed with a remark like: "The chorus of sympathetic Trachinian maidens enters and seeks to console Deianeira." True, but how do they do it? The ode both begins and ends with the splendid imagery of sparkling Night who for ever brings forth blazing Day, and then again lulls him to sleep. There is a second astronomical image: as the Great Bear circles endlessly around the Pole, so do joy and sorrow endlessly succeed each other in the lives of men; for which reason Deianeira, after so many years of anxiety for Heracles, can surely look now for years of peace and joy. Besides (they say), he is a son of Zeus, and who has ever seen Zeus regardless of his offspring?

It is a familiar thought in Sophocles' work; it recurs very impressively in the *Ajax*: a steady rhythm runs through the lives of men. This poem is the background against which the succeeding action is played out. In the regular course of things, Deianeira and Heracles should now enjoy peace. We feel sure that in this instance the natural rhythm is going to break down – but why? This is the question that we should be asking ourselves, not "Which of the two is the central character?" As the action unrolls itself we hear, successively, of what Heracles has done or is doing: to Iphitus (of which Zeus did indeed take sharp notice), to the total population of a city, some of whose pitiful survivors presently fill the orchestra – Heracles doing this because Iole's father would not give her to him as his mistress – to a loyal wife, to an innocent messenger, and, finally, to his son, in forcing him to marry a woman whom he abhors. Then, "Nothing is here but Zeus": it is what *would* happen; these are the reasons why the natural rhythm breaks down here. Our universe is precarious enough at best; for instance, we often act in ignorance and effect results that we never intended. It has its own way of working, but it cannot sustain moral violence of this kind.

The *Ajax* is composed on a similar scale. Ajax is a strong character, but in the play there is one far stronger: Athena, who typifies here, we might say, the inexorable demands of life, which Ajax thinks he can set aside. The idea of rhythm permeates the play – the instability of human fortunes. It appears not only in Ajax's grand – and tragically ironic – speech about Night and Day, Summer and Winter, but also in the repeated ideas that today's friend is tomorrow's enemy, that no man is good all the time. This play too has its impressive background: not Ajax's hut, but the presence of Athena, with Ajax mad, and cruel. She tempts Odysseus to exult over his fallen enemy; he says: "No; enemy though he is, I pity him in the disaster that holds him fast in its grip, thinking of myself no less than of him. For I can see that none of us who walk the earth is more than an insubstantial shade." (We should remember this later, when Agamemnon scornfully says to Teucer: "What? *you* defy *me*, for one who is a man no longer, only a shade?") Athena gravely approves: "A single day can raise one man on high and cast another down. Do not be puffed up if you are stronger or richer than another. It is the *sophrones* whom the gods cherish." The quality of the *sophron* is understanding; in this play, in particular, knowing how to behave in the face of the vicissitudes and the demands of life. Odysseus has it; so too has Tecmessa, instinctively perhaps rather than consciously. She, as she gently tells Ajax, suffered a reversal incomparably worse than his, but she accepted and made the best of it. He was always rigid, and now is broken. What is more, he has exposed all those near him (so it is assumed) certainly to grief, perhaps to danger too.

That is the point of his ironic speech. It is not merely that he is deceiving Tecmessa and the chorus in order to gain solitude. When he says that he is moved to pity, he means it; he means it too when he says that now he sees that as Night gives place to Day and Winter to Summer, so he too must yield; but he sees it and feels pity only now, when the knowledge is too late to help him; and when he says "yield", his two Greek verbs really mean "get out of the way", "give place". Therefore, he "gets out of the way": it is all he can do now, to save his honour, cost what it may to those near and dear to him.

Why does Sophocles continue? Not because he is yet only at v. 865 and at least another four hundred verses are wanted. Not because Sophocles wishes to "rehabilitate" the character of his tragic hero. That, if it happens, is only incidental: Ajax's merits are recalled, by Odysseus, but there is no attempt to palliate his crime; and our last, posthumous glimpse of him is instructive. Odysseus has won for his old enemy (who was torturing him to death in the opening mad-scene) the common decency of burial, against the judgment of Agamemnon; generously, he offers Teucer friendship in place of hatred, and Teucer accepts it gladly; then he asks to be allowed a share in the burial-rites, but that Teucer reluctantly refuses, "lest it anger the spirit of the dead man". Teucer cannot presume that Ajax, in death, could match the generosity of Odysseus.

This is hardly "rehabilitation", but it is the point on which the play ends, so finely: Odysseus has to walk away alone, the only one in the play, bar Tecmessa, who knows in what spirit the vicissitudes of life are to be confronted. Not Menelaus: Sophocles makes this man of limited intelligence say: "These thing go by turns. That fellow was always insubordinate; now it is my turn to think big"; therefore he will throw the body out, for the animals to eat. But here, as in the *Antigone,* and at the end of the *Iliad,* death is the ultimate fact, and burial is the tribute that we owe to our common humanity. Agamemnon, like Creon in the *Antigone,* would deny that tribute for reasons of State; but Sophocles says here what he says there: "No; the claims of humanity — or the Laws of the gods — must come first."

There is no problem over the unity either of this play or the *Trachiniae,* once we emancipate ourselves from the constrictions of "tragedy of character" and the tragic hero.

But surely there can be no doubt over the *Electra* and the *Oedipus Tyrannus,* each of which is dominated from first to last by one towering figure? Quite so, but the odd fact is that the more we focus our attention on the tragic hero of each play, the harder it becomes to make real sense of it. Let us take the *Electra* first. The role of Electra is as long, and as exacting, as we shall find anywhere. It is reasonably true to say that she is at the centre of the play throughout. It is also reasonably true to say of it what Richmond Lattimore does in an introduction to a translation: "Critics are left to come to the most various conclusions, including the conclusion that there is no conclusion." That is true, but surely rather queer.

The difficulty is that the detailed and exciting study of Electra's character and situation lead up to the vengeance that she and Orestes take upon their mother and Aegisthus, and that there the play stops dead, with no hint of any further punishment or purgation for the matricide: no flight for Orestes, no Erinyes, nothing. Does it really make sense to suggest, as some do, that Sophocles contrived this for the sake of showing what such an Electra would have been like? that it is a study in heroism?

Theoi also are concerned in the action – a fact sometimes overlooked and sometimes misinterpreted. Orestes has been called "the god-commanded matricide"; quite wrongly, since Orestes makes it plain in his first speech that the idea was entirely his own; that he went to Delphi only for practical advice, which the god gave him: "Kill them not by open show of force, but by stratagem." That advice he follows. In fact, the idea of stratagem, or guile, is made so prominent in the play that Lattimore has called it "The Liars' drama". But although no god has commanded Orestes, or Electra, and no god lifts a finger to help them, the presence of *theoi* in the action – Apollo, Zeus, Hermes, and even the Erinyes – is suggested time after time, unless indeed we can persuade ourselves that all this is no more than pietistic trimming, of a singularly ungodly kind, since the end is to include matricide. So that if we do decide that the *theoi* are to be taken seriously in the play, we have two problems to resolve. First, since Sophocles was going to show, with his brilliant and convincing study of character and situation, that his Electra and Orestes intended vengeance, and were well able to achieve it, why did he interweave gods in the action, especially as they do nothing to help or hinder – for this Orestes does not give the impression of one who would never have thought of "stratagem" if a god had not put the idea into his head? Second, since for some reason he wanted Apollo to preside over the action, how could he represent him, the pure god of Delphi, as one who could encourage Orestes to kill his mother, and suppress the Aeschylean idea that this was a crime for which atonement of some kind must be made?

Our difficulties, naturally, are entirely home-made. Sophocles had no interest in puzzling his audience, leaving them to come to "the most various conclusions". If we protest that gods should not countenance matricide and therefore cannot understand this Apollo, the reason is that we are bogged down in our word "religion", and have not understood that what the *theoi* represent may be something good, or something bad, but in either case something that is true. When the Greek said: "Zeus gives two evils for every good thing", he was not criticising Zeus, but stating an obvious fact of experience. If on the other hand we are so dazzled by the vividness and depth of the character-drawing (as can easily happen) that we try to interpret the play in terms of heroism and explain away its gods as best we can, then we are reducing the play to about half its size – perhaps less, since the ending, now, leaves us with the feeling that we are standing on only one leg.

The play is permeated with the idea of Dike: not "Justice", but "what regularly happens". Some have said that Sophocles, in this play, has abolished the Erinyes, the agents of Dike: it is not true, for when Orestes and Pylades have entered the palace to kill Clytemnestra, and Electra soon follows, the chorus sings: "Look! there go the hounds that unerringly follow the trail of crime" – in other words, the Erinyes. In this play they do not pursue Orestes: they *are* Orestes.

There were the ancient crimes: murder, adultery, usurpation, confiscation. The character-study of Electra is indeed absorbing and exciting for its own sake, but if we are satisfied with that, we "come to most various conclusions" – naturally. The *theoi* are in it too, including the Erinyes. Every detail in this portrait of Electra, including the ferocity that she displays at the end, is devised to this end, that we should see how the old crimes and their continuing effect impel this Electra to dedicate herself, at any cost, to their reversal; and the same is true of Orestes. The presence of the *theoi* does not mean that the vengeance is heroically glorious or morally edifying, only that it is what may be expected. They slew by guile (v. 197), it is by guile that they are slain; Orestes drives Aegisthus in to be killed on the very spot where he had killed Agamemnon. It is Measure for Measure; grim – but what do you expect? Clytemnestra, frightened by her dream, makes sacrifice to Apollo and offers up her viciously blasphemous prayer. As soon as it is finished, in comes Orestes' old slave with his circumstantial story which will lure her to her death. We know that the story was made up by Orestes, but how can we not take it also as Apollo's answer to that prayer? Later, when Orestes and Pylades have entered the palace, Electra too makes sacrifice to Apollo, and she too prays: "Aid our purpose, and show all mankind what chastisement the gods inflict on wickedness." That prayer too is answered by Apollo.

In short, if critics have come to the most various conclusions about the play, the reason is either that they have not come to terms with Sophocles' "religion", or that they are excessively preoccupied with the persons in the play, or both, so that what was designed as a powerful statement of a universal truth is reduced to the level of an exciting revenge-play which indeed contains a marvellous "portrait of a lady" but does not really make sense.

Then there is the tragedy of King Oedipus. As usual, we have no lack of interpretations from which to choose: it is a play about father-hatred, mother-love, and incest; about the search for identity; about the peril of trying to know too much; about the ideal leader of his people who risks his all to save his city; it is the typical Greek play that enforces the typical Greek doctrine that Man is subject to Fate, and that what he is or does makes no difference; it is a superb *tour-de-force* for the theatre but has no further claim on our attention, since the action consists of a series of coincidences that no one can take seriously. In fact, "Critics are left to come to the most various conclusions": a fact that suggests – as with certain other plays too – the absence of critical controls. Yet they exist. It may be rude, but is it otherwise wrong, to say that no interpretation is worth listening to unless it gives a reasonable answer to a series of precise questions that can be asked about the composition of the play?

First, which are we talking about, the play or the Oedipus myth? The answer is obvious, yet the question seems important. It is not going very far into paradox to say that there was no such thing as the Oedipus myth, only particular versions of the Oedipus myth, which could be startlingly different. Was it part of the Orestes myth that Orestes was pursued by the Erinyes? As we have seen, it depends on whose version we are reading. We are inclined, I think, to underestimate the freedom with which the Greek poets treated myth, and to overestimate the degree to which the Athenian audience "knew the story beforehand". Was it part of the Oedipus myth that Iocasta killed herself on learning the truth? She does in Sophocles' play, but in Euripides' *Phoenissae* she is alive years later.

That free handling of myth is important for our control of the *Tyrannus* for this reason, that we know enough of Aeschylus' version of the Oedipus myth to know that Sophocles turned it not upside-down but nearly inside-out. Of Aeschylus' trilogy only the third play survives, the *Seven against Thebes*. It is generally assumed, and reasonably, that in the first play, *Laius*, Aeschylus used the story of Chrysippus, the son of his guest-friend Pelops: Laius abducted the lad and used him so abominably that in shame he hanged himself. What we know for certain is that Laius, three times, received a solemn warning from Delphi to beget no son of his own, for a son would bring destruction on Laius and the whole house. That would give the normal tragic foundation: sin followed by punishment. Even if we discount Aeschylus' use of the Chrysippus story as conjectural, we still have the wanton disregard of the triple warning. So too in Euripides' play: Iocasta says there that Laius begat the child "when heated with wine and giving way to pleasure". We have only to read what Iocasta says about it in the *Tyrannus* to see that Sophocles has made it, morally, a totally different story. Here, the prediction comes to Laius, "perhaps not from the god himself, but from his ministers", as Iocasta scrupulously says, in the baldest and bleakest terms. Indeed, what she says about it does not exclude the hypothesis that the fatal child was conceived already. Further, if there is any Divine Plan in the event, Sophocles never hints at it. In short, Aeschylus' Oedipus myth had a rational foundation – and Sophocles removed it; an odd and challenging thing for the author of the *Ajax, Antigone,* and *Electra* to do. What is irrational, unjust, bewildering, in the play was put there by Sophocles; we cannot blame "the myth".

This may prove to have a bearing on the ever-popular idea that the play has to do with ineluctable Fate. No other extant tragedy does, and it is fairly clear that Aeschylus' Laius-trilogy did not. Therefore a certain scepticism seems to be in order.

We know what are the consequences of regarding *Hamlet* as the tragedy of the Prince of Denmark, just *that*. The action of the play concerns, almost exclusively, two noble houses of Denmark, and at the end not a single member of either house is left alive. The play has been called "the tragedy of a man who could not make up his mind"; on which a gloomy colleague of my own commented: "Shows, doesn't it? how important it is to make up your mind." The *Tyrannus* too is larger than the tragedy of King Oedipus; like Hamlet, he has his partners in the same disaster: Iocasta and the two girls. Their ruin is integral to the play: Sophocles has certainly not taken pains to make Iocasta's death inconspicuous, and the two children are introduced towards the end for no evident purpose except that Oedipus may tell them that for no fault in them, their young lives are already blasted. As for Iocasta, addicts of *hamartia* used to pretend that she is being punished for her blasphemy about divine prophecies. But she has not been blasphemous; here her only fault is that she firmly believes something that she had no reason to disbelieve – that the child had been destroyed. What drives her to her death is the fact that years earlier she, the widowed Queen, in no unusual way, married, or was given in marriage to, the new King – a marriage against which, at the time, no possible argument could have been found. But a perfectly reasonable action kills her. *Exit* Hamartia; *enter* sheer Unreason. She, the two girls, and Oedipus himself, are all innocent victims of – what?

Such are the lines on which Sophocles has remodelled the Oedipus myth. Now we will look at the play. It is said to be well-constructed, but some parts of the structure are decidedly odd.

The action of the play begins at v. 1. That is by no means unusual, but it seems necessary to record the fact, since the play is often treated as if it began away back in the past – just as the *Oresteia* is often treated as if it began with Thyestes' seduction of Atreus' wife. But the *Oresteia* is not a dramatising of the story of Atreus' life, nor is the *Tyrannus* the story of Oedipus. We should not overlook the fact that an audience cannot witness a play backwards nor inside-out. It begins with the presentation of Oedipus as the devoted and exceptionally intelligent King who is doing all he can to save the city from a devouring plague. Some six hundred verses later, the ideal King is behaving like the typical Tyrant, sentencing to death (or exile), on his sole authority, a kinsman whom we know to be innocent, and whom, in the first scene, he was treating with confidence and courtesy. Why should Sophocles contrive this? The intervening scenes are often called, reasonably, the beginnings of the Discovery, but why should they lead to a noisy climax like this, with Oedipus on the verge of committing a monstrous crime? It has been said: "It shows what Oedipus was like; how he came to fulfill the prophecies." That will not do. All that the audience knows about him at the moment is that he was the ideal King, and when, later, it learns Sophocles' version of the past story, it certainly will not receive the impression that the predictions were fulfilled because Oedipus was a man of tyrannical temper. No; the scene does not help explain the past story (of which yet we know nothing), and – what is more surprising – it affects the future course of the action not at all. It is alluded to only once, when Creon dismisses it in two verses as a matter hardly worth mentioning (vv. 1422 f.). Why then did Sophocles invent it?

Some two hundred verses later he does something even more disconcerting. Oedipus has been terribly frightened and is led in by Iocasta. Sophocles writes an ode for his chorus, and it begins with a solemn prayer for holiness and the observance of the eternal Unwritten Laws. "And what has that to do with the menace now impending on Oedipus and Iocasta?" The question rises in our minds automatically, and the only possible answer is: "Nothing whatever." Sophocles has done his best to make clear that the predictions have been fulfilled by the fortuitous actions – good, bad, or indifferent – of half a dozen separate people. One, certainly, was guilty of gross hybris, but it was not Oedipus; it was the boorish charioteer who tried to hustle an innocent pedestrian off the road.

The two middle stanzas of the ode are no less disconcerting. They begin with a ray of light: "It is hybris that begets the tyrant." Certainly we have seen Oedipus behaving like a tyrant towards Creon, but we are at once lost in darkness again, for the man of hybris is described as one of vaulting ambition, full of arrogance, reckless of Right, a pursuer of unjust gain, a sacrilegious contemner of holy places. None of this makes intelligible reference to our tragic hero, and certainly none to Iocasta, whose only fault so far – to say it again – is that she believed something that she had no reason not to.

Finally, to complete our bewilderment, this chorus of loyal Theban citizens is made to pray that the oracles be "manifestly" fulfilled, although this must mean that their admired King shall, sometime, be proved to have killed his father and married his mother; and their astonishing reason for making the prayer is that if the oracles fail, "religion" is finished. Was Sophocles so arid and inhuman a theologian as this?

What we might have expected of an ode written for this moment in the play is, shall we say, anxious comment about the affair at the Three Ways and anxious speculation about what the slave, the survivor of it, will say when he arrives. What we have is utterly different, and demands explanation. Further, since Sophocles had no interest in offering obscure puzzles to his audience, the explanation should be perfectly straightforward. Such an explanation is available, though it involves our giving up one or two inherited and cherished opinions, but let us first complete the examination-paper which interpreters of the play should be required to pass. So far the questions have been: (i) Why did Sophocles remove the intelligible moral foundation of the story? (ii) Why did he contrive that apparently gratuitous condemnation of Creon? (iii) Why did he write this almost unintelligible ode? The next question

concerns Iocasta's prayer and sacrifice, an exact parallel to the middle
scene in the *Electra*, except that Clytemnestra's prayer was abominable
and she deserved everything that came to her, while Iocasta's is entirely
innocent and she deserves nothing. Why could Sophocles treat both
Queens alike? The last question concerns the ending. A synopsis of the
play printed in a certain theatre program finished by saying: "So, at
the end, Thebes is delivered from the plague and Oedipus leaves the
city for ever." The facts are, of course, that the last allusion to the
plague occurred as far back as v. 666, and that Oedipus does not go
into exile. At least one modern director has improved on Sophocles
by devising such a tragic, spectacular and indeed logical *finale* – the
blinded King groping his way out of the theatre and out of his native
city into hopeless exile – as Teiresias had fortold. How did Sophocles
come to miss it?

That is our last question, and part of the answer is that Oedipus is
not the tragic hero in the sense that he is the focus of the play and that
his catastrophe is "the moment of truth". Immediate exile is what he
demands, three or four times, and Creon will not grant it – until he has
first taken the advice of Delphi. The end of the play, possibly "the
moment of truth", is that Oedipus has to return into the palace and is
told: "Do not expect to control everything."

We moderns find it difficult to believe that for Sophocles, and his
Athenian audience, it is not really a play about Oedipus, but about
something further. That is the reason why we find the central ode inexplicable: the chorus *must* be singing about either Oedipus or Iocasta
or both; the only question is which? – and to that, there is no reasonable answer. Yet we know that when the Herald has told his appalling
story to the chorus of the *Agamemnon*, those sage consellors, left to
sing an ode, make not the slightest reference to the storm but instead
sing about Helen – and we have seen why. (Incidentally, the way in
which that storm is allowed to disappear from the play once it has done
its work is very like the way in which the plague is allowed to fade out
in the *Tyrannus*.) We know that in the *Antigone*, when the Guard has
brought his unwelcome news to Creon and has gone, the chorus, left
alone in the theatre, does not anxiously speculate who has done it, but
with apparent irrelevance begins to sing about the Ascent of Man. Yet
as the ode draws to its conclusion we see the point: that marvelous
civilization is precarious; man must obey the dike of the *theoi* and the
laws of the land – which are presumed to be in harmony. That, so to
speak, is what the play is about.

Here too, when Iocasta has led Oedipus into the palace, chorus and audience have the theatre to themselves. Here too the poet leaves the immediate dramatic situation in abeyance, for the moment: he composes an ode that sharply contrasts two opposing ways of life, the religious and the irreligious. That, so to speak, is what the play is about. But how?

Deliberately, as we have seen, Sophocles has removed that foundation in reason which the myth had in Aeschylus' trilogy. His detailed treatment of the story is in accordance: there is no reason why Oedipus or Iocasta — or, prospectively, the two girls — should suffer like this, except that things so fall out. We are shown *how* it occurred; there is never a hint *why*. It is a picture of a totally irrational universe, one to make a mockery of anything like religion. But since we know his other extant plays that a belief in a universal order, Dike, was at the very heart of Sophocles' "religion", we had better amend the foregoing sentence and say: it is a picture of that aspect of our universe in which it seems irrational, unjust, cruel. We well know that this aspect exists: "Who did sin, this man, or his parents, that he was born blind?" It was unconventional of Sophocles to write a play about it; we are familiar with Poetic Justice, but here is Poetic Injustice, in an extreme form. It is only polite to assume that Sophocles may have had reason for doing this unconventional thing, and it should be possible to deduce the reason from the play itself — provided that we do not frustrate ourselves with fixed ideas of our own that may be wrong, about Fate, Oracles and the like. Perhaps one such has been removed already, the idea that where the third ode begins, it will inevitably comment on the present situation of Oedipus and Iocasta.

Does divine prophecy imply divine constraint, or only prediction? In the *Antigone*, Teiresias the diviner prophesies to Creon what the angry gods and their Erinyes are going to do to him. It happens exactly as foretold, but it happens through the spontaneous actions, fully motivated by Sophocles, of Antigone, Haemon and Eurydice. In this instance it is very clear that the prophecy in no way compels but only predicts, and its dramatic function is clear enough: since the event was forseeable, in the unnatural behaviour of the birds and the hot fat from the sacrifice, some general principle, some natural law, is operating. That, or something like it, is (I suppose) the normal function of prophecy in tragic drama, Shakespearian as well as Greek.

So far as the Tyrannus is concerned the objection is obvious: how can anything like a regular law be operating in these predictions? Yet

that is the whole point, and it is here that we find the answer to some
of those awkward questions: the one about Iocasta's sacrifice, and the
one about Oracles and Religion. As we all know, the customs and ideas
of Foreigners are often odd and occasionally stupid, but when they are
Ancients as well, there is hardly any limit to the oddities that we are
ready to impute to them. Yet I would hazard the opinion that if
Sophocles had privately assured friends that for him the validity of
"religion" stood or fell with the verity of Delphic prophecies, they
would have suspected his sanity, much as Shakespeare's friends would
have done, surely, had he told them in the Mermaid that he believed in
magicians who could raise a storm at sea at the drop of a hat. What
evidence we have about the Delphic oracle suggests that people normally went there for practical advice or for moral support or sanction,
and that the god – for obvious reasons – was reluctant to "prophesy",
except in carefully ambiguous terms: "Heads, I win; tails, you lose."
Delphi was indeed a holy place, and its oracular responses deserved
respect, since the controllers of the oracle were men of wide experience
with unusually wide contacts; but if we take quite literally that stanza
about Oracles and Religion, we are (I suspect) relegating Sophocles to
the ranks of the intellectually underprivileged among contemporary
Athenians. The card-index is useful to the critic, but other possessions
are more valuable.

Fortunately, we have only to pay attention to what happens next.
Immediately, Iocasta comes out and offers up her prayer. Like everything else that she does in the play, it is entirely innocent: she prays
only that what divine Omniscience had foreseen shall, somehow, not
come to pass – and even Aristotle, who was not strong on gods (except
for the Unmoved Mover), agrees that "we credit the gods with the
power of seeing everything"; for which reason, he says they are a great
convenience to the playwright. At once the news comes (as she naturally thinks) that Oedipus' father has died in his bed; whereupon she
draws the logical conclusion. Yet another divine prediction has failed;
therefore chance rules; therefore there is no room for *pronoia*, taking
thought beforehand, so that the wise policy is to live at random, to act
as seems best. She is not wicked, only terribly deceived.

So, even in this play divine prediction is a symbol of a regular Order
in the universe, inasmuch as Sophocles is using it as a denial of a
random universe. To say that we can see neither rhyme nor reason in
what happens to these people is only to say what Sophocles himself
says, with much more emphasis, throughout the play. But the dominant

imagery is Blindness. We cannot *know* enough; our reasonable plans can be frustrated by unpredictable events. Who would have expected that Laius' slave would take pity on the baby and disobey orders? Laius is not the only man to bet on a certainty and lose. It was becoming smart doctrine in Athens that Chance obviously does rule, not the gods, who doubtlessly exist but take little notice of what goes on among men; for do we in fact notice that the good prosper and the wicked do not? The traditional laws of morality are so much humbug. Take no notice of them; stand on your own feet; act exactly as you judge best. (The evidence for this trend is conveniently assembled in the fourth chapter of Bernard Knox's *Oedipus at Thebes*.) Sophocles' answer to this is that our best judgment may not be very good when at any moment we may be ignorant of the only fact that really matters, and when unforeseeable and remote contingencies may upset the most intelligent plans. But he says something further.

Of course the innocent sometimes fall into inexplicable disaster. We all know that – even though Aristotle thought that no dramatist should admit the fact. Of course life can seem to us, from time to time, irrational and cruel. But not always, even to our limited vision; and to build a philosophy of life on the assumption that the Eternal Laws are only transitory humbug is disastrous. The third ode was not composed in a moment of artistic insanity, nor is it a composition to be explained by scholastic ingenuity: it is the heart of the play. The first stanza is Sophocles' affirmation of faith in a moral order, made in the teeth of appearances which he has defiantly made as glaring as possible. The two stanzas on hybris give a picture of the violence of chaos to which we deliver ourselves if, in our short-sighted, pseudo-intellectual folly, we reject every thought of a moral order. The final stanza is not the mumbling of a pious fundamentalist; it is truth, straight from the shoulder: if the course of things cannot be foreseen by Omniscience, then the universe is random; we might as well do one thing as another (in our inevitable blindness) – and God help us!

It is a superb play, as strong intellectually as it is emotionally and technically – which, I suppose, is the normal condition of great art. But one of our examination-questions has not yet been attempted, the one about the ending.

Since the mercy of God is infinite, those who have devised a more effective ending may be granted forgiveness – though perhaps repentance may be required. Sophocles has devised a masterly reversal of situation: Creon is now King; Oedipus is abased. He seems to do nothing with it. If we say that Oedipus, even in his ruin, towers above the mediocre Creon, or that he is more splendid than ever in his fall, we are relying on hope rather than on the text. The culmination of this exciting play, the last bit of stage-action, is that Creon, not in the least vindictively but quite firmly, takes the two girls from their father's embrace, and Oedipus must accept it: "Do not hope to control everything."

The ending is not spectacular. It is better than that: it is thoughtful. If we can set aside what we should hope for in such a complete Reversal and look at what we actually find, points of interest emerge. In the earlier scene the question at issue was unclear and uncertain, as the chorus says (v. 656 ff.); in the later it is as clear as daylight, as Oedipus keeps on saying. In the earlier, Oedipus is quite in the dark, but he is intelligent enough to combine the scattered clues into complete certainty, and neither the respect due to the seer and to a loyal kinsman, nor the prudential warnings of the chorus, nor Creon's oath nor his reasoned defence nor even his challenge that Oedipus should ask a simple question of Delphi that would settle the matter – some of this will deter him from committing what would have been a fearful crime. He refrains only out of deference to Iocasta and the chorus, still convinced that he is right (vv. 669-672). That was his hybris, the hybris that "breeds the tyrant". It has nothing to do with his past story; it is the certainty of a man who is in fact in the dark, but is so sure of himself that he sweeps aside all restraints, moral or prudential. The later scene shows the complete contrast. Although everything seems clear, Creon, in so serious a matter (vv. 1442 f.), will not act before seeking the better information that is available to him. Oedipus would not go to Delphi; Creon will.

One point remains. In this play there is no trace of that "double determination"; but for the predictions, nothing at all would have happened. There is one other extant play in which, similarly, the action is made to depend on a direct, unmotivated, divine *fiat*: the *Philoctetes*. Here the action is set in motion by a prophecy that the Trojan war is to end at a certain time and by the hands of two named men. It may well seem incredible, but it is the solemn fact, that this has been taken to prove that Sophocles and the Greek tragic poets in general believed that human affairs were controlled by a quite arbitrary Fate. The poets did not forsee readers of this kind. In each case the divine predictions, like Prospero's magic, and the Sun-god's chariot which incurred Aristotle's disapproval by rescuing Medea the murderess, are dramatic in-

ventions of the kind natural to a race which had not burdened itself
with an orthodox theological system, having nothing like a Church or
authoritative sacred writings – for Greek myth was very far from being
that.

The predictions of the *Tyrannus* do not involve theological belief;
they are an *ad hoc* invention. We have seen in them one dramatic purpose: what divine Omniscience has foreseen can not be fortuitous. The
event may have no meaning discernible by human reason, but our
vision is limited. Sophocles is using the validity of the predictions as a
denial of the doctrine of Chance. But they serve another purpose too.
Laius and Oedipus, both resolute men, and one of them highly intelligent, are (by an exceptional dramatic license) told explicitly that a
particular form of ruin awaits them. Each is left entirely free to deal
with the menace. Each does what he judges to be reasonable and sufficient. Each is frustrated by unforeseeable and uncontrollable circumstances. (It is modern critics, not Sophocles, who suggest that Laius
was wicked in trying to thwart the Divine Will; Sophocles' point is
simply that his plan didn't work.) "Do not aspire to control everything." The universe we inhabit is not random. It can be terrifying, as
we know, but is based on Order; and who are we, that we should
presume to understand the whole? According to Thucydides (140),
Sophocles' friend Pericles observed that chance is the name we give to
what we cannot explain otherwise. Sophocles seems to have agreed.
The play seems to concede everything to the proponents of the random,
quite amoral, universe – as Plato's Socrates will sometimes begin by
seeming to concede everything. Then it turns on them; it defiantly af-
firms the validity of the moral laws, exposes the folly of the new-fangled
brash immoralism, and points out that a modest caution is the only safe
guide – not of course that any policy can positively ensure safety. The
Greeks knew their Gods!

This survey of the *Tyrannus* has been long; not, I hope, unduly long,
in fact unduly short, from some points of view. Its bearing on the theme
of this paper is clear, I trust. King Oedipus is probably the first character that comes to mind when we think of the Greek tragic hero. No
harm in that, if we are using the term in only a casual way; but if we
mean by it that it was the person and fate of Oedipus that filled
Sophocles' mind as he was composing it and should fill ours as we
witness it, we mutilate its amplitude and make important parts of its
structure unintelligible.

One last question. If it has been shown that neither Aeschylus nor

Sophocles built his plays around the tragic hero, and since it is admitted that Euripides did not, when (in antiquity) did he make his appearance, if indeed he did?

I think he did, in the fourth century, and for an intelligible reason. Most of the evidence is provided by Aristotle's *Poetics*. Let it be set down with all possible brevity.

The foregoing argument has implied, all the way through, that the classical dramatists of the fifth century consciously constructed their plays with reference to some general statement, or intuition, about human experience rather than to the persons of the drama. That may be anathema to us, as is the Greek notion that the poets are the "teachers" of the people; but we should reflect that they had no other "teachers": no church, no sacred writings, and (as near as makes no difference) no prose-writing and no books. Traditionally, public poetry had been the only public means of contemplating the serious aspects of life: "Art for art's sake" would have sounded silly and trifling. But by the end of the century things were changing, and poetry lost what philosophy was gaining.

Aristotle remarks that the modern tragic poets were drawing their subjects from a much smaller range of myth than the "classics". He is good enough to give us the reason: they were confining themselves to the stories of those families in which fearful things were done. He himself seems to be in sympathy with this. In his chapter on the *pathos*, the deed of violence, he takes it for granted that it is "tragic" only when it occurs between kinsmen. Tragedy, it seems, has lost its deep perspective and has become sensational, though Aristotle, as a philosopher, would philosophically limit that sensationalism. As for the fifth-century drama that we know, it is clear that, oftener than not, the *pathos* does occur between kinsmen (though not in the *Prometheus, Persae, Ajax, Philoctetes, Trojan Women, Hecuba*), but no one would say that this was primary in any fifth-century play that survives; only secondary. Now, deeds of horror are primary; there is nothing beyond.

This is the reason why, in that same chapter, Aristotle gives a low place, second from the bottom, to that kind of *pathos* which, as he says, was customary with "the old poets", his chosen example being Medea's murder of her children. This he finds *miaron*, "repugnant". Naturally, if what you now require is a "strong scene" which, however, should respect the decencies. Even more surprising is that the mode that he ranks first is one that we should not call "tragic" at all, illustrated by the *Iphigeneia in Tauris*: Pity and Fear in abundance, in the first part of the play; then the thrilling discovery, and then the eminently satisfying ending.

In short, the shrinkage in the range of usable myth corresponds naturally with the shrinkage in the poets' intellectual and moral ambitions. The *theoi* have dropped out; only the human characters remain, doing the most exciting things. The reign of the tragic hero has begun.

It may be that this history repeated itself with tragedy and the theory of tragedy from the early seventeenth century, and in similar circumstances, but we will not examine that here.

ELDER OLSON

"MIGHTY OPPOSITES":
REMARKS ON THE PLOT OF *HAMLET*

I have often wondered what a student would suppose *Hamlet* to be like, as a play, if he were never permitted access to the text or to a performance but forced instead to read the entire body of criticism and commentary upon it. That huge mass of discussion, full of interpretations, hypotheses, and judgments so diverse, so dissonant – could he penetrate it to gain some notion of the play about which it centered? I fear he could not; and while some may take such diversity of comment as a mark of the richness of the work, I take it rather as a mark of the irresponsibility of commentators. It seems to me a test of the soundness of critical discussion that it should give an accurate idea of the work it discusses; a body of criticism which does not do so must be in proportion unsound.

The extreme variety of interpretation seems to be due principally to two causes. The first is that critics have, by and large, failed to establish proper controls in failing to distinguish adequately between facts, inferences, and value judgments, and hence between warranted and unwarranted inferences and value judgments. The second is that in the history of its discussion the action of the play was first reduced to Hamlet's actions only and then Hamlet was taken out of the play, to be explained and analyzed as a real rather than a fictional person, in terms of natural rather than artistic considerations. In consequence interpretation and discussion were extended far beyond the relatively narrow limits of matters appropriate to tragedy. In counteracting the first of these causes, we may clarify what happens in individual scenes; in counteracting the second, what happens in the plot as a whole.

In establishing what occurs in individual scenes, we may pass over the question of the reality of the Ghost. Every device accessible to a dramatist is used to assure us of his reality, including permitting us to see and hear him, and the play offers no foundation for doubt on the matter. There are, however, three important questions concerning the

Ghost, and to fail to resolve them properly is to risk gross errors of interpretation. These are the problems of precisely what accusations the Ghost makes, of what he asks Hamlet to do, and of whether his statements are true and his demands just.

The Ghost makes two accusations. No one in his senses can mistake the first: in clear language and in full detail the Ghost charges Claudius with having poisoned him and with having given out a false report of the manner of his death. The second accusation, however, offers some difficulty because of its ambiguity, and its exact nature must be determined by inference. It involves Hamlet's mother, and its ambiguity is such that it might refer simply to her "o'er-hasty marriage". Indeed, a good many critics have so understood it, and in consequence pondered problems of Hamlet's inadequate motivation and excessive emotion. The charge can in fact mean three different things: that Gertrude married improperly in marrying her husband's brother, and that too rapidly; that she committed adultery with Claudius prior to the death of the elder Hamlet; and that she not merely committed such adultery but was implicated in the murder as well. Now, the first interpretation is clearly untenable. It is preposterous that the Ghost should inform Hamlet of what he already knows all too well (there needs no ghost come from the grave to tell him this) and that Hamlet should respond to such stale news with shock and indignation ("O most pernicious woman!"). The metaphor in which the charge is couched is worth noting:

> But virtue, as it never will be moved
> Though lewdness court it in a shape of Heaven,
> So Lust, though to a radiant angel linked,
> Will sate itself in a celestial bed
> And prey on garbage. (I, v, 53-57)

The analogy involved here is identical with that in Iachimo's charge of adultery in *Cymbeline*, I, vi, 47 ff.:

> The cloyed will, —
> That satiate yet unsatisfied desire, that tub
> Both fill'd and running, — ravening first the lamb,
> Longs after for the garbage.

The point is put bluntly and literally by Hamlet in V, ii, 64: "whor'd my mother". The second and third interpretations are thus the only reasonable ones; the latter is Hamlet's own until the closet scene.

We have, then, a prince whose king and father has been murdered, whose mother has been seduced by the murderer, possibly even induced to participate in the murder, whose throne has been usurped by the murderer, whose father's ghost has returned to demand vengeance, who is "prompted to [his] revenge by Heaven and Hell"; and we may well wonder at critics who can manage to doubt whether Hamlet has "the motive and the cue for passion" and who never progress beyond Gertrude's first and erroneous conjecture that Hamlet's behavior is in response to his father's death and her o'er-hasty marriage. Indeed, the whole point of the play is that with such extraordinary motivation, Hamlet does not act.

What sort of action is required of him? It is no simple command that the Ghost gives. Hamlet is to avenge the murder and, apparently, the adultery ("Let not the royal bed –"). The manner of revenge is evidently left to his choice, with the provision that he is not to taint his mind nor contrive against his mother. For a man like Hamlet, in Hamlet's circumstances, the execution of these demands is no easy task. Hamlet is no Iago, who "for mere suspicion . . ./Will do as if for surety". He must be certain of the justice of his cause, to kill even a man whom he detests as much as he does Claudius. He must determine what act of vengeance is appropriate and just. He must keep the foul grounds for vengeance in mind in order to act, and if he does keep them so, how shall his mind not be tainted? He must dwell upon the crime of uncle and mother and take vengeance upon one but leave the other to Heaven. Surely there is much here to "puzzle the will".

Finally, are the Ghost's statements true, and his demands just? The demands are just – according to the conventions of the play – if the statements are true; that they are true is attested, so far as the murder is concerned, by the King's aside in III, i, 48 ff., by his behavior at the play, by his very explicit statement of his crime as fratricide, as well as his reasons for committing it, in the prayer-scene. It has been offered in objection to this view that the King does not react to the dumb-show, but this objection fails to account for the passages just mentioned and the fact that he *does* react to the play – indeed, it is his recognition of the image of his crime that sends him to remorseful prayer. The accusation of adultery is confirmed by Gertrude's response to Hamlet's charge in the closest scene (III, iv, 66-67), a charge employing a metaphor in basis the same as those already cited from the Ghost's speech and from *Cymbeline*. Her aside in IV, v, 177 ff. offers further evidence. In addition to his accusations, the Ghost claims to be the spirit of Hamlet's father. Hamlet may doubt the truth of that, and presently does, but we may not.

Since, then, the Ghost speaks truth, we may bend his remarks back upon Act I, scene ii to understand it in retrospect. In the light of what we now know, what kind of court is this? It is a court in which deception rules, in which seeming and being, appearance and reality, that within and outward show, have no necessary relation to each other; in which, consequently, nothing and no one can be surely trusted, and in which, consequently, one must plot and spy, pose and lie. This fact is the very axis of the play: all actions, Hamlet's as well, turn upon it. We are not given this fact fully in the scene, but we are given a good part of it. The first fifteen lines of the King's opening speech contain a pack of lies. The elder Hamlet obviously was not a "dear" brother, for Claudius murdered him. Since he did murder him, there was no such thing as "an auspicious and a dropping eye", etc. Moreover, Claudius' counsel to Hamlet, which has so greatly impressed Wilson Knight, is in fact an attempt to get Hamlet to doff his mourning because it reminds him of his crime. Beneath the guise of kindly counsel, the King's real feelings are betrayed by his indignation:

> But to perséver
> In obstinate condolement is a course
> Of impious stubbornness, 'tis unmanly grief.
> It shows a will most incorrect to Heaven,
> A heart unfortified, a mind impatient,
> An understanding simple and unschooled.
> For what we know must be and is as common
> As any the most vulgar thing to sense,
> Why should we in our peevish opposition
> Take it to heart? Fie! 'Tis a fault to Heaven,
> A fault against the dead, a fault to nature,
> To reason most absurd. . . .

This is strong language, considering that the "fault" rebuked is grief for a beloved king and father "but two months dead".

Furthermore – why does Shakespeare show us the granting of Laertes' request – something we might readily have gathered from scene iii – if not to underline the refusal of Hamlet's? And why is Hamlet not permitted to return to Wittenberg, where he would be well out of the way and might wear all the mourning he chose without troubling anyone? Is it simply that since Gertrude desires her son to be near her, the King in honeymoon fashion indulges her desire? Or is it that Hamlet must be kept where he can be watched? Again, when Hamlet pointedly accedes to his mother's request rather than the King's,

Claudius accepts the snub as "a loving and a fair reply"; can he possibly think so?

These last points need not be labored; there is other evidence in abundance of the hypocrisy, lying, distrust, and spying prevalent at the court. Act I, scene iii presents us with a brother advising a sister not to trust her lover, the sister in turn advising him to follow his own precepts about chastity, the father giving counsel to the son upon whom he will later set a spy, and finally, the father also advising the daughter not to trust her lover. Act II, scene i shows us the father setting the spy upon his son; the spy is to lie in order to uncover the truth. Much that is subsequent in the play is illustrative of how one may "by indirections find directions out".

The discrepancy between seeming and being, pretense and truth, constitutes, as we said, the axis of the play. Rosencrantz and Guildenstern pretend to be Hamlet's friends to forward the King's aims; Ophelia pretends to be alone; the players are to be used as a pretended entertainment of Hamlet, with the real purpose of sounding him; the Queen pretends to be alone in her closet; the voyage to England is a pretended mission; the final duel is a pretense. The note is struck with Hamlet's first long speech: "Seems, Madam! Nay, it is." Indeed, the whole speech is a development of the opposition. The note is struck many times thereafter; in Hamlet's first soliloquy, in which he compares his mother's apparent love for her husband with her real lack of it; in the themes of scene iii, as we saw; in the first five lines of Hamlet's speech to the Ghost in scene iv and in Horatio's words, lines 69-74; in "my most seeming-virtuous queen", "one may smile, and smile, and be a villain", and "put an antic disposition on", all within scene v. We may perhaps leave this point; to cite all of the instances would be to cite a great part of the text.

In the uncertainties of this court, Claudius and Hamlet are at stalemate. Claudius can do nothing to Hamlet beyond keeping him at court. Hamlet is loved by the people and by Gertrude, a circumstance that keeps Claudius from overt action even when he has the best of reasons for it (IV, vii, 9 ff.). At this point, although he may be annoyed by Hamlet, he has no reason whatever for action; he needs only to pretend a paternal affection. Hamlet, in turn, however much he despises Claudius, must suppress his real bitterness and disgust; however much he may be sickened by a world of sham and pretense, in which solemn vows and shows of affection are meaningless, he can do nothing but hold his tongue and wish for the release of death. He is, moreover, alone and friendless until the advent of Horatio; there is no one to whom he can unburden his heart. Can he trust Ophelia when his mother's professions of love could so quickly be proved hollow? (It is this thought, doubtless, that underlies his behavior toward Ophelia as she describes it in II, i.)

At the outset, then, Hamlet and Claudius are in equilibrium and inert. Even with news of the appearance of his father's ghost, Hamlet can at most merely "doubt some foul play"; till he definitely knows something, his soul must "sit still". It is only when the Ghost informs him that he is in a position to act. And here he makes his first mistake. He has two courses open to him: action immediate, direct, and open, taken without thought, or action calculated – and therefore delayed, and therefore needing to be kept secret. He chooses the latter. It is not strange that he should have, in view of his nature, and indirection is a plausible course in a court so full of indirection. What would have happened had he chosen the former? We are shown what would have happened in the episode of Laertes' assault on the palace; indeed, the chief function of the episode is to illustrate this, for Laertes might have been brought to conspire with the King in a dozen different ways. The King is but shakily set on his throne. Laertes is merely a noble, his father was merely Lord Chamberlain, his actions are founded on mere rumor and suspicion, and yet he is able immediately to raise a mob of followers who wish him for king – a mob so considerable and formidable as to overcome the palace guards and win into the very presence of the King. How would it have been then with Hamlet, a greatly beloved prince, with a King for his father, with witnesses at hand to attest to the appearance of his father's ghost?

But Hamlet chooses calculated action, which implies secrecy, which implies plots and stratagems, as well as pretense. His basic stratagem is of course feigned insanity; we see him considering it tentatively in I, v, and he puts his plan into effect in the interim between Acts I and II. In feigning he is simply playing the favorite game of the court, and using it to turn the tables, so to speak. Why insanity? Thus ran the old story, of course; but Shakespeare never follows a story simply to follow it. In truth we do wrong to the piece by raising the question; it is an essential detail to alter which would be to alter everything else; everything else is predicated upon it, it is a donnée. Even so, Shakespeare has done something to establish its probability. Clearly it was suggested by Horatio:

> What if it tempt you toward the flood, my lord,
> Or to the dreadful summit of the cliff
> That beetles o'er his base into the sea,
> And there assume some other horrible form
> That might deprive your sovereignty of reason
> And draw you into madness? Think of it.
> The very place puts toys of desperation,
> Without more motive, into every brain
> That looks so many fathoms to the sea
> And hears it roar beneath.

There is no doubt that these words made a great impression upon Hamlet. The expressed distrust of the Ghost becomes the reason for his initial delay and for his decision to use the play as a test. While the play is certainly a test of Claudius' guilt, it is primarily a test of the genuineness and veracity of the Ghost, which Claudius' reaction simply confirms. The question whether

> The spirit that I have seen
> May be the Devil, and the Devil hath power
> To assume a pleasing shape. Yea, and perhaps,
> Out of my weakness and my melancholy,
> As he is very potent with such spirits,
> Abuses me to damn me.

is resolved with

> I'll take the ghost's word for a thousand pound.

Although the feigned madness is properly treated as a donnée, there are certain advantages in the pose for one in Hamlet's circumstances; perhaps they are worth considering even though they have no warrant in the text. To act naturally while possessed of such knowledge and purpose as he has would be very difficult, as Chambers and others have observed, and the merest slip would expose him to suspicion; the pose obviates both the difficulty and the risk. More importantly, the mad are without rational purpose; what better disguise for a man with a purpose? Even more importantly, the mad are in a certain sense free, in that they may do anything and everything at any time and cannot be called to account for it, whereas the sane may be forced to explain actions dictated by reason.

Of the assumed madness we are shown – with one exception, the fight in Ophelia's grave – the verbal rather than the physical side. That there was a physical side we know; the King remarks that neither "the exterior nor the inward man / Resembles that it was" (II, ii, 6-7) and speaks of him as "Grating so harshly all his days of quiet/ With turbulent and dangerous lunacy" (III, i, 34), and there are other indications. We have nothing to support this, however, in the represented actions – nothing of Saxo's and Belleforest's antic heroes. Shakespeare's Hamlet does not besmear himself with filth and ashes, sharpen sticks and hooks, pretend to be a cock in the Queen's chambers, or cut Polonius' body to pieces, boil them, and feed them to the hogs. Yet physical manifestations of "madness" there undoubtedly were; although they are part of the plot, they are not part of the scenario, that is, are not represented on stage.

This raises the question of what other parts of the plot may have gone unrepresented; for the moment, however, we must look into Hamlet's madness as it is set before us. Consider all of Hamlet's speeches throughout the play. There is no hint of madness in any of the asides, in any of the soliloquies; there is none in his speeches to Horatio or any other whom he trusts. To whom are his "mad" speeches addressed? To his enemies or to those whom he does not trust. In what does his "madness" in those speeches consist? In actual excess of rationality, in sheer brilliance of wit, in passages of thought connected by a thread so subtle as to escape detection by inferior minds. Speeches between which we can see no connection we assume to be disconnected; so it is with those who think Hamlet mad. Sometimes – very seldom – they have inklings of the connection, like Polonius in II, ii, 211 ff. or Claudius in III, i, 171-172. But the connection is always present. Hamlet uses the device of deliberate misunderstanding, based upon puns or other equivocations, to balk questions:

Pol. What do you read, my lord?
Haml. Words, words, words.
Pol. What is the matter, my lord?
Haml. Between who?

He uses fantastic paradoxes and sophistries:

Haml. . . . Farewell, dear mother.
King. Thy loving father, Hamlet.
Haml. My mother; father and mother is man and wife, man and wife is one flesh, and so, my mother.

He uses "metaphysical" conceits, as in this passage where he is simply capping conceits with Rosencrantz and Guildenstern:

Haml. . . . were it not that I have bad dreams.
Guil. Which dreams are indeed ambition, for the very substance of the ambitious is merely the shadow of a dream.
Haml. A dream itself is but a shadow.

Ros.   Truly, and I hold ambition to be of so light and airy a quality
           that it is but a shadow's shadow.
Haml.   Then are our beggars bodies, and our monarchs and outstretched
           heroes the beggars' shadows.

He uses in addition irony, innuendo, a kind of super-Euphuism with
Osric – in brief, every conceivable device to frustrate the inquisitive.

How can this be real madness? Those who think Hamlet really mad
do so because they import their own definitions of madness into the
play, as some think him merely neurotic or perfectly sane because they
import their own definitions of neurosis or sanity. All of this is completely illicit. The play defines one test of madness for us:

> Bring me to the test,
> And I the matter will re-word, which madness
> Would gambol from. (III, iv, 142-4)

This is a test that Hamlet certainly can pass.

Moreover, the feigned madness of Hamlet is sharply contrasted with
the real madness of Ophelia. Her thought consists only in short passages of association, centering chiefly on the two recurrent themes of
death and faithless love. Compare Lear, who is also mad; in his mad
period there is the same shuttling back and forth between fixed themes.
Compare Othello when his passion drives him to the brink of madness;
you will find the same thing. But Hamlet – if we are to abide by the
evidence of the play – is sane. That "wounded name" which his dying
voice asks Horatio to clear can involve only three things: his "madness", his killing of Polonius, his killing of the King; and that name
can be cleared only by explanation of his real sanity, of his motives for
pretense, of what occasioned his killing of both men.

Hamlet, then, must be considered sane. But, as we saw, he made a
wrong choice at the beginning; had Laertes (or shall we say, Macbeth
or Hotspur) been in his shoes, we should have had a one act play. He
is a bookish man, as the metaphors of his first speech after encounter-
ing the ghost make clear, as, indeed, his writing in his tables makes
clear, for he records the unforgettable. He is a thoughtful, deliberative
man; he can act, indeed, but – at first – not without thought. It is a
great irony of the play that his first commitment to the Ghost is

> Haste me to know't, that I, with wings as swift
> As meditation or the thoughts of love
> May sweep to my revenge.

It is precisely meditation and thought that forbid him haste. Shakespeare's major tragic figures fall into error, not through flaws, but through their virtues. A man of virtue is thrown into circumstances in which his virtue is his undoing. Hamlet is being asked, most solemnly, to do something in opposition to his fundamental nature; he responds in accordance with his fundamental nature. What a difference there is between that "Haste me to know't" and, at the end of that very scene,

> The time is out of joint. Oh, cursèd spite
> That ever I was born to set it right!

We may spend too much thought upon this question, however, for it is not the true question of the play. The question is not one of *delay because of* — and this is where most critics have gone astray — but *delay as cause*; that is, of what happens *in consequence of delay* when action should have been immediate. Hamlet later learns this:

> Rightly to be great
> Is not to stir without great argument,
> But greatly to find quarrel in a straw
> When honor's at the stake. How stand I then,
> That have a father killed, a mother stained,
> Excitements of my reason and my blood,
> And let all sleep. . . .

In his major works Shakespeare has the convenient habit of stating clearly and repeatedly the basic probability of his play. He states it in the speech of the Player King:

> I do believe you think what now you speak,
> But what we do determine oft we break.
> Purpose is but the slave to memory,
> Of violent birth but poor validity. . . .
>
> What to ourselves in passion we propose,
> The passion ending, doth the purpose lose.
> The violence of either grief or joy
> Their most enactures with themselves destroy.

He states it again when Claudius speaks to Laertes:

> *King.*   Laertes, was your father dear to you? . . .
> *Laer.*   Why ask you this?
> *King.*   Not that I think you did not love your father,
> But that I know love is begun by time,
> And that I see, in passages of proof,
> Time qualifies the spark and fire of it.
> There lives within the very flame of love
> A kind of wick or snuff that will abate it.

And nothing is at a line goodness still,
For goodness, growing to a pleurisy,
Dies in his own too much. That we would do
We should do when we would; for this "would" changes
And hath abatements and delays as many
As there are tongues, are hands, are accidents,
And then this "should" is like a spendthrift sigh
That hurts by easing.

Hamlet himself is made to state it in the soliloquy of III, i; a soliloquy which, despite general opinion, cannot possibly be a meditation on whether he ought to take his own life, for he has dismissed that question in his first soliloquy. It is instead a meditation on the way in which thought ("conscience") can baffle all enterprises, even great ones; and the point is argued from two examples, the first of which has nothing to do with suicide but with the problem of whether to remain passive or to take action under misfortune and of which is the nobler course. The second, while it involves suicide, is in perfectly general terms: even with the inducement of release from an intolerable life men hesitate to kill themselves for fear of unknown consequences (it is the generality of the consideration, incidentally, that permits Hamlet to speak of the "bourne" from which "no traveller returns" despite the fact that he has seen one return). The conclusion is very clear:

Thus conscience doth make cowards of us all;
And thus the native hue of resolution
Is sicklied o'er with the pale cast of thought,
And enterprises of great pitch and moment
With this regard their currents turn awry
And lose the name of action.

We have now worked out some of the chief difficulties of individual scenes; the rest may be made clear as we proceed. Suppose we put Hamlet back into the play, and back into his proper role in the play.

Hamlet and Claudius have generally been treated as static figures in static relation. This is of course the consequence of abstracting them from the play, so that all acts and changes become merely evidence of traits entering into a description of character; all kinetic elements become, as it were, telescoped into stasis, and plot becomes merely the gradual revelation of something which is itself stationary. To see how this violates the play we need only to consider their respective speeches in succession. At the beginning Claudius – though his speeches are untrustworthy, as we saw – is prepared to be gracious to Hamlet, and publicly acknowledges him as his "son" and successor to the throne.

When we next see him, in II, ii, he has been sufficiently troubled and puzzled by Hamlet's "madness" to send for Rosencrantz and Guildenstern. He is by no means content with Gertrude's conjecture that its cause is "no other but the main"; he wishes to discover whether it is "aught to us unknown," and grasps eagerly at Polonius' hypothesis. When this hypothesis is disproved, he begins to doubt the madness itself ("what he spake, though it lacked form a little /Was not like madness") and fears that what Hamlet is hatching in his mind "will be some danger". It is at this point that — no longer wishing Hamlet to remain at court — he devises the plan of the voyage to England. When Polonius proposes the interview with the Queen, the King agrees, for "Madness in great ones must not unwatch'd go." Struck to heart by the image of his crime in the play scene, he realizes that his secret is known, reacts with fear, fury, and remorse, and prepares the document that is to send Hamlet to execution in England. After the death of Polonius he expresses his feelings toward Hamlet in the soliloquy which closes IV, iii: "like the hectic in my blood he rages." We need go no further; that there is change is manifest.

The changes in Hamlet are, quite naturally, far more various and extensive. There are, to begin with, all of his changing relationships to other personages of the play. Horatio he seems to trust increasingly: if his confidence in I, v, is somewhat qualified (though this may be due to the presence of others), by Act III, scene ii, two months later, he has told Horatio at least something of the Ghost's words and of the circumstances of the murder, and now asks aid in ascertaining the King's guilt (59-92); shows further trust in IV, vi; has confided all by V, ii, 80, including the matter of his mother's adultery (l. 64); and ultimately entrusts Horatio with the telling of the whole story. In his relationship with Ophelia Hamlet moves from distrust on purely general grounds — from, that is, a mere generalizing on his mother's inconstancy ("Frailty, thy name is woman!") to distrust founded on particulars in III, i. The long perusal of her face during his visit to her chamber seems to be the effect of a desperate hope that she is as true within as she is fair without (compare the "Ha, ha! are you honest? . . . Are you fair?" of III, i), and his sigh seems to indicate abandonment of that hope. There is no need to suppose with Coleridge and others that some stage-business betrays the presence of the King and Polonius in the "nunnery" scene, nor is there any indication that Hamlet detects it. Hamlet cannot trust her and so must play the madman. He does so from his very first words to her; it is only in his soliloquy that he speaks tenderly. She gives him particular grounds for distrust in this scene, for while she reproaches him with unkindness, it is she who has denied him access; furthermore, though pretending to read and meditate, she has come provided with all the gifts he has given her. Rosencrantz and Guildenstern he obviously views with increasing distrust. He greets them cordially enough at first, but either suspects or has learned that they were sent for. Once he has brought them to admit that they were summoned, he seems briefly to trust them, for he is apparently at point to reveal the secret of his madness (II, ii, 396) when Polonius interrupts. They must have revealed his selection of the play, perhaps even his interpolation of a speech, to Claudius; otherwise the King's great "choler" and being "much offended" with Hamlet is unintelligible. If so, the "choler" itself would show Hamlet that they had betrayed him. At any rate, he voices his distrust in the recorder passage; later, he would trust them as he would "adders fang'd"; ultimately, he can dismiss his engineering of their deaths with "they are not near my conscience". Laertes he seems to have no great connection with at first. His fury in the graveyard he explains himself ("sure, the bravery of his grief did put me/ Into a towering passion"), and it is understandable in view of his preoccupation with outward show and "that within which passeth show." He repents and decides to court Laertes' favor. The "Give me your pardon" speech of V, ii has been called hypocritical; what is overlooked is Hamlet's need to persist in his role as madman. If hypocrisy is looked for, it may easily be found in Laertes' ensuing speech. He readily forgives Laertes at the end. In his relationship with Gertrude, finally, Hamlet moves from an initial disgust with her inconstancy to horror at her adultery and possible complicity in the murder. Once he has realized her innocence in the latter and has seen her conscience at work, he entrusts her with the secret of his "madness", offering her both mental and physical proof of his sanity (III, iv, 139 ff.). It must be noted that she never betrays Hamlet; in her narrative to Claudius she conceals much and lies about most of the rest. Hamlet has succeeded in making her feel "those thorns that in her bosom lodge", for she is still plagued by guilt in IV, v, 17-20.

There are also changes in Hamlet himself. He changes in his attitude toward death: it is at first something greatly to be desired; in the graveyard scene he discovers that it has another side; later, it is "that sergeant . . . strict in his arrest", even though it is a way to "felicity" and though to live is to "in this harsh world draw thy breath in pain". He changes in his view of his task: he is first sure that he has grounds for revenge, then doubts his grounds, then confirms his grounds, then seeks for the appropriate act of revenge (the prayer scene), and in between meditates on the "event" or consequence of action. He changes in his view of human action itself. He first sees himself as a solitary agent who must plot; presently realizes that others are plotting against him also, and thinks he must plot more deeply still — "delve one yard below their mines/ And blow them at the moon"; and finally, after the English voyage, comes to understand that "our deep plots do pall", that rashness is praiseworthy, that divinity and Providence have a part in all human actions and fortunes (V, ii, 6-11; 48; 230-235) and that "readiness is all". Had he been earlier what he is at this point, he would not have delayed.

Hamlet's actions, thoughts, and feelings are not intelligible by themselves; they can be understood only in the context of the actions of others — in particular, of course, the actions of Claudius. For Hamlet and Claudius are protagonist and antagonist, hero and adversary. The plot of the play is a protracted duel; Hamlet himself recognizes that what he is engaged in is a matter of "the pass and fell incensèd points / Of mighty opposites" (V, ii, 61-62). In this duel Claudius makes six passes, each of which Hamlet meets with parry and counterthrust. These "passes" or stratagems utilize every conceivable instrument against Hamlet: friends, mistress, mother, even Hamlet himself, in that they involve his predilections for drama and fencing and indeed, in the supposed mission to England, his very rank. The stratagems have, to be sure, different purposes, according to the state of Claudius' knowledge; the earliest are merely attempts to discover the cause of Hamlet's madness, whereas the later ones — those which follow on the play scene — have deadly intent.

Each pass produces a situation at once advantageous and disadvantageous for Claudius, as each counterthrust does for Hamlet. Thus the first pass — the use of Rosencrantz and Guildenstern to sound Hamlet — fails in its purpose, and informs Hamlet that the pair are working in the King's interests and that his pose of madness is under scrutiny; on the other hand, it eliminates the easy hypotheses and sharpens the King's interest in causes "to us unknown". Hamlet's counterthrust — in this instance as in the next, the baffling of his interrogators by persisting in his pose — foils Claudius' intent, but it also convinces him of the need for further investigation, and leads him to accept Polonius' proposal to use Ophelia. This device in turn fails, but it permits him to reject the hypothesis that love is involved, to suspect the madness itself, to surmise that danger is involved, and thus to hatch the plan of the voyage to England. Hamlet's counterthrust, if it foils the King, also exposes the Prince to closer scrutiny and hence greater danger; the guise adopted to shift attention from his actions is actually drawing attention to them. The third pass – the stratagem of sounding Hamlet through his amusements – also involves both success and failure: if it exposes the King to Hamlet's counterthrust, the riposte which it provokes reveals Hamlet's knowledge of the murder. At this point the opponents stand on equally firm ground, prepared for action, for while Hamlet has proved the veracity of the Ghost, the King too has found a cause for prompt and definite action. After Hamlet fails to kill him at prayer – another matter of seeming and being, by the way, for the King is only apparently praying – the initiative passes to Claudius. So it is with the other three stratagems and their counter-stratagems: the conversation with the Queen, the voyage to England, the final plot with Laertes, all involve mingled success and failure on both sides.

In a curious way the situations of protagonist and antagonist parallel each other, for each seeks a sure ground for action, contemplates what action should be taken once the ground is established, with the hampering proviso that certain consequences must be averted; each, moreover, is at certain points in possession of knowledge which the other is unaware that he possesses; and, as we just saw, each by his actions produces results both more and less than those looked for. The whole plot, were we to exhibit it in detail, would be seen to be one of extreme complexity; were it fully represented on stage, the play would perhaps be twice its present length.

But Shakespeare does not choose so to represent it; indeed, his extreme abridgment of it in his representation has been at the bottom of many problems of interpretation. We have already observed that Hamlet's physical antics as a madman have been suppressed – for, among other reasons, the very good one that they would have tended to endanger his tragic stature, perhaps even convert him into a comic figure. But many other things are suppressed. What happened – aside from Hamlet's "going mad" – in the interval between Acts I and II? What were Hamlet's thoughts and feelings, what were the reactions of others in that period? What led Hamlet to suspect that Rosencrantz and Guildenstern were sent for? What, step by step, produced his increasing distrust of them? Did they betray his selection of the play and his writing of a speech to Claudius? At what point did Hamlet take Horatio into his full confidence? How and when did Hamlet gain knowledge of

the projected voyage to England and the "letters seal'd?" Etc., etc.
Not all of this is important; some of it undoubtedly is. But, given full representation of the plot, the melodramatic elements would have swamped the more serious ones. With the internal obstacles of thought and passion obscured — for both Hamlet and Claudius labor against internal as well as external obstacles — the play would have turned into a mere adventure story. It bears some resemblance, in fact, to *The Mark of Zorro,* for Zorro also assumes a pose to disguise his real powers and purposes. Shakespeare, however, forewent the superficial excitements of a savage contest to study the issues, problems, and passions which underlie action. In so doing, he gave his play tragic dimension.

JAMES H. CLANCY

HEDDA GABLER: POETRY IN ACTION AND IN OBJECT

How easy is a bush supposed a bear!

Or so it may be supposed in Shakespeare's *The Winter's Tale*; indeed, in all major examples of theatre art – the actual becomes the virtual, the real object is transformed in the imagination.

If such a metamorphosis is one of the accomplishments of the theatrical poet, critical judgment has paid it little attention. This is especially true in that great period of "realistic" drama climaxed by the major prose works of Ibsen. Here the major critical approaches have been ideational (philosophical, sociological, psychological) and not until recently have we had the beginnings of a criticism that places specific emphasis upon the physical attributes of Ibsen's plays as a contribution to their poetic configuration.

Brian Johnston, in his essay on "The Metaphoric Structure of *The Wild Duck*", notes that "With a less suggestive, less richly metaphoric language at his command than Shakespeare, Ibsen yet arrived at a Shakespearean complexity and depth supplementing verbal metaphors with visual metaphors."[1] This brilliant *aperçu* is, unfortunately, not developed and the rest of the essay, as with most of the product of the metaphoric-symbolic school, spends itself upon the sea of myth and generic symbol that links this play (and how much else!) to the central Western European experience. It is as if we were to explicate Solness by a demonstration of his descent from Adam and Eve.

This use of the metaphor as a critical apparatus is not so much mistaken as it is misleading. Rather than distinguishing the work in hand by its particularity, it generalizes it until the work is apt to become featureless. It is a criticism of reduction rather than a criticism of distinction. It leads us away rather than in.

The renewed critical interest in Ibsen, welcome after the dry years, suffers from this suggested lack of specificity, due in part, no doubt, to the fact that the theatre, as an art form *sui generis*, has been little

[1] *Contemporary Approaches to Ibsen* (Oslo, 1965), 73.

examined. Its verbal and ideational patterns have been combed for meaning and suggestion, but a method of examining its whole form, which includes the use and import of space and object, has yet to be thoroughly worked out.

This is clear when such a critic as M. C. Bradbrook notes that Ibsen, after writing *Brand*, gave up poetry: "The world gained a dramatist, but Norway lost a poet."[2] This is true, however, only in one sense, and that a most literal one. The dramatic poems *Peer Gynt* and *Brand* become in time the dramas *Rosmersholm* and *Hedda Gabler*, where the full theatrical language is used to create a poetry of the theatre.

In this move to abandon poetic language in order more fully to write a modern poetic drama, Ibsen was quietly moving in the direction more flamboyantly exploited by his brilliant and erratic contemporary Strindberg. Both developed the use of the non-verbal elements of the theatre to create an atmosphere of meaning and a sensed but not fully explicable vitality. In this they were contributing to the revolt that took place in the later part of the nineteenth century against a reliance upon the discursive and descriptive power of language that had dominated literature and serious drama since the Age of Reason. The result of this revolt is clearly seen today in the more rarefied branches of science where language is no longer expressive of the higher rational functions. It is also seen in the art forms that utilize language, where language's discursive tendencies have made it more and more suspect for its failure to convey the subterranean forces that shape so many aspects of man.

The theatre, frequently the most conservative because the most truly vulgar of all the art forms, has naturally participated in this shift away from a complete dependency upon verbalization. Despite the efforts of such diverse literary talents as von Hoffmansthal, Eliot, Lowell and others, the chief aesthetic accomplishment of the modern theatre has been to realize a poetry which employs language only as one of many means. In doing so, what it has lost as literature it has gained as art. In attempting to recreate its own poetic, the modern theatre agrees with Edwin Arlington Robinson's statement that "poetry is language that tells us . . . something that cannot be said". The definition needs to be qualified only by the addition that the language of the theatre is composed of more than words, that its vocabulary and its syntax include silence as well as sound, reason as well as the irrational, movement, stillness, darkness, light, color, pattern, action and object: all of the multifarious effects of sense and mind that play upon the human imagi-

[2] *Ibsen the Norwegian* (London, 1948), 10.

nation and allow it to create an essential, a virtual act.

To ally Ibsen with such a definition may seem perverse, and indeed would be were the intention to prove the Norwegian a primitive Artaud and to establish a direct line of descent from *Hedda Gabler* to *The Royal Hunt of the Sun*. Ibsen was not an advocate of Total Theatre, though in developing the non-verbal poetry in his middle plays he participated in the movement that has led to the concept of theatrical totality.

A brief examination of the spatial and object import of *Hedda Gabler* may be suggestive here and serve as an indication of the kind of examination of theatre pieces that would be useful in order to build up a body of material that might serve to establish a more precise vocabulary for dramatic criticism.

I will discuss first the physical environment inside of which the play circulates: the scenic arrangement suggested by Ibsen which controls the physical action of the play. To do this we must first look at Ibsen's description of the setting as it prefaces the opening of Act One (in Eva LeGalliene's translation):

A large handsomely furnished drawing room, decorated in dark colors. In the back wall a wide opening with portieres that are drawn back. This opening leads to a smaller room decorated in the same style as the drawing room. In the right-hand wall of the front room is a folding door leading to the hall. In the wall opposite, on the left, a glass door, its hangings also drawn back. Through the panes can be seen part of a veranda and trees in autumn foliage.

Then follows a description of the placement of most of the furniture. For our purposes we will ignore the famous stove and note only the piano placed "above the glass door". Again back to Ibsen's description:

Against the back wall of the inner room a sofa, a table, and a couple of chairs. Above the sofa hangs the portrait of a handsome elderly man in the uniform of a general.

To summarize and repeat: the major features of the physical setting are a large room with folding doors in the right wall leading to the hall, a glass door in the left wall leading to the garden, and an inner room opening through an arch in the back wall, this room large enough to have a sofa against its back wall with a portrait of "a handsome elderly man in the uniform of a general" hanging directly over it.

Ibsen's stage directions for the use of this setting are not of the novelistic nature that were to be popularized later by such writers as

Barrie and Shaw, but his sparing use of brief but specific directions may perhaps be taken as an indication of their importance. Only the most vital placements and movements are recorded by the author.

First let us note that the door to the hallway and thus to the "front door" of the house is, for our purposes, blocked. It is used by everyone in the play; everyone, significantly, but Hedda. She uses the door in the right wall only once: to escort Thea Elvsted to the front door. All the other major characters use the door to the hall as a means of entering or leaving the house. For them it is a normal exit to the world that lies outside Secretary Falk's Villa. Its very normality bars its use by Hedda. The one time that she uses it is to accompany Thea to that outer door which Thea may use but which Hedda, once she is secreted within the cave she has made for herself, is never to broach. No other significant direction is given concerning the use of the door in the right wall.

Ibsen's manipulation of the other major features of the setting is more detailed. Here he demands positive actions by Hedda rather than her meaningful but negative reaction to the hall door.

First let us turn our attention to the "wide opening" in the back wall and the inner room to which it gives access. We note that Jörgen Tesman's initial appearance is to the *"inner room from the right"*. Opposed to this, Hedda, when she first appears, *"enters from the left through the inner room"*. As we check through the following action we will see that in the inner room Tesman always uses the right entrance (or exit), Hedda always uses the left entrance (or exit) and she, except for one notable exception, is the only one to use the left exit. Between these two entrances, you will remember, hangs the picture *"of a handsome elderly man in the uniform of a general"*: General Gabler, the father, the owner of the pistols.

At the end of Act One this physical meaning is summarized: Jörgen has failed in his expectations of an immediate appointment; Hedda sees the prospects for which she married Jörgen failing and she says, as she *"walks about the room"*:

Hedda: Well, at least I have one thing to amuse myself with.
Tesman (*Beaming*): Thank heaven for that. What is it, Hedda, eh?
Hedda   (*At center opening – looks at him with suppressed scorn*): My pistols, Jörgen.
Tesman: Your pistols!
Hedda   (*With cold eyes*): General Gabler's pistols. (*She goes out through the inner room to the left.*)

Tesman follows her only to the center opening, eyed by the picture under which Hedda has been standing; as he calls after her he does not dare enter the territory that Ibsen has marked as Hedda's own.

Other uses of the inner room and of the area into which Hedda retires reinforce this physical image of the cave (or of the womb, if one wishes to be more Freudian). The piano (Hedda's "old piano") which we noted as part of Ibsen's original setting, has been removed by the second act to the "inner room": Hedda must secrete within her own area those things which she identifies as part of her private life.

It should also be noted that Eilert Lövberg's first temptation comes from the inner room: when Hedda makes arrangements for the entertainment of Eilert, Judge Brack and Jörgen, she talks to the servant Berte "*in a whisper and points to the inner room*". Berte arranges the glasses and decanter in the inner room, and like Lady Macbeth to Duncan, Hedda points to the inner room and invites Eilert to join the other men there for the final temptation. The visual image of Brack and Tesman in the inner room, at the very entrance to Hedda's mystery, while Hedda titillates the sensibilities of Eilert outside the cave is another summary statement of the meaning of the play in what might be termed physical poetry.

Again: at the end of Act Two, Hedda "*almost drags Mrs. Elvsted toward the center opening*". She is assimilating Thea's relationship with Eilert here; doing with Thea in excitement what she always desired but never permitted Eilert to do to her in those hushed and palpitating evenings Hedda spent with him in the past. When, in Act Three, she sends Thea to sleep in her bedroom – the only character, remember, other than Hedda herself who exits left from the inner room – we have a concise and evocative physical statement of Hedda's perverse sexual relationship with Eilert.

The image of the cave, so briefly sketched above, does not bear its complete meaning, however, until it is seen as an antithesis to another physical image, the glass door in the left wall of the set. Let us note how Ibsen uses this door.

In Act One, Aunt Julie has opened the door wide shortly after her entrance. When Hedda enters, she wants the curtain drawn across it because it lets in "*a whole flood of sunshine*". Later in the act, when Jörgen suggests that Aunt Julie look at Hedda to see how she has "filled out" and states that though this development may not be apparent to Aunt Julie he has "certain opportunities" to note more accurately, Ibsen says that Hedda "*stands at the glass door*" as she impatiently says, "You have no opportunities at all, Jörgen –".

When Miss Tesman leaves, promising not to let a day pass without seeing her, Hedda "*flings back the curtains of the glass door and stands gazing out*".

At the beginning of Act Two, Hedda is discovered at the glass door, loading a pistol, which she shoots in the direction of Judge Brack as he comes toward the house through the garden.

Later in the act, when Jörgen brings up the subject of Aunt Julie, Hedda bitterly comments: "Oh, those eternal aunts!" Jörgen asks her what she has said and Ibsen notes that when she replies "Nothing – nothing – nothing" she is "*Going to the glass door*".

In Act Two, when Judge Brack presses Hedda about the possibility that she may have a child, the image of the door and the cave are brought together. Judge Brack has asked Hedda, "Why should you deliberately turn away from duties –?" and Hedda "*At the glass door*", has answered "Be quiet, I tell you! I sometimes think there's only one thing in this world I'm really fitted for." The Judge comes "*nearer to her*" and says, "What's that, if I may ask?" And Hedda, "*looking out*" the glass door (for freedom, for escape, for release?) replies: "Boring myself to death! Now you know it. (*Turns, looks toward the inner room, and laughs*) Ah! I thought so – here comes the professor!" Carefully Ibsen notes that Jörgen "*enters from the right through the inner room*". Jörgen comes from Hedda's area, but not from that final labyrinthine recess into which no one but a distorted mirror image of Eilert Lövborg is allowed to penetrate. The cave and the door have been fully juxtaposed.

Other instances of Ibsen's use of the glass door could be noted; perhaps only one more is necessary. At the beginning of the last act, Hedda is seen pacing back and forth in the dark room. She "*goes up into the inner room and off left. A few chords are heard on the piano*". When she re-enters the room she "*goes to the glass door, pulls the curtains aside a little and peers out into the darkness*". Some part of us may recall that at the opening of the first act we had seen through the same door morning light and autumn foliage. Quite literally, by the last act, although she has repeatedly gone to the window in moments of stress, there is no escape for Hedda except into darkness. And this may not be into the literal night that lies outside the glass door. The intervening acts have shown us that this is the entrance of Judge Brack when he wishes to demonstrate his intimacy with the Tesman household. Hedda's only escape that way is through the projectile flight of a bullet, not aimed at removing the Judge, but ejected in an emotional spasm of erotic frustration.

In this brief account of the physical setting Ibsen gives to *Hedda Gabler* and of some of the uses that he makes of it, I hope enough has been suggested to make it evident that Ibsen's physical construct is in itself one of the major poetic images of the play, is, in fact, a visual metaphor of one aspect of the play. The physical action that this construct enforces (if his stage directions are respected) constantly presents differing refractions of this central image. The cave and the door are never forced upon our attention as they have been in this paper, but they manage through an unconscious pressure to distill and at the same time extend the realistic surface of the play and thus be two of the non-verbal devices that help give *Hedda Gabler* its poetic form.

Lest, however, it seem that this interpretation be only another effort to apply a diluted Freudianism to a major playwright, another form of poetic device used by Ibsen should be noted. The recessive character of Hedda's cave cannot help but invite sexual interpretations, for this is one of the major themes of the play as presented for rational consideration through the dialogue. Ibsen's use of a physical object to underscore treatment rather than theme presents him as a theatre poet in a somewhat different light.

In the last act of the play, when Tesman and Mrs. Elvsted are speculating about how they might save Eilert's book now that both he and his manuscript have been destroyed, Thea suddenly remembers a fact of vital importance. As Ibsen specifies, she *"searches in the pocket of her dress"* as she remarks: "Look! I have kept all the notes he used to dictate from –". She then hands Tesman *"a bundle of scraps of paper"*.

This object, this property introduced late in the play near what might appear to be its tragic climax, is as clear an example of an object distilling the essence of the treatment of a play as the physical setting already noted is an example of the distillation of one of the play's major thematic movements.

As with the cave, Eilert's notes have their antithesis. Upon Tesman's initial appearance in the first act he is seen to be carrying an empty suitcase, but one which he explains had been full of notes for his work. Jörgen, who writes upon such subjects as the Domestic Industries of Brabant during the Middle Ages, needs a suitcase to carry his notes. Eilert, whose first book was an outline of civilization and whose new book deals with the Future (in two parts: the civilizing forces of the future; a forecast of probable lines of development!), needs only the number of notes that may without notice be carried in a lady's pocket! The contrast of the two methods of work is a neat demonstration of comparative psychology on Ibsen's part, but the introduction of Eilert's actual notes at the time that Ibsen has Thea produce them goes far beyond this. A saturnine, even comic, atmosphere is injected into the increasing seriousness of the situation. With that bundle of notes, Ibsen seems to say, either the Future or Eilert's book is pretty thin.

William Archer wrote of the improbability of Thea's having these notes with her at the time, but the absurdity lies in the actual physical presence of the notes themselves. It is not psychologically improbable that Thea would have kept with her Eilert's "*bundle of scraps of paper*": many cling to fetishes of a much odder sort. Ibsen introduces the notes for us to *see*; our eye discovers their absurd physical insufficiency. Their existential presence is, in terms of the theatre, a poetic device of the first order. As with most such devices it leads us in more than one direction: either Eilert's book was a windy expansion of very little; or else it was a poetic prophecy and Tesman and Thea are the last who could reconstruct it. Their futile afflatus is nowhere more strongly and more acidly marked.

If a defense of such an interpretation of Eilert's notes is needed, it may be found in the jottings that Ibsen entered in his notebook shortly before the first draft of his play was made.[3] I will cite only two of these jotted memoranda. In the first, Ibsen clearly states his attitude (at least at the time of the jotting) toward the possibility of Jörgen and Thea rewriting Eilert's book:

Neither he nor Mrs. Elvsted understand the point. Tesman reads in the manuscript that was left behind about "the two ideals". Mrs. Elvsted can't explain to him what E. L. meant. Then comes the burlesque note: both T. and Mrs. E. are going to devote their future lives to interpreting the mystery.

It is evident that the idea of the comic is central in Ibsen's mind as he considers this episode. He has not yet, however, made it poetic. One further citation will demonstrate how the craftsman might work who wishes to make this point rationally clear. The following jotting is mainly in the form of a speech written out for Hedda to say in the fifth act:

Hedda: How hugely comic it is that those two harmless people, Tesman and Mrs. E., should try to put the pieces together for a

---

[3] "Notes for *Hedda Gabler*", translated by Evert Sprinchorn and A. G. Chater, in *The Modern Theatre*, edited by Robert W. Corrigan (New York, 1964).

> monument to E. L. The man who deeply despised the whole business –.

Now skip to the play as written. Hedda's proposed speech is gone and with it the somewhat dogmatic precision with which it presents Ibsen's attitude towards his invention. Instead, the theatrical poet presents to our sight *"a bundle of scraps of paper"*. Robinson's "something that cannot be said" has been expressed by a theatrical object that has two of the chief characteristics of the poetic: concision and extension. What Ibsen's attitude has lost in rational clarity and precision it has gained in expansion and in depth. For a rhetorical device of language, Ibsen has substituted a poetic device inherent in the theatrical form. He has moved in a direction increasingly followed in the modern theatre and apotheosized in Bert Brecht's poem, "Weigel's Props".

Ibsen's use of space to shape meaningful action and his use of objects to essentialize an attitude are not, of course, the whole of his poetic method, but in his so-called realistic plays they are two major devices that he learned to use in a masterful fashion and that justify his claim, made throughout his lifetime, that he had always been and always would be a poet. His greatest poems were the plays of his central period, when he curtailed the poetic language of his youth to develop the full diapason of the theatrical instrument.

SOME NOTES ON MUSIC AND DRAMA

1.

For a number of years now I have been writing and helping produce plays here and there through the land dealing with the life of the American people – sometimes the folk life but most often having to do with leading characters and events important in the history of our nation. Nearly all of these plays have been produced in outdoor amphitheatres built especially for their staging – for instance, the Waterside Theatre on Roanoke Island, North Carolina, for *The Lost Colony*, the Lake Matoaka Amphitheatre in Williamsburg, Virginia, for *The Common Glory*, the Old Kentucky Home Amphitheatre at Bardstown, Kentucky, for *The Stephen Foster Story*, the Pioneer Amphitheatre in Palo Duro Canyon for the play *Texas*, the Tuscawaras Valley Amphitheatre in Ohio for *Trumpet in the Land*, and so on. (The majority of these plays happily have succeeded and have continued summer season after summer season through the years. *The Lost Colony* is now in its 30th year, *The Common Glory* in its 23rd.)

In working at these "symphonic dramas", as I finally named them, I found myself again and again having to call on every phase and facet, every ingredient of theatre art in order to put my storyline across in full amplitude and expressiveness – dialogue, poetry, scene design, sound, dance, costuming, pantomine, mental speech, film, masks, choreography, song, puppetry even, and especially lighting, and more especially music.

In the process of these workings I did a great deal of thinking and searching and reading about the theatre as an art creation, as a sensitized, integrated whole, if you will, or, as Richard Wagner, Max Reinhardt, Adolphe Appia, Gordon Craig and others considered and tried to envisage it, a *Gesamtkunstwerk* – a total art work.

2.

Years and years ago – about the time I began writing plays in earnest – I had the good fortune of using up two Guggenheim Fellowships in

Europe studying theatre there. My study was mostly in Germany which at that time was the leading theatre country on the continent, although I did some study in France especially as to Paul Claudel. I saw the work of Erwin Piscator, Max Reinhardt, the salient and imaginative Gordon Craig, the Russian director Alexis Granowsky, and many others. Of them all Granowsky impressed me most. He had just brought his Jewish Moscow State Theatre troupe from Russia to Berlin for a short season. His plays were of Jewish folk life, and all of them were saturated with music.

I was in the full fervor of writing American folk plays at the time and had found myself again and again using folk tunes in these pieces, most of them one-act, and so I was especially interested in the way Granowsky used native music in his dramas. Through a friend I got in touch with him and arranged a meeting. The night before he and I got together I had seen his music drama *Two Hundred Thousand*, a play dealing with a humble Jewish citizen who had won 200,000 rubles in a lottery and with the newfound wealth cut a real splurge and was carried away for a while in public fervor and adulation before he relapsed to his former state of humility and poverty.

I expressed my enthusiasm to Granowsky for his work, and he was pleased. I guess he needed to have some praise from anybody he could, for his audiences had been very small. In fact, at one of his music-drama showings I counted only thirty-four people in the auditorium. Folklore apparently was not appreciated by the German theatregoers at that time, or maybe already there was brewing some anti-Semitic feeling in the city.

"This is the kind of music drama, Herr Granowsky," I said, "that I have been looking for."

"Yes," he said in his careful English, "I think the musical play offers greater opportunity for the theatre artist than any other. Actually these folk pieces I have been producing are not music dramas in the sense that, say, Richard Wagner used the term or even Adolphe Appia described in his tone-word-drama (*Wort-Tondrama*). They are plays with music. Someday," he went on, "somebody will perhaps hit on the creation of the true music-drama, a drama in which music is of its soul and essence even as words, the dialogue, the action, are of it."

And then we talked about the use of musicalized pantomine, of sound effects, of masks and so on. But constantly the word "music" popped up.

"By the use of music," he said, "all sorts of conventions and needs which otherwise might slow up the story, obstruct action or even cause a production to tend toward disintegration can be avoided. Shortcuts in scenery, in properties and staging methods can be obtained. It is easier to go straight to the heart of your story, to reach its inner expressive nature and even suggested symbolism, its most vital meaning, with music. That is, if you use the right kind of music. You say you liked my production of *Two Hundred Thousand?*"

"Very much," I said, "and tonight I am going to see your *Travels of Benjamin the Third.*"

"Yes, it too is in the same style as the *Two Hundred Thousand*, and my other folk dramas with music. Have you anything like this in America?"

"No, we haven't yet," I said.

And then he went on to say that if ever he was forced to leave Russia, he would like to go to America and there begin his theatre career all over again. (Later he had to leave Russia but he retired to Paris where he died.)

"Of all the nations on earth," he said, "the United States is richest in dramatic materials, in subject matter for plays. Yours is a land of boundless energy and color and imagination, of emotions, of flaring impudence, yes. In short, yours is the most creative nation on the globe. I know the names of a number of American playwrights – O'Neill, Anderson, Sherwood, Howard, Rice, Barry. Do any of them make any great use of music?"

"No, they don't."

"Too bad. You have a lot of native music, don't you – folk music, among your people, especially among your Negroes?"

"Yes, yes, plenty."

"Have you used music in any of your plays?"

"Yes, in nearly all of them – but only simple folk tunes, some folk dances, old hymns. But so far I have never tried my hand at a full-length drama with music."

"You should, you should," he said with some emphasis. "I have often wondered," he went on, "why your country has never produced a theatre of the Negro people. Surely you could create a great musical dramatic art in the United States from them, with them. These most gifted people are full of music. I have been able to get several published volumes of their spirituals and folksongs. What a rich storehouse!"

"A few small experiments are being made in Negro drama," I replied, "in Harlem, in Cleveland, in Chicago, but only small experiments. Nothing big has yet been done."

"Let us hope in time there will be," he said rising to conclude our interview.

"Yes, let us hope," I said.

.3.

On my return home from Europe I had to go to Hollywood to make some money to pay off my theatre-studying debts and to provide for my family, and in the movies which I wrote I tried to use as much music – and native music at that – as I could. I kept thinking of the time when I might do a full-length play, preferably of the Negro people, in which I could work out a solid theory about the relation of music to drama and put it into practice.

In between Hollywood stints I finally got a play written[1] about a Negro section of the little town, Chapel Hill, North Carolina, in which I lived. In trying to tell the story of these people I felt from the beginning the full power and richness of the music with which they themselves were filled, and I poured it into my story. I had nearly one hundred characters in my play, for I was intent on a sort of epic account of a people, of a race, with a few main characters highlighted in and along the center of the storyline, they being the main bearers of the narrative. And as I worked away, weaving and interweaving these characters onward, bringing them onto the stage and moving them away, I felt myself much like a composer creating a score for, say, some one hundred instruments, or even as a conductor directing the orchestra which played the composition after it was written. And as I say, there was this music, this music – folk songs, hymn singing, love ditties, dance pieces and the like – the vibrant heartbeat music of a people.

I sent the script with its written-out melodies to my agent in New York, and he got it sold to a producer. This producer came down to Chapel Hill and studied the Negro village for atmosphere and stage-setting. Then time went by. No production. The producer's option lapsed. Another man bought it. The same story. Finally Margaret Hewes, the mother of the drama critic Henry Hewes of *The Saturday Review*, bought the play and produced it in 1934 at the Cort Theatre

---

[1]   The play to which Mr. Green refers is *Roll, Sweet Chariot*, "a series of dramatic episodes acted against a background of choral and orchestral music". [Editor's note.]

in New York on Forty-eight Street. By the time of the opening I had drenched the piece with music, securing Dolphe Martin, a talented composer, to amplify the native melodies and give them voices spilling down even into the orchestra pit. We put eighteen singers there, with timpani and a clarinet framing them, as it were, and all intoned vocables as background harmony and mood evocation for the action on the stage.

We had a resounding flop. I had to draw out of the bank what little Hollywood money I had left to help pay off the salaries of the loyal Negro actors.

And that was that.

4.

In 1937 I had the chance again to try out the use of music in drama far away from Broadway, and this time in a much more auspicious environment. With the help of the Federal Theatre and its dynamic director, Hallie Flanagan, we were able to open *The Lost Colony* on Roanoke Island in an outdoor theatre built by CCC Camp boys and credulous neighbors. In this play I got nearer to the dream of true music-drama than I had before. Here the music not only was interwoven with the history and action, but sometimes in its own self-expressiveness it helped to provoke story movement and action. We had wonderful musical instruments in both the chorus of singers and in the sonorous cathedral-like organ, hidden away among the trees, and sometimes these would grieve over some part of the tragedy which was appearing on the stage or give forth in jollity when jollity was the doing there. For instance, in a little scene where the comic character, Old Tom, flirts water from a bucket in teasing drops at his Indian squaw-love, the theatre music backed up each hand-flirt with a punching liquid note, and the effect was hilarious and charming. So it was that the play, the story throughout, received a greater resonance as well as a greater intensity of meaning and emotion by the use of music.

Gradually I began to see, or thought I saw, the coming actualization of the true theatre art work, the veritable *Gesamtkuntswerk* – a drama in which not only the music was married in a true copulation with the word (the syllable, the gesture, the act) but the word married with it, each becoming its intenser and purer dramatic self because of the marriage.

For, see how the note makes the word glow, fires it with a new radiance, a loveliness beyond what it is in its natural self. Behold there, music and its power making for theatre entrancement in all things – in all elements of the stage and staging. For music is the natural poetry sounding in the world – the first, the most direct, the pure emotional art of man's creative life – art in which each particularization of itself brings a universal effect and significance. Is it not so? Or as Hegel puts it, "Music is the one art which speaks directly to the soul."

Through music, then, we can change the prosiness of our daily life, change it into a provenance of beauty. It is not for nothing that, say, soft soothing music is provided in restaurants for the factual business of chewing and swallowing food, or that a brass band can fire up the whole landscape with glee and high spirits at a football game, or military music can send the patriotism and saber-drawing of the listeners to heights of frenzy.

And so it is that when this great art is added to, is wedded in and of drama, a new fire and fervor, a new intensity and beauty result.

5.

Now in opera as everybody knows, the word, the libretto, plays second place to the note, to the music, and the actor is absorbed into the singer – just as in Wagner's operas, for all of that great man's contention of equality and balance, the singer is enslaved to and overpowered by the orchestra.

The action in an opera is primarily action in music, musical action. Here the conflict of wills – the luring and rebuffing, the yearning and the hating, the hoping and lamenting – all is done essentially in music and with just enough of storyline continuity and statement in the libretto to take care of the narrative needs and demands of the audience.

Consider the situation and the words flowing from the scene in Mozart's *Don Giovanni* where the Don sets out to seduce flighty and feminine and adorable little Zerlina. The love as expressed here musically in the duet *La ci darem la mano* is incomparable, whatever the words used. The two voices caressing each other in the melody, drawing apart, yielding to each other, even for a moment intertwining, ever increasing the warmth of the courtship, give expression to masculine ardor and female surrender in terms – to use a cliché – impossible in any art other than music. I think so.

And though opera can be considered drama carried to musical excess, the principle involved is the same. It is a matter of balance, of
proportion, of musical accord in the play.

It is this added loveliness, this matchless intensity that music can
bring to drama when properly used. Think but for a moment too of
those delicious, even sublime, bits in Shakespeare when the lyric word
and the action rise emotionally until they pass into music, into melody
– little Ophelia mad and singing her song or Desdemona her willow
lament. Then the heart of the listener, of the spectator, overflows.
Without music there would not be this overflowing.

And so it is.

In an address given at Yale University many years ago the great
French dramatist Paul Claudel discussed the use of music in drama –
and he made great use of music in all of his huge and over-written
plays – and gave an illustration which is to the point here. There is a
scene in his fine play, *The Tidings Brought to Mary* (*L'Annonce Faite
à Marie*) in which the father of the family, preparing to set off on a
long journey, breaks bread for the last time with his children and his
servants gathered around the table. In the first production of the play,
Claudel reports, the scene was dead. He felt a "shudder run along" his
spine, he said, as if he had heard a false note. The director M. Gemier,
"prompted by his vast dramatic experience did not hesitate a moment.
'We must have some music,' he exclaimed. They set going a glockenspiel
of some sort," Claudel said, "and the scene passed off triumphantly,
the sound of the bells at once conferring upon it the atmosphere, the
ambience, the dignity and remoteness which the words alone in their
thinness and bareness were unable to provide. And the cinema of course
offers many instances of the same kind. Any pantomine or dumbshow
is simply impossible without music." So spoke Paul Claudel.

6.

I remember as a young man going to a showing of the silent motion
picture *The Birth of a Nation* – a landmark piece in the history of the
movies. The film had such an effect on the audience that I recall it
vividly to this day.

The theatre was crowded when I got there, but I finally managed
to get a seat in the balcony. The lights went down, the orchestra of
some twelve or fifteen pieces in the pit began to play the score written

for the story. Then things began to happen. Soon there on the screen in front of our eyes not more than twenty yards away we saw brave armies fighting as only the brave can fight. We heard the roar of cannon in the timpani, the neighing of horses in the sound effects, saw the bleeding and the dying, the fluttering of flags and banners held aloft by dedicated and dying hands, and all the while the beat and surge of the orchestra whipped our souls fiercely and fervently along.

Now like a breath the tumult and the turmoil are gone, the rumble and cannonading die out, and a beautiful vision entrances us, the music announcing it, bringing it on. There stands the hero, the dauntless and without-reproach Little Colonel and his exquisite Southern sweetheart saying a fond farewell, and the music of the violins proclaims the eternal fidelity, the piteousness of their love.

Then with a flick the scene has changed again, and we see the dark sliding figure of the villain prowling around a vine-clad cottage. And the evil of his nature and his dire intent are intensified for us in the notes of the bassoons and the low vibrato of the drumstick against the drumhead.

So the story went on unfolding in dumbshow, captions and musical sound, telling the hopes, the loves, and the dangers that beset these our heroic characters. The audience sat one moment in breathless anxiety, another moment it was applauding the short triumph of virtue, innocence and honor. And when at last the robed and wind-blown figure of the Ku Klux Klansman on his horse showed in a medium close-up on a hill and the bugle in the orchestra cried out with its high note that a stern and powerful force of righteousness was risen to defend the innocent ones from all villains of whatsoever creed, color or circumstance, a frenzy ran among the audience like fire among wintry broomstraw. There were yells and shouts, clenching of fists, and loud unashamed oaths.

One woman directly in front of me sprang up in a holyroller hysteria and screamed, "Kill 'em! Kill 'em!" and then like a lady in a play or protracted gospel camp-meeting fell with a fainting thud to the floor. The ushers hurried up and carried her out, but even as they went, she opened her recovering eyes and looked longingly back toward the screen. . . .

Not until years later did I realize that without the bugle note the lady would not have fainted. It was then I began to have my first understanding of the place of music in drama.

SAM SMILEY

THOUGHT AS PLOT IN DIDACTIC DRAMA

One of the perennial questions asked about art is whether it should teach or give pleasure. Proponents of the didactic viewpoint, taking their cue perhaps from Plato or Jean-Paul Sartre, argue that art should be used to educate, arouse, or convince. Their opponents claim, perhaps with supporting quotations from Aristotle or T. S. Eliot, that the best art is an end in itself. In our own age of crisis and confrontation, playwrights and others interested in formulative principles of drama are again concerned with the problems of using theatre for purposes other than purely aesthetic ones.

A comparison of plays by Albert Camus, LeRoi Jones, or Max Frisch with plays by Tennessee Williams, Neil Simon, or Harold Pinter can reveal that some excellent contemporary dramas have a dominantly rhetorical purpose while others have a primarily imitative focus. *The Just Assassins* by Camus and *The Chinese Wall* by Frisch are clearly didactic plays; *A Streetcar Named Desire* by Williams and *The Homecoming* by Pinter are certainly mimetic plays. Among contemporary dramas, then, it is possible to identify some as persuasive, or instrumental, and others as more purely aesthetic, or non-instrumental.

In this second half of the twentieth century, with its social unrest and political turmoil, drama is once again, as in so many ages of the past, being used as a weapon. The plays of Rolf Hochhuth and Peter Weiss, for example, attest that effective drama can be made on the basis of a didactic intent. Because of the renewal of social concern among contemporary theatre artists and because of the increasing incidence of ideological commitment on the part of dramatists, it may be valuable to consider some of the significant principles applicable to didactic plays, and to define the didactic as a distinct species of dramatic art.

Although studies of the inherent nature of mimetic dramas abound, few analyses indeed have been made of the structural nature of didactic dramas. Several studies, for instance, treat didactic poems and novels, such as those of Spenser, Dante, Bunyan, and Sartre. There are even good structural studies of the plays of certain great playwrights who occasionally or frequently wrote didactically – e.g., Euripides, Shaw, and Brecht. These latter studies, however, do not attempt to identify the nature of didactic drama *per se*. Although some of them contain internal criticism of plays, they usually deal more with an individual author's subject matter, his social and psychological motivations, his style of expression, or his attitudes toward theatrical aesthetics. A few critics have written brief pieces about didactic drama as articles or in books that treat other subjects. R. S. Crane has briefly noted that in spite of the current vogue for didactic forms in lyric, novel, and drama our "resources for dealing with the problems raised by such works in other than a casual and undiscriminating way are still very meager", and he suggested that the causal method of analysis be applied to such new species as are emerging.[1] In an article about the dramaturgy of Brecht and Camus, James Clancy has written that today's dramatists are writing "a new drama of ideas" to show man as "the instrument rather than the product of change".[2] Eric Bentley has contributed to the growing body of material about didacticism with his essay defining the theatre of commitment and discussing what he calls activist, or polemical, drama.[3] Elder Olson has made an important contribution, too, by distinguishing mimetic poetry and didactic poetry as two broad species of verbal art.[4] In a discussion of unity and probability in drama, Hubert Heffner has stated that "certain modern didactic plays may be largely or wholly unified only in terms of thought".[5]

The utilization of thought is, in fact, the crucial matter in distinguishing a didactic drama from a mimetic one. In a mimetic drama – such as Shakespeare's *King Lear* or Pinter's *The Birthday Party* – *action as plot* is the controlling element of the play. Such a play's basic principle of unity is action, a series of human changes that form the core of the drama itself. A playwright admits to a mimetic play all other elements – character, thought, diction, melody, and spectacle – only

---

[1] R. S. Crane, ed., Introduction, *Critics and Criticism: Ancient and Modern* (Chicago, 1952), 18-21.
[2] James H. Clancy, "Beyond Despair: A New Drama of Ideas", *Essays in the Modern Drama*, ed. Morris Freedman (Boston, 1964), 173.
[3] Eric Bentley, "The Theatre of Commitment", in *The Theatre of Commitment: And Other Essays on Drama in Our Society* (New York, 1967), 190-231.
[4] Elder Olson, "William Empson, Contemporary Criticism, and Poetic Diction", and "A Dialogue on Symbolism", both in *Critics and Criticism*, 65-68 and 588-592.
[5] Hubert Heffner, *The Nature of Drama* (Boston, 1959), 343.

insofar as the action requires them for its beginning, middle, and end. In a didactic play, however, thought takes over as the controlling factor; it replaces action as the organizing element. *Thought as plot* furnishes the unity in such didactic plays as *Awake and Sing!* by Clifford Odets and *Blues for Mister Charlie* by James Baldwin. In other words, a mimetic drama focuses on and is controlled by a series of actions; a didactic drama, however, focuses on and is controlled by a complex of thought. This is not to say that a didactic drama cannot have action, character, diction, melody, and spectacle. Didactic dramas obviously contain events, characters, and words. But thought dominates all the other elements. Didactic drama is dianoetic, or thought-controlled.

This discussion requires that some attention be given to a definition of *thought* in order more clearly to distinguish how it operates in various kinds of plays. Thought can mean a power, an action, or a product. First, most human beings have the *power* to think, to reason, and to imagine. Second, when a person thinks, his mind initiates a *process* of recognition, recall, and formulation; as a rational action, thought is cogitation. Third, thought as a *product* is an idea; ideas can be intentions, plans, opinions, beliefs, or even abstract principles. Ideas can appear in the minds of human beings as sensations, as images, and as conceptions actually or potentially present to consciousness. Thought as a power can be measured; as an action it can be identified; but only as a product can it be concretely recorded in words. That thought can exist in these three ways – as power, action, or product – has special significance for how thought applies to drama.

A play does not have the human power of thought; a play is after all an object, not a human being. Even though characters in a play may be represented as having powers of reflection, they possess such powers only symbolically, or because of the actors performing them. In most plays, however, thought is an element that is material to character. In this guise, thought is sometimes defined as anything represented in a play that occurs inside the characters – including sensations, feelings, attitudes, desires, deliberations, and decisions. Thus, as a contributive element of drama, a definition of thought as action, or process, is the most appropriate. Characters often engage in the actions of feeling, considering, reasoning, or deciding; such actions reveal the natures of the characters and directly affect the course of events. Additionally, thought as product applies to most plays – in two ways. First, a play usually contains thoughts as products; such thoughts, or ideas, appear explicitly in the words of the characters or implicitly in

their physical actions. Also a play normally stimulates thoughts, or
ideas, as products in an audience; these are, of course, thoughts external
to the play itself.

There are important differences, then, between thought as an element
in a drama and thought as a power, a process, or a product associated
with, but external to, a play. Note the limitation of the terms *in a
drama*. The thoughts that a playwright has about a drama he is writing
are not necessarily identical with the thoughts that appear within that
drama itself. A playwright may or may not succeed at incorporating a
certain idea in his play. Nor are the thoughts that members of an
audience may conceive as a result, or in reaction to, a drama automatically the same as those the play actually contains. There are, therefore, three loci of thought in relation to drama – in the playwright, in
the play, and in the audience.

To understand thought in drama, one should realize that formulative
thoughts about a drama and interpretive thoughts stimulated by a
drama are not the same as the material or structural thoughts in a
drama. To differentiate the didactic play from the mimetic one, it is
important to distinguish between learning from drama and teaching by
drama. A person may learn from any drama, but only didactic drama
is created with the primary intent of teaching or persuading. The confusion of learning from a play and teaching by a play leads to a study
of the location and operation of thought in drama. To consider any
thought in relation to any particular drama is first to ask: What exactly
is the thought under consideration? And where does this thought truly
originate, in the mind of the beholder or in the play? When attempting
to understand any play, an observer must carefully identify the thoughts
that actually exist in the play, and not confuse them with thoughts that
a play may more fortuitously excite in himself or in an audience.

Also appropriate to an investigation of thought in drama are the
following definitions of *theme* and *thesis*. Although some critics of the
drama employ the word *theme* when writing about drama, too often it
has a vague or confusing meaning. The most precise and useful definition of theme in drama is as the subject matter of a play. Thus, the
theme of John Osborne's *Luther*, for example, is the life of Martin
Luther. Theme may also mean the topic of a play. But why not use the
word *topic* itself? Theme as topic is the definition that proves particularly confusing because the topic of a drama is an ideational area or a
problem, not a central thought or an idea. Thesis is less often misused.
A thesis in drama is a singular ideological proposition which a play

advances or illustrates. Unfortunately, some critics unjustly label many didactic plays as thesis plays, but only the most obvious and simplistic propaganda pieces are truly so. The best conceived plays of the didactic sort advance a thought complex rather than a single idea. Too often *theme* and *thesis* replace the more functional and specific words *topic, thought,* and *idea.*

Before proceeding further with the investigation of thought as plot in didactic drama, it will be useful briefly to consider the elements of plot and thought as they often occur in mimetic drama.

Plot in a mimetic drama is the organization of situations and events that comprise the action of the play. A playwright can arrange the materials of a drama and thus formulate a mimetic plot in an infinite variety of ways. Some mimetic plays contain strong stories – as does Williams' *A Streetcar Named Desire,* for example – at the hearts of their plots. Story is a special type of plot consisting of such elements as balance, disturbance, obstacles, crisis, climax, and resolution; although most plays contain some of these elements, only the plays that contain them all can properly be identified as having a story organization. Story is a particular kind of sequence of events and may or may not be identical with overall plot. Other plays feature such plot arrangements as a series of misunderstandings culminating in a discovery that corrects them (e.g., *Comedy of Errors* by Shakespeare), or a sequence of discoveries leading to a reversal (e.g., *Oedipus the King* by Sophocles), or a string of crises building to a climactic decision or catastrophe (e.g., *Ghosts* by Ibsen). Some mimetic plots consist of causally related events, as in Eugene O'Neill's *Beyond the Horizon*; others utilize loosely related episodes or even configurative, non-logical patterns or situations, as in Strindberg's *The Ghost Sonata.* Mimetic plots vary widely from such horizontally causal arrangements as the one in *Look Back in Anger* by John Osborne to the configurative and vertical organization in Samuel Beckett's *Waiting for Godot.* In all mimetic plots, however, the emphasis insofar as structure is concerned rests upon the action itself and upon the requisite characters as agents. Mimetic plots follow the action of human change.

Thought in mimetic drama stands as material to character and plot. This is not to say that the meanings any person may derive from a mimetic play are unimportant. The meaning gleaned from a mimetic play, however, usually varies from spectator to spectator. Thought operates as a working part of a mimetic play, while meaning occurs more in the spectator than in the play itself. More specifically, thought in mimetic drama may be defined as anything that goes on inside a character. All the sensations, feelings, ideas, and decisions of any character are actually the materials of that character and ultimately the motivating factors for his actions. Thought appears in a mimetic play in such details as reactions, soliloquies, arguments, deliberations, and moments of decision. But an entire play usually displays some overall thoughts as well. An entire mimetic play can be considered as one complete "speech" that "says something" as an idea to an audience. But the "something" that any mimetic plays "says" is not likely to be the same for any two people who hear and see it. The most important thing to note in this context is that thought in mimetic drama acts primarily as material to character and plot, and in this special sense it is subsidiary to them.

If plot in mimetic drama is organized action, and if thought in mimetic drama is material to character and plot, what then is different about plot and thought in didactic drama? An answer to this question is best discovered through an inductive examination of didactic plays themselves. A study of how didactic plays have actually been organized is more revealing than speculation about how they might or ought to be organized. All the following ideas about thought in didactic drama have come from the examination of a large number of didactic plays.

The controlling ideas chosen by playwrights for activist dramas are apparent in finished plays. The following four plays provide initial examples: *The Brig* by Kenneth Brown, *Viet Rock* by Megan Terry, *The Deputy* by Rolf Hochhuth, and *The Investigation* by Peter Weiss. The complex of thought within each such didactic play is not usually difficult to discover. The thought complex is bound to a dynamic and structural *line of intention*. In *The Brig*, the line of intention is to depict man's inhumanity to man, especially as encouraged by military and prison conditions. *Viet Rock* is an exhortation against war in general and against the Viet Nam war in particular. *The Deputy* is an accusation of Pope Pius XII for his allegedly inhumane position of neutrality in relation to the Nazi horror during World War II. *The Investigation* censures the evil of those who enacted atrocities in Nazi prison camps during the same war. The majority of didactic plays, in fact, follow one of these four lines of intention: to depict, to exhort, to accuse, or to censure.

Such functional verbs connect with the subjects of individual plays or with the actual ideas as stated by dialogue within plays at the time of climax and resolution. The key operative ideas act as the formal controls of the plays themselves. The four verbs mentioned above can describe both the process of formulation in the mind of a playwright and the formulative pattern in his completed play. A playwright who chooses to write didactically combines a persuasive intention with a certain subject in order to compound a thought complex; then he selects a series of events and a group of characters that will most effectively fulfill his intention and communicate the central thought. Thus, the ideational intention of the playwright, provided he is successful in the writing, becomes an organizational line of intention within the finished play.

Examples of plays written according to the four basic didactic lines of intention abound. The following four paragraphs present illustrations from American leftist plays of the 1930's.

To depict: Lillian Hellman depicted the viciousness of capitalists in *The Little Foxes* and *Days to Come*. The latter play demonstrates the degeneracy of the capitalist who wanted a strike broken with no violence. The former shows how greed can lead not only to wealth but to the destruction of lives and how capitalistic exploitation can overwhelm individuals. *Brass Ankle* by Du Bose Heyward and *Hymn to the Rising Sun* by Paul Green present the plight of the Negro during the depression era, but they offer no particular solution. *Golden Boy* and *Rocket to the Moon* by Clifford Odets exhibit the misfortunes of middle-class people struggling under economic burdens; Odets shows how some people react by choosing increasing immorality, some by psychological withdrawal, and some by a revolutionary awakening. Other ideas depicted in a like manner during the thirties are that slums produce criminals (*Dead End* by Sidney Kingsley), that fascism is evil and must be opposed (*The Gentle People* by Irwin Shaw), and that ethical decisions in the medical profession should supersede financial ones (*Men in White* by Sidney Kingsley). All these plays point to the principle of depiction as one type of organizational line in didactic drama.

To exhort: The central idea in *Bury the Dead* by Irwin Shaw is that if common men refused to fight, war would be impossible. In this play, six dead soldiers stand up in their graves to protest the evil of war, and after refusing the requests of others that they lie down again, they exhort their living comrades and all the poor people of the world to join their protest. *Johnny Johnson* by Paul Green and *Peace on Earth* by George Sklar and Albert Maltz are also deliberative arguments against war. Both show an honest man beset by the evils of an insane world. The solution in *Johnny Johnson* indicates that every man should

decide to oppose war as an individual, but in *Peace on Earth* the answer is that if everyone joins the workers' movement then war can be
averted. *If This Be Treason* by John Haynes Holmes and Reginald
Lawrence is another anti-war play. Its organizing idea, although the
story employs some historical information, is this: If the common people
of any two countries about to engage in war were given a choice, the
populace on both sides would always choose peace, not war.

Further examples of exhortative drama in the thirties are the Living
Newspapers. Each Living Newspaper presents the conditions of a social
problem and advances some possible solutions to that problem. *Triple-
A Plowed Under* explains the then current national agricultural problem
and hints that if workers and farmers joined forces and together applied political pressure, then something could be done that would help
them both. *One-Third of a Nation* deals with housing problems in New
York City, especially in slum areas, and indicates that governmental
intervention is necessary.

Also among the plays of exhortation during the Depression were
the strike plays: e.g., *Waiting for Lefty* by Clifford Odets, *Stevedore* by
Paul Peters and George Sklar, *The Cradle Will Rock* by Marc Blitzstein, and *Marching Song* by John Howard Lawson. Each of these
follows an organizational pattern that shows oppressed people in miserable circumstances, a decision to join in a strike, and the action of a
strike itself. All the strike plays present the ideas that there is a class
war between workers and bosses, that everyone should help the workers, and that a strike as miniature revolution is the cure. These revolutionary pieces are the most directly and obviously persuasive of all
the didactic dramas of the thirties. *Marching Song* contains most of
the propagandistic features of the strike plays, and it also is one of the
few plays of the period that follows almost exactly the organizing
criteria of socialist realism as set forth by the leftist critics of the period
and the theorists of the Communist Party. The formula requires that a
"good" worker be converted to Communism because of the oppression
of "evil" capitalists, that private distress is the result of "the system",
that workers ultimately conquer the bosses, and that a strike is a "rehearsal" for revolution. All the above mentioned exhortative dramas
might be called plays of protest.

To accuse: The plays in this group accuse either individuals or society
as "the system". In *We, the People* by Elmer Rice, a variety of oppressed and exploited common people blame both society and its
leaders for economic and social injustices. This play is nearly a dic-

tionary of the schisms of the time. The final speech generally states the controlling idea; it is a long persuasive oration made by one of the major characters. Speaking directly to the audience, a character named Sloane claims that no social system which destroys the right of its citizens to live in liberty has a right to continued existence. Then Sloane appeals to the members of the audience by telling them that they are the "people" of America who must cleanse the country, put it in order, and transform it into a decent place in which decent people can live. Elmer Rice also wrote *Judgment Day*. This play accuses the fascist movement, then in 1934 first arising in Europe, of being unjust, dishonorable, and corrupt. Also, it condemns the countries where fascism was taking hold. In such countries, the play asserts, justice is dead and liberty no longer exists. Another accusative play, one that points to the injustice, social prejudice, and economic oppression supposedly influential in the American legal system, is *They Shall Not Die* by John Wexley. *Precedent* by I. J. Golden follows the factual story of labor leader Tom Mooney in order to demonstrate that some laws are so archaic and outdated as to be vicious; too many laws, the plays says, indicate a system in which human life has less value than foolish rules of procedure written in statute books. Paul and Claire Siften indicted the capitalistic system, which allegedly caused a nationwide employment crisis, in their play, *1931 –*. Most of these plays of accusation contain trial scenes as the crucial moments of confrontation, decision, and persuasion.

To censure: Some didactic plays written during the thirties contain organizational patterns amounting to a line of censure. Most of these deal primarily with one of three sorts of topics: (1) individuals representing an economic class; (2) groups, movements, or political parties; or (3) ideological attitudes. Sometimes, of course, a play touches all three areas. *Black Pit* by Albert Maltz is, structurally, the best of the group. This play censures an individual who symbolizes all those who turn against the workers' movement. It examines the motives of a coal miner who turns informer during a strike situation. In presenting this man's fall, Albert Maltz came the nearest to writing a tragedy of any of the didactic playwrights of the decade. The idea the play proposes is that no matter what the cost – loss of job, home, family, even life – workers must remain faithful to the common cause. Two plays by Clifford Odets, *Paradise Lost* and *Awake and Sing!*, censure the idealism and the lethargy of the entire middle class. He characterizes individuals as representatives of the degeneracy, impotency, and evil of the class. He points to some people, however, as worthy of admiration, because they are capable of a resurrection and because they are willing to join the workers to make a better "tomorrow". During the thirties, Odets expressed an interest in constructing his plays so that they would be "immediately useful".[6] *Success Story* and *Gold Eagle Guy* are examples of other authors' plays that heap blame upon individuals who represent the rapacious ideals of capitalism. John Howard Lawson's *Success Story* features the idea that every man has a choice to follow the narrow radical path or the broad capitalistic highway. Sol Ginsburg, the focal character, chooses the gold-paved road and thereby ruins his life. Capitalistic success, the play says, is nourished by the sorrow of others, but it provides only a living death. *Gold Eagle Guy* by Melvin Levy pictures a sailor-become-capitalist. The process of climbing to financial power dehumanizes him, and the play demonstrates that the adoption of the capitalistic ideology has psychological effects likely to destroy a person's ethical values. John Howard Lawson also wrote two other plays of censure. *The Pure in Heart*, the success story of an actress, says that those who succumb to the commercial system are destroyed by it. *Gentlewoman* is more deeply rooted in the issues of the Depression. The accusation in this play is of capitalism itself. The heroine faces inevitable doom because of her connection with the decadent system. *Panic* by Archibald MacLeish bitterly decries an individual capitalist, a business magnate panicked by a stock market crisis. *Margin for Error* by Claire Booth straightforwardly censures the heartlessness and evil of the Nazi Party of Germany in the late thirties, and of the national representatives of the Nazi government. *Till the Day I Die* by Clifford Odets exposes Nazi fascism as bestial and praises Communism as the hope of the future. It is the most violent play of this group. The plays of censure depend as much on plot arrangement as upon invective for their means of persuasion.

The mere categorization of didactic plays according to these four lines of intention is not the point here. Rather, it is important to recognize that various didactic plays do, in fact, possess differing persuasive principles. Only by studying such plays individually, of course, can one justifiably group them or differentiate them according to structural principles.

A significant connection exists between *rhetorical arrangements* and *didactic structures*. One can align every persuasive play within one of four lines of rhetorical organization. Each of the four dramatic types,

---

[6]   Clifford Odets, Preface, *Six Plays* (New York, 1939), ix-x.

as discussed in the foregoing paragraphs, corresponds to a traditional type of speech as persuasive presentation. First, a play that depicts a condition is similar to an informative speech; both provide information about a subject and perhaps point to the salient issues of a problem. Second, a play of exhortation is like a deliberative speech; both urge the acceptance of an attitude or a policy on which to base future action. Third, a play of accusation resembles a forensic speech; both utilize facts about people and events in order to weigh the justice or injustice of a past action. And fourth, a play of censure parallels a negative epideictic speech; both blame some person, group, or institution for unfortunate conditions in the present. In all four types – whether poetic or rhetorical, play or speech – the object is persuasion.

That three of the four rhetorical types serve a particular function in relation to time also has a connection with the structural principles of didactic drama. Exhortative, or deliberative, plays point to the future. Accusative, or forensic, plays concentrate on the past. And censurous, or epideictic, plays focus upon the present. Such distinctions should be made with care, however, because any didactic play is to some degree likely to draw upon the past, to illuminate the present, and to recommend ideas for the future. The three time designations are useful mainly for an identification of where the author of the didactic play placed the chronological emphasis of the controlling thoughts. With such an identification, one can better understand the function of the thoughts within the play and the recommendations which the play advances to the audience.

One other point needs to be made about time in relation to the organization of a didactic drama. As in mimetic plays, the *chronological progression* in didactic plays varies widely. In Bertolt Brecht's *The Private Life of the Master Race*, for example, each small episode of the play follows its antecedent in performance, but how much time elapses between most of the scenes is irrelevant and unidentifiable. Time is thus more abstract in that play than in a play like Odet's *Awake and Sing!*, in which time is realistically progressive and carefully identified. A few other examples will indicate the varying treatments of time as found in didactic plays. The characters in *No Exit* by Sartre find time both progressive and eternal. Megan Terry wrote *Viet Rock* with little regard for straightforward time sequence; she built the play in "transformational" units – the actors briefly portray first one set of characters, then another, and another until the end. The scenes are not connected in time. There is, in fact, little discernible difference in di-

dactic plays as compared with mimetic plays in the use of time se-
quences. In both sorts of drama, authors handle time so differently
from one play to another that few generalizations are possible. One fact,
however, is often characteristic of the chronological arrangements in
didactic plays. In most such plays, time is usually rather arbitrarily
handled. By comparison with most mimetic plays, the leaps in time
within most didactic plays are more likely to be made for the sake of
persuasion than for the sake of causal progression of the action.

As long as this discussion has touched upon didactic drama as it may
relate to traditional rhetorical forms, it appropriately should mention
the traditional dramatic forms as well. How does didactic drama connect, if at all, with the traditional forms of mimetic drama – tragedy,
comedy, and melodrama?

A temptation immediately arises, perhaps, to say that didactic dramas
because of their persuasive, or propagandistic, natures are quite unlike
mimetic tragedies, comedies, or melodramas. But this is not true. Although didactic melodramas, for example, are not exactly like conventional melodramas, still the two sorts of melodramas have many
structural features in common. A mimetic melodrama contains the
emotive powers of fear and hate – fear for the sake of the protagonist
and hate of the antagonist. Its action is temporarily serious and follows
a pattern involving a threat, scenes of conflict, and a relatively happy
resolution. Most well constructed melodramas have a double resolution,
including the reward of the hero and the punishment of the villain. In
a didactic melodrama – *The Gentle People* by Irwin Shaw makes an
excellent example – the same features are apparent, but they serve a
controlling thought rather than merely existing for their own sake. Most
didactic plays are more likely to resemble melodramas than either of
the other two forms. Typically, the hero of such a play believes in and
verbalizes the basic thoughts of the play. His "evil" opponent usually
articulates opposing views. As one character threatens another – usually
the villain persecutes the hero – the playwright can easily identify them
as representatives of conflicting ideologies, one bad and the other good.
When the writer draws audience sympathy for the hero with the "right"
ideas and encourages audience antipathy for the villain with the "wrong"
ideas, then the ideas themselves are made to be sympathetic or not.
Furthermore, when the protagonist with the favored ideas wins in the
end and is rewarded, the audience learns that such ideas are functional
and beneficial. Or if the normal melodramatic ending is wrenched – as
in *The Little Foxes* by Lillian Hellman – and the villain wins, then the

audience can understand that perhaps they themselves must do something about such evil in the world. Playwrights sometimes use a third kind of ending in didactic melodramas. Such a melodrama can conclude with an unresolved, or open, ending. As in Brecht's *The Good Woman of Setzuan*, the play forces the audience to decide how to settle the conflict, solve the problem of evil presented in the play, and resolve the action. An open ending impels the audience to make a choice not only about the play's problem but also about similar problems in life.

Comedy, too, is a likely sort of form to be taken over by a didactic playwright. Many of the plays by both Aristophanes and George Bernard Shaw, for example, are overtly didactic. Because comedy arises from ridicule, the didactic playwright can employ comic means to ridicule the ideas and characters he dislikes and to favor the ideas and characters he likes. Often, didactic plays simply ridicule certain ideas without at all bothering to advance others; in such cases, the play is built upon a *negative* thought complex. Both *The Cradle Will Rock* by Marc Blitzstein and *Viet Rock* by Megan Terry are comedies that utilize such negative thought complexes.

Compared with melodrama and comedy, tragedy is far less likely to be the form chosen by didactic playwrights for their persuasive pieces. But some writers have composed serious didactic plays that employ many of the structural features of tragedy. *Black Pit* by Albert Maltz, *Mother Courage* by Bertolt Brecht, and *Blues for Mister Charlie* by James Baldwin are apt examples. In such dianoetic plays as these, an unremittingly serious action illustrates the thought which the play favors. The central characters in didactic tragedies are likely to face a moral or ethical decision which, when verbalized, precisely presents both the favored didactic thoughts of the author and an opposing thought complex. In the didactic plays that most resemble mimetic tragedies, the major character is likely to choose the "wrong" thoughts and follow the "wrong" course of action, and thus he brings about his own fall. The audience is expected to learn from his example what *not* to do when faced with a similar decision.

Didactic dramatists do not, then, eliminate action from their plays, nor do they avoid the emotive powers so essential to the mimetic forms. On the contrary, every didactic play to some extent employs action and emotional powers in order to persuade. The action becomes a didactic exemplum, and the emotional arousal serves a persuasive function. Didactic dramatists use the mimetic forms for didactic purposes.

Aristotle pointed out that *suffering, discovery,* and *reversal* are qualitatlve elements in mimetic plots. These elements also appear in didactic dramas, not so much as contributing factors in the action as means to persuasion. In didactic plays, major characters usually suffer because of persecution by characters who live by "bad" ideologies, because they have not yet made the "right" decision, or because they themselves are "evil" and are living according to the "wrong" ideals. The major moments of discovery in rhetorical plays usually have to do with a character's recognition of the "right" ideas, of those ideas which the play itself is attempting to propound. In many didactic plays no true plot reversal occurs, but in those that have one, the reversal also advances either the organizational thesis or points out the action which the play recommends to the audience. John Howard Lawson's *Marching Song* holds examples of all three of these plot elements; it uses each for didactic purposes. Bertolt Brecht's *The Good Woman of Setzuan* does too, even though it ends with a question.

Two other principles named by some as significant in dramatic structures can also be found in persuasive plays. These are *conflict* and *decision*. If anything, these are even easier to identify in thought-controlled plays. In such works, conflict is simply the struggle between the forces of "right" who favor the ideas at the heart of the play and the forces of "wrong" who favor opposing ideas. The conflict is as much one of ideologies as of characters. Insofar as decision is concerned, didactic dramatists make sure that key characters make "right" ones or "wrong" ones as measured by criteria that are aligned with the thought complex which the entire play advances.

Another organizational principle often operative in didactic plays, the final one to be mentioned here, is that of *rhetorical arrangement*. Some didactic plays more nearly follow the form of oratory than do any of the mimetic forms of drama. Instead of a causal sequence of events, they employ a logical arrangement of persuasive materials. And in fact, they are best understood as speeches that begin with an introduction of the problem of the play and that proceed to state the thesis, to offer proof, and finally to conclude with a peroration that summarizes the argument and urges a particular action upon the audience. *The Chinese Wall* by Max Frisch depends heavily upon such a rhetorical pattern.

Although most of this discussion has focused on the identification of structural principles in didactic drama, it is worth mentioning that there are three basic critical approaches useful in an analysis of persuasive plays. In a paper for a conference on rhetoric and poetic, Oscar

G. Brockett identified the three approaches. He explained that a didactic work – or a mimetic one for that matter – can be discussed as expression, as instrument, and as object.[7] Each of these approaches would no doubt furnish some important information about a particular didactic drama. First, since a didactic play is the *expression* of some person or group of persons who live in a certain time and place, information about such antecedent circumstances would enhance one's understanding of a given play. A knowledge of an author's personal views and intentions can help illuminate his play. Also, an understanding of the milieu from which the play came may heighten one's understanding of the play. It would, for example, enlarge anyone's view of the didactic plays of the thirties to know about the economic and social turmoil of that era. Second, since any didactic play presumably can fulfill an instrumental purpose, a critic can appropriately examine such a play as an *instrument* of persuasion, i.e., from a rhetorical viewpoint. Didactic plays can be judged, thus, by an analysis of them as instruments containing the means to persuasion and by an examination of their success or failure at effectively persuading an audience. The instrumental approach is likely to provide information about the play that is quite different from that found by the biographical-environmental approach. The third critical attitude, perhaps the most objective and certainly the most structurally oriented, will reveal still another kind of information. To study a didactic play as an *object,* one containing parts organized into a whole, can be called the internal approach. Even though an author may have written a didactic play for an instrumental purpose, and even though it may function with some success rhetorically, it can nevertheless be analyzed as an artistic whole, as an art object possessing materials and a form. As this discussion has indicated, didactic plays usually contain devices and connections that are clearly rhetorical, plus devices and structural relationships that are mostly poetic. The best didactic plays may, indeed, achieve a high place on the scale of artistry and aesthetic value. Some of the didactic pieces of Euripides, Aristophanes, Shaw, Sartre, and Brecht, for instance, demonstrate the aesthetic potentials of didactic drama. Many critics, however, prefer not to employ the term *didactic* when speaking of the great thought-controlled plays; they rather use such terms as *philosophic play, problem play, dialectic play, play of ideas,* or *play of commitment.* Regardless of the term applied to such plays, a large

[7]   Oscar G. Brockett, "Poetry as Instrument", *Papers in Rhetoric and Poetic*, ed. Donald C. Bryant (Iowa City, Iowa, 1965), 15-25.

number are obviously didactic because their plots are ordered to propound a complex of thought or even a simple thesis. In such plays,
thought, not action, comprise the form of the whole, and the best way
to discover the basic thought and to discern the overall form is by
means of an internal, or structural, analysis.

Two matters remain for the conclusion of this investigation of thought
as plot in didactic drama: first, a summary statement about how thought
works in a dual capacity in every didactic play, and second, the definition of didactic drama as a distinct species.

In a mimetic play, thought stands as material to character; it is the
substance within each of the characterizations in a play, the basis upon
which the characters say or do whatever words or activities the play
contains. It is the sub-text which actors eventually perform, i.e., the
detailed ideas that the words represent. In a didactic play, thought
functions in a like manner, as the particularized matter of each character, as material to the whole. But also in didactic drama – and this is
the crucial difference between it and mimetic drama – thought of a
different sort operates as the architectonic part. Thought in this guise
acts as the control of the entire play, the form of the whole. Thought is
the plot of a didactic play. Functioning so, a thought complex, a series
of ideas, or a thesis determines what will be said and done in the play.
All the situations, events, characters, and detailed thoughts in the play
are there primarily for the sake of the overall thought complex rather
than for the sake of a credible and progressive action. Thought performs dual roles in didactic drama, as the material of character and as
the control of the action.

A didactic drama is a different kind of art object than a mimetic
drama, despite their apparent similarities. The first difference has to do
with final cause; the purpose of a didactic drama is a function – persuasion. The materials of a didactic drama are more similar to those
in a mimetic drama; they consist of the feelings, sayings, and doings of
characters who exist within delimited circumstances. The formal cause
of a didactic drama is not primarily a pattern of human action, but
rather a thought complex – ideological and persuasive. The manner of
a didactic play is rhetorical; its style depends upon many more principles of rhetoric than does the style of a mimetic play. Didactic drama
is the presentation of a thought complex in words arranged dramatically
for the purpose of persuading an audience. Thus, a didactic play can
be studied both as rhetoric and as poetic, as an act of persuasion and
as an object of art.

NORMAN PHILBRICK

THE SPY AS HERO: AN EXAMINATION OF *ANDRÉ* BY WILLIAM DUNLAP

If one analyzes the corpus of the dramatic writings of William Dunlap, the conclusion must be made that he was, if not by any means a distinguished playwright, certainly a more than competent one.[1] His work, to be sure, is uneven, and it follows a sometimes derivative, sometimes imitative pattern. It is sentimental, moralistic, indulges frequently in excesses of the purple writing and Gothic atmosphere characteristic of its time, but its faults are often overcome by the sincerity and intensity of the writer as well as the technical control exercised by a playwright who was essentially an experienced man of the theatre. He sometimes wrote hastily so that his actors would have something to perform and to stave off financial disaster both for himself and his company. He might have become a significant force in the creation of a native American drama had he had the time and leisure to pursue his passion for the theatre, but he was burdened by management and had to struggle against agonizing odds to keep from financial ruin – and failed to do so. It is a wonder that he was able to write as much as he did and to have to his credit a number of successes during his career.

André, unfortunately, was a failure, but there were extenuating conditions, causing its rapid demise, and these are related to the subject matter and the political environment of the time when it was produced in 1798. In examining the play, one is struck by its merits more than by its faults. Its worth as an example of early native drama and its superiority to many other plays of the eighteenth century, both English and American, should be emphasized. *André* is far from being a jerry-built, incompetent piece of work. One is impressed by its clarity, its several scenes of emotional validity, the slow but effective progression

---

[1] According to his biographer, he wrote at least twenty-seven original plays, made twenty-seven translations from the French and German. In addition there are ten plays doubtfully attributed to him. Oral Sumner Coad, *William Dunlap* (New York, 1917), 284-293.

of its plot, and the honesty of its patriotic sentiments. The characters are not fully realized, but neither are they cut-out figures played against the explosions of chauvinistic effusions.

One of the chief weaknesses of *André* lies in the choice of a spy as hero, and Dunlap does not attempt to avoid the issue of the shocking nature of André's crime against a nation. He does mitigate it, however, and he obviously felt justified in doing so because of the character of the spy-hero and the romantic aura surrounding him. It is my purpose to review all the circumstances, both positive and negative, which affected the success of *André* in order to reach conclusions as to why it failed.

In his preface to the play, published in early April, within four or five days of its opening on March 30, 1798, Dunlap remarks that he had chosen the subject nine years earlier but had not completed the drama because of a "prevailing opinion that recent events are unfit subjects for tragedy". He was eventually convinced that the story "would excite interest in the breasts of an American audience. ... If this play is successful it will be proof that recent events may be so managed in tragedy as to command popular attention; if it is unsuccessful, the question must remain undetermined until some more powerful writer shall make the experiment."[2]

Referring to *André* in 1832, Dunlap says, "Mr. Hodgkinson's partner in the management had now finished another tragedy called *André* – a most unfortunate subject for the stage, at a period so near the time of the event dramatized."[3] Thus he reiterates the single reason he can ascribe to the failure of his play, but there are also a number of other conditions which resulted in the collapse of *André*.[4]

[2] [William Dunlap.] *André; a Tragedy in Five Acts* (New York, 1798), iii, v-vi. It should be noted that the play, as printed, also includes "Authentic Documents respecting Major André; consisting of Letters to Miss Seward, The Cow Chace [an original poem by André], Proceedings of the Court Martial, etc.", enlarging the publication to 139 pages. All quotations from the play and the various documents are from this edition, referred to in the footnotes as *André*. The second edition of the play, published in London in 1799, omits the Letters to Miss Seward, excises certain passages unfavorable to Great Britain, and carries on the title page the rubric: "As now performing at the Theatre in New York" – an obviously incorrect statement. *André: a Tragedy in Five Acts* (London, 1799).
[3] *A History of the American Theatre* (New York, 1832), 221.
[4] The success of a play in the eighteenth century was, of course, based on different standards from those of today. If a play achieved a run of nine nights, it was a "hit", even if those nine performances did not run consecutively. Both the English and American theatres housed repertory companies, and "the success of a new piece must be judged, not by length of its initial run, but by the number of performances it had throughout the entire season and by the number of seasons it was later revived .... new plays then were more expendable". James J. Lynch,

Before reviewing them, it should be noted that Dunlap's explanation of his failure is not without validity. He observes in the preface that

In exhibiting a stage representation of a real transaction, the particulars of which are fresh in the minds of many of the audience, an author had this peculiar difficulty to struggle with, that those who know the events expect to see them *all* recorded; and any deviation from what they remember to be fact appears to them as a fault in the poet; they are disappointed, their expectations are not fulfilled, and the writer is more or less condemned, not considering the difference between the poet and the historian, or not knowing that what is intended to be exhibited is a free poetical picture, not an exact historical portrait.[5]

In his analysis of the particular predicament facing the writer of an historical play, Dunlap argues that the artist must often change the record to make it accord with his aesthetic purpose, and his reference to the "prevailing opinion" that recent history is not fit subject for tragedy harks back to neo-classical canon and later neo-Aristotelian interpretation, and he echoes the old controversies between the historian and the poet who have much in common; the former, however, adds little embellishment and narrates what has happened whereas the latter adds imaginatively to his sources and invents fictions which must have at least the appearance of truth.

Dunlap's concern about the use of the distant past for dramatic treatments reflects a prevalent attitude of playwrights. Britons particularly, were becoming increasingly aware of the expansion of their empire and had begun to look to their antecedents; the theatre attested to this self-conscious preoccupation. In addition to the successful revival of many of the Shakespearean chronicles – *Richard III, King John, Henry VIII,* the more popular among them – new plays were written, the subject matter of which extended from ancient and Anglo-Saxon times to the Elizabethan and Stuart periods. (There were at least three treatments of the Elizabeth-Essex tragedy, and Havard's melancholic *King Charles the First* was often revived.) A number of these revivals and new "history dramas" were produced in America. Dunlap might well question the advisibility of choosing an historical event only eighteen years old.

In America during the Revolution the only original works of the

---

Box Pit and Gallery (Berkeley, 1953), 11. *André* ran three nights only and might have been taken off after the second night if Dunlap had not been the manager and author and sought a third performance for the customary author's benefit.
[5]   *André*, p. iii.

time were propaganda pieces, both anti- and pro-British. They were historical, concerned with immediate current events – a journalistic kind of writing, a newspaper report immediately dramatized – and two of them were presented at least once for school audiences – *The Battle of Bunker's Hill* (1776) and *The Death of General Montgomery* (1777) by Hugh Henry Brackenridge. *The Patriots* by Robert Munford, written between 1777 and 1779, could have been given by amateurs at a country house in Virginia.

From the Revolution until 1797, there were no original plays concerned with American historical occurrences. Dramas treated the social scene or combined comments on society with some overtones of political controversy, such as *The Father; or, American Shandyism* by Dunlap (1789), *The Politician Out-witted* by Samuel Low (1789), and *The Contrast* by Royall Tyler (1790). On February 17, 1797, a year before the appearance of *André,* the company at the Haymarket Theatre in Boston presented *Bunker-Hill; or, The Death of General Warren,* by John Daly Burk, celebrating an event which had occurred only twenty-two years before. *Bunker-Hill* was a success, and it must have given Dunlap pause a year later when he surveyed the ruins of his own venture into American history.

Bunker-Hill is the first example of a native drama, in the sense that the subject was American, becoming an outstanding popular sensation in spite of its condemnation by the more intelligent professional theatre people and citizens of good sense, among them President John Adams.[6] It was called "the most execrable of the Grub-Street kind" by the manager of the rival Federal Street Theatre,[7] and Dunlap comments in a letter to his co-manager, John Hodgkinson, when *Bunker-Hill* appeared later in New York that the play "was performing to a mere rabble, amounting to a house of about 200Ds – and even they execrated it".[8] A statement not quite true.

The piece cleared two thousand dollars for Burk in Boston, and in New York he added to his income from the play. It continued to be popular until the middle of the nineteenth century, being often revived

---

[6] The only possible exception was the production of *Tammany* by Anne Kemble Hatton, in 1794, but that piece, dreadful as it was with its patriotic extravagances, received tremendous support from the "Republicans", vociferous members of the extremely democratic Tammany Society, and the Jacobin element in New York. The play was a four days' wonder.

[7] *A History of the American Theatre*, 161. Letter from John B. Williamson to John Hodgkinson, quoted by Dunlap.

[8] Dorothy C. Barck (ed.), *Diary of William Dunlap*, 3 vols. (New York, 1930), I, 144.

for celebrations of the Fourth of July after it was dropped from the regular repertory. Charles Blake in his *Historical Account of the Providence Stage,* published in 1868, comments on the tenacious survival of this "miserable compound of fustian".[9] Fustian it was, full of rant including a sentimental, although unconscious parody of the love and honor theme, a hyperbolical distortion of the character of Warren, the glorious spectacle of the Battle of Bunker's Hill and the death of Warren, but above all, infused with a feverish patriotic emotionalism designed to appeal to the mob and the Jacobin tendencies of the lower classes. Dunlap might well have had *Bunker-Hill* in mind when in 1817, he re-wrote *André* in praise of that same unruly rabble and titled it *The Glory of Columbia Her Yeomanry!*

André is far superior to Burk's shoddy effort, and by its literary merit, it should have succeeded. Dunlap's excuse for its failure – that it was too close to the actual event – has some justification, but there were other more obvious reasons for the collapse of a well-intentioned endeavor.

Of major importance was the choice of subject. At first sight the story of André has within it many ingredients of a dramatic romance, as Brander Mathews notes in his introduction to *André.*[10]

There is the young, handsome André, if not innocent, at least extremely gullible; his Nemesis, Benedict Arnold, embittered and villainous, Peggy Shippen Arnold, the traitor's wife, certainly infatuated by André and involved in the intended betrayal of America. The plot is also ready-made for dramatization: the intrigue of spies, the plans for the surrender of West Point, the use of André as an instrument in the proceedings, the incredible mismanagement of the whole affair, the accidental capture of André, his subsequent trial and execution.

Unfortunately for Dunlap, the realistic aspect of the business made it impossible to treat the subject romantically or sentimentally, although he attempts to do so. André was involved in a heinous crime, the results of which might have led to the collapse of the Revolution and the eventual triumph of Britain. Dunlap did foresee, however, that he might have difficulties if he dramatized all aspects of the conspiracy. Consequently, he restricts his treatment of the event, beginning his play after the capture and trial of André, just the day before his execution. The playwright concentrates on the nobility of his hero-spy, emphasizes

[9] John Daly Burk, *Bunker-Hill; or, The Death of General Warren* (Providence, 1868), 58.
[10] (New York, 1887).

the efforts of his friends to save him, presents the anguish of Washington who must place his country's honor above his own love of humanity. Revealing the collapse of the plans for rescue, Dunlap raises the hope that André may be allowed to die like a gentleman rather than a common criminal, but that hope is destroyed, and the spy is brought to the final catastrophe of an ignominious death. To these circumstances Dunlap adds the fiction of an ill-fated romance between André and Honora Sneyd, the latter arriving at the last moment from England in an attempt to persuade Washington to pardon her lover. (Honora had been a sweetheart of André's but she had married in 1773 and had died in April of 1780, five months before André's execution. He retained a sentimental memory of her and kept her miniature, which he had painted, on his person, in fact concealing it in his mouth when captured.) In the play the pathetic separation of the lovers is made more poignant by the device of Honora's going mad when she cannot save André. There are then all the possibilities of an eighteenth-century tragedy in the grand manner – with a touch of Gothic thrown in.

Aware, however, that he is basing his drama on an actual occurrence and troubled by the fact that many of the participants in the affair are still alive, Dunlap cautiously threads his way through the historic facts of the case. He ignores some of them entirely, refers only slightly to others, and bases most of his evidence on the documents he has collected for publication with the first edition of the play.

To summarize briefly the historical events preceding the action of the play which have some bearing on the drama itself: the wretched affair began in 1779 when Benedict Arnold, commander of the American troops in Philadelphia and generally respected as one of the heroes of the American defeat at Quebec under Montgomery, decided with the concurrence of his wife to betray his country and go over to the British. The couple, through an intermediary, approached André, then with the British in New York, recently having been appointed head of British intelligence by General Clinton. Eventually Arnold succeeded in securing from Congress the command of West Point on August 3, 1780, having already promised Clinton that he would surrender the fort.

Matters reached a climax on September 21, when Arnold met the disguised André on the banks of the Hudson to discuss final plans for the great betrayal. In the play André relates the subsequent events to Bland; the details correspond to a letter he wrote Washington on September 24, 1780, published with the first edition of the play.

ANDRÉ

On ground, unoccupied by either part,
Neutral esteem'd, I landed, and was met.
But ere my conference was with Arnold clos'd,
The day began to dawn; I then was told
That till the night I must my safety seek
In close concealment. Within your posts convey'd,
I found myself involv'd in unthought dangers.
Night came. I sought the vessel which had borne
Me to the fatal spot; but she was gone.
Retreat that way cut off, again I sought
Concealment with the traitors of your army.
Arnold now granted passes, and I doff'd
My martial garb, and put on curs'd disguise!
Thus in a peasant's form I pass'd your posts;
And when, as I conceiv'd, my danger o'er,
Was stopt and seiz'd by some returning scouts.
So did ambition lead me, step by step,
To treat with traitors, and encourage treason;
And then, bewilder'd in the guilty scene,
To quit my martial designating badges,
Deny my name, and sink into the spy.[11]

The "returning scouts" were John Paulding, Isaac Van Wart and David Williams. Because of their capture of André, they had become by 1798 American heroes, particularly so to the common man — for they were sturdy homespun militiamen — and they were well rewarded by Congress (some doubts remain today about their unadulterated patriotism), but Dunlap, giving a nod in the direction of the pit and the gallery where their "peers" sat, expresses the general acceptance of their patriotic motives:

He [André] offer'd bribes to tempt the band that seiz'd him;
But the rough farmer, for his country arm'd,
That soil defending which his ploughshare turn'd,
Those laws, his father chose, and he approv'd,
Cannot, as mercenary soldiers may,
Be brib'd to sell the public-weal for gold.[12]

André was allowed a trial before a Board of General Officers at which he admitted freely that he had come ashore without a flag of truce, not under one as both Arnold and Clinton contended in letters to Washington. By his own words André condemned himself, and there

---

[11] *André*, 22-23.
[12] *André*, 12.

was no recourse for the Board except to condemn him to death.[13]

The relief of the American command that Arnold's intended betrayal had been aborted was obviously great, and Congress ordered a day of national thanksgiving. Thus should have ended the whole business. The affair, however, was an international sensation, and from the day of his execution André was memorialized and adulated. There were several reasons for this intense hero-worship.

Dunlap in his play makes full use of the André legend, which grew with the years. (Unfortunately, by 1798, it had begun to tarnish somewhat, as will be discussed later.) As eye-witness accounts of the trial and execution became common knowledge, the character of the spy emerged as being more important than the event, and it is that aspect of the business which invigorated the sad romantic history of the mighty fallen – the bright promise of unlimited prosperity, the attractive artistic and intellectual figure brought to a shameful death. Nobility was recognized in André, his fatal flaw lay in his ambition, as he confesses to Bland in the play. The hubris, attending his rise to power, gave him the human quality, making possible sentimental tears over his fate.

There is one aspect of the case, however, which added possibly just that extra component needed to increase sympathy for André, and which Dunlap uses effectively for the same purpose. It is André's request that he die a soldier's death and not be hanged as a common felon or murderer.

Among the documents relating to André printed with the first edition of the play is the letter written to Washington in which he asks that his last moments be softened by sympathy towards a soldier, that the mode of his death be adapted "to the feelings of a man of honor" who is "a victim of policy and not of resentment", and with dignity pleads that he may be informed "that I am not to die on a gibbet".[14]

Washington, however, was adamant, and in the light of history for good reason. If André were shot instead of being hanged – the fate of

[13] As Alexander Hamilton observed, in the conventions of war, and if nothing underhanded was intended, André would have come ashore under a flag with a passport in his own name. He had no flag, and he was designated in the passport as "Mr. Anderson". Yet even if there had been a protective flag, as Hamilton notes, it would have been a mockery because its purpose was to corrupt an officer (Arnold) to "betray his trust" – the irony being that the officer in question was eager to betray the whole American cause. A flag thus used would have no validity and would make other arrangements extremely doubtful. André saw the reality of the situation and exploded the myth at his trial. *The Papers of Alexander Hamilton*, Edited by Harold C. Syrett and Jacob E. Cooke (New York, 1961), II, 469.
[14] *André*, 104-105.

spies – it would suggest that the Commander-in-Chief had some dubiety as to the absolute guilt of the prisoner; furthermore, to be shot rather than to be hanged was an officer's prerogative – a privilege, if one can call it that – of class. Such a change might have created a precedent and certainly would have weakened the morale of the American army.

The decision of Washington shocked the aristocratic world. In England Anna Seward's *Monody* expressed this point of view:

> Th' opprobrious tomb your harden'd hearts decreed,
> While all he ask'd was as the brave to bleed!
> No other boon the glorious youth implor'd
> Save the cold mercy of the warrior-sword!
> O dark, and pitiless! Your impious hate
> O'er-whelm'd the hero in the ruffian's fate!
> Stopt with the felon-cord the rosy breath!
> And venom'd with disgrace the darts of death!
>
> Oh Washington! I thought thee great and good,
> Nor knew thy Nero-thirst of guiltless blood!
> Severe to use the pow'r that fortune gave,
> Thou cool determin'd murderer of the brave!
> Lost to each fairer virtue, that inspires
> The genuine fervour of the patriot fires! [15]

In Washington's camp there was also anger over the decision, made vocal by Alexander Hamilton. Although Hamilton reluctantly agreed that André should die, he abhorred the method. He loudly expressed himself on that subject to his colleagues and wrote his sentiments in a number of letters, thinly veiling his antagonism to Washington for his treatment of André.

Dunlap, in the Preface to *André*, notes that in 1780 there was a "diversity of opinion which agitated the minds of men at that time, on the question of the propriety of putting André to death", and he feels justified in using the opposition to André's fate in the person of young, tempestuous Bland. Consequently, wishing to add cubits to André's fame, the playwright dramatizes the written request to Washington, pleading for an honored and "privileged" death.

There is one service Bland can perform.

BLAND.

Speak it.

---

[15] Walter Scott (ed.), *The Poetical Works of Anna Seward*, 3 vols. (Edinburgh, 1810), 85. Miss Seward, indulging in poetic license, seems to have been confused over the manner of André's death.

ANDRÉ

O, think, and as a soldier think,
How I must die – The *manner* of my death –
Like the base ruffian, or the midnight thief,
Ta'en in the act of stealing from the poor,
To be turn'd off the felon's – murderer's cart,
A mid-air spectacle to gaping clowns: –
To run a short, an envied course to glory,
And end it on a gibbet. –

Let me, O! let me die a soldier's death,
While friendly clouds of smoke shroud from all eyes
My last convulsive pangs, and I'm content.[16]

Having raised this particular point, thus increasing the nobility of André in an age when war had a romantic aura, Dunlap drops the subject. Later, when André asks Bland if he made his request to Washington, Bland says that he was so emotionally overcome while pleading for André's life that he forgot to speak of the mode of death. It is fairly obvious why the matter is not brought forward again. Dunlap was in an ambivalent situation – by making André a hero, he had to be particularly careful of his treatment of an American idol – Washington. It would have been folly to have made Washington a villain, and yet Dunlap needed a protagonist and an antagonist. By the nature of the event, however, and the personnel involved, with all the national ramifications, he had almost written himself into a corner. In omitting a confrontation between Bland and Washington over the subject of the hanging – a scene which could have been highly dramatic – Dunlap avoided even the remote possibility of casting Washington in an unfavorable light. As to the major question – André's being sentenced to death as a spy – Washington had the majority opinion on his side; the manner of execution was an entirely different concern and in that circumstance there could have been some criticism of Washington, yet Dunlap makes it clear that the Commander-in-Chief, although acting from duty, was not insensitive to the human issues involved.

Thus Washington is treated with dignity, and it is to the credit of Dunlap that in his characterization of the greatest of American heroes Washington rises above plaster sainthood. He has a stern sense of justice, a rigidity where his duty is concerned, but he recognizes the virtues in André. Speaking of himself, Washington says:

[16]   *André*, 23-24.

Think'st thou thy country would not curse the man,
Who, by a clemency ill-tim'd, ill-judg'd,
Encourag'd treason?

And of one man, André, weighed in the balance of a nation:

I know the virtues of this man, and love them.
But the destiny of millions, millions
Yet unborn, depends upon the rigour
Of this moment. The haughty Briton laughs
To scorn our armies and our councils. Mercy,
Humanity, call loudly, that we make
Our now despised power be felt, vindictive,
Millions demand the death of this young man.
My injur'd country, he his forfeit life
Must yield, to shield thy lacerated breast
From torture.[17]

Among the younger officers of Washington's suite there were others in addition to Hamilton who felt that Washington had betrayed his class. Lying close to the heart of the resentment against Washington was the character of the human sacrifice – André himself.

In spite of the sentimentality attached to the André affair, the romantic aspects of the tragedy of a young man destroyed in his prime by forces too great for him, there was no doubt that he was a singularly attractive person with many potentials for future promise. He was charming, full of good humor; he was an excellent military man and also excelled in artistic accomplishments beyond those usually expected of a gentleman. His interest in the theatre was enthusiastic – he acted in Philadelphia and New York during the British occupations, and he staged in the former city one of the most elaborate pageants ever seen in America (in honor of General Howe, who was returning to England). André painted scenery for the celebration, prepared costumes and participated in all the events. André also painted scenery for the South Street Theatre in Philadelphia – a backdrop of a landscape, which, ironically, was used in 1807 for *The Glory of Columbia Her Yeomanry!*, representing in that production the place where André was apprehended by his America captors.

These accomplishments were his contribution to his society, but they do not entirely explain his appeal to both men and women. His open nature, a kind of infectious gregariousness drew people to him. There was also about him an innocent integrity; he could accept no evil in

[17] *André*, 31-33.

men without a palliative. His letters abound with enthusiasms and the right touch of sincerity. It was his manner of leaving life which has caused the most comment, and any description of the way in which he ennobled his own execution contains expressions of the highest praise for his courage, dignity and cheerfulness. Dunlap makes full use of the excellent character of the man and paints a hero just slightly more than life-size. His portrait is not idealized to such a degree that André appears to be a cardboard figure. To achieve the three-dimensional quality of the man, the playwright uses Bland, his close friend, as a dramatic counterfoil. Bland is tempestuous; André remains composed. Bland seeks excuses for André's conduct; André admits his errors. Bland betrays sentimental weaknesses in his character; André is an example of the typical reasonable man of the eighteenth century. He speaks sadly of his heinous offence, contrasting it to his own high standards:

> I . . . dared act against my reason . . .
> against my conscience . . . Oft have I
> said how fully I despis'd all bribery
> base, . . . But now my deeds will
> rise against my words.[18]

He admits that the honors given him by Clinton had turned his head, that he was tempted by avarice and ambition and that he has mistaken the encouraging of treason and conniving with traitors as a duty, but he now realizes that it was only dissimulation or rationalization motivated by ambition which led him step by step to degradation. He thus is portrayed as a tragic protagonist with a fatal weakness – in the best tradition of neo-classical dramatic literature.

If, then, in spite of the remembrance of the controversy dividing men eighteen years before the play was produced, Dunlap succeeded in convincing his audience that a spy could be a hero and at the same time added to the honor of Washington, and if Dunlap's explanation that the events were too recent for tragedy is questionable, what other conditions were present, militating against a theatrical achievement of promise?

When *André* was produced at the New or Park Theatre on March 30, 1798, the building had been open only two months. It was a handsome edifice, seating about 2,000, designed so that there was an unbroken view of the stage without the usual obstructing pillars to support the boxes. The acoustics were good, and there were high praises

[18]   *André,* 20-21.

sung to the remarkable scenery: "The scenery was of itself worth a visit to the theatre." [19]

Unfortunately, as seems to be the nature of theatre structures, the estimated cost of $42,000 rose to the actual cost of $130,000, plunging proprietors and both managers – Dunlap and Hodgkinson – into excessive debts. In addition to this sorry state of affairs, the theatre, opening to a full house and excellent receipts, almost immediately began to lose money, so that within two weeks Dunlap was fearful that he would have to close the theatre. He was saved from that disaster when Thomas Abthorpe Cooper came to the New York company, having been recently acclaimed in Philadelphia, where he had arrived from England with an excellent reputation for his work in the provinces. His *Hamlet* presented at the Park on February 28 was a great success, and it was hoped that he would save the jeopardized theatre. Once again Dunlap's hopes were dashed, because Cooper proved to be an uneven attraction, although it was not entirely his fault. The professionalism of the times was such that standards of performance varied from obvious inexperience and amateurism to good solid acting – generally second-rate and rarely brilliant, although Cooper, when he exerted himself, could be outstanding. Cooper had a rival in John Hodgkinson, manager and actor. There was considerable dissension among the company; Dunlap constantly attempted to placate them with compromises, judicial decisions and even threats. One of his weaknesses was that he could not be ruthless; he was a gentleman and expected others to behave as he did.

The first night of *André* was nearly a fiasco for two reasons, one theatrical and the other political. The theatrical misadventures began almost as soon as the managers announced that *André* would be produced. Dunlap, as he stated in his preface, had abandoned the idea of the play in 1789, but on November 25, 1797, while in Boston, he notes in his diary, "Write on André". Upon returning to New York, he continues to work steadily on the play and has a rough draft ready by February 20, 1798, which Cooper reads.[20]

The leading characters are André, and his friend, Bland, "a generous and amiable youth". Washington and M'Donald are next in importance, and the other officers are minor roles, as are the women, Mrs. Bland

[19] Brooks McNamara, *The American Playhouse in the Eighteenth Century* (Cambridge, Mass., 1969), 139. Mr. McNamara quotes from *The Daily Advertiser* of New York for January 31, 1798.
[20] *Diary*, 174-225.

and Honora. The two younger children of Mrs. Bland complete the cast.

Dunlap suggests to Cooper that he play Bland, but the latter would prefer the part of M'Donald, a sturdy American patriot, slow to anger, the *raissoneur* of the piece. No reason is given for this inclination on Cooper's part. Bland should have appealed to Cooper because it would have given him an opportunity to display his abilities – he had just been highly praised for his Hamlet – yet Bland, written in one key, may have seemed too full of histrionic cliches. Hodgkinson was chosen for André from the first, a selection which could have antagonized Cooper, who considered Hodgkinson inferior. Curiously enough, Dunlap notes in his diary that Hodgkinson told Cooper that André was the worst part of the three – Bland, M'Donald and André.

Dunlap reports that Cooper praised the play, that Dr. Timothy Dwight, Mrs. Dunlap's brother-in-law and President of Yale, "approves the sentiments attributed to André and Washington", and Hodgkinson, evidently satisfied with the play, is hopeful that it will be profitable for the theatre where expenses are far exceeding receipts.

On March 27, Dunlap reads *André* to the cast. The night before, Hodgkinson and Cooper had appeared in *Zorinski* by Thomas Morton. Cooper, falling into a non-professional habit which was to become more serious as time elapsed – that of being imperfect in his role if he did not particularly care for it and thus spoiling the scenes of others – antagonized Hodgkinson, and the two actors quarreled. The morning of the reading of *André* the dispute continued. That afternoon Cooper wrote Dunlap, desiring that *André* be postponed, but Dunlap was not able to grant the request, because he did not have money to pay salaries at the end of the week – and he would rather see the play "poorly presented than put off". Apparently, there were three rehearsals of *André* before it opened on the evening of March 30 – two the day before and one on the day of performance. For well-known stock pieces in the repertory this schedule would not have been unusual, but with a new play and with Cooper's known weakness in not memorizing lines, the business was chancy, as well it proved to be.

In spite of the disaster Cooper's negligence caused in contributing to the collapse of *André*, Dunlap, recalling the incident when he wrote his history of the American theatre, is amused in retrospect by the circumstances. He reports:

Our friend Cooper was at this time rather in the habit of neglecting such *parts* as were not *first*, or exactly to his mind. Young Bland was not the hero of the piece, and very little of the author's blank verse came *un-amended* from the mouth of the tragedian. In what was intended as the most pathetic scene of the play, between Cooper and Hodgkinson, the first, as Bland, after repeating, "oh, André – oh, André," . . . approached the unfortunate André, who in vain waited for his *cue*, and falling in a burst of sorrow on his neck, cried, loud enough to be heard at the side scene, "Oh, André – damn the prompter! – Oh, André! What's next, Hodgkinson," and sunk in unutterable sorrow on the breast of his overwhelmed friend, upon whose more practised stage cleverness he relied for support in the trying scene.[21]

Even with the deficiencies of Cooper, the drama was "much applauded"; it had new scenery and costumes and had been physically produced with all the care which Dunlap could lavish on it; it was not his fault that Cooper, particularly, failed him. It was a mistake to allow the play to be given when under-rehearsed, yet Dunlap was desperate for a success. The receipts were $817.00 – "a temporary relief", as Dunlap states in his history.[22] *André* might have recovered from the initial mistakes of the opening night, for audiences were unfortunately accustomed to inept performances, especially in an untried work.

There are then a number of reasons why *André* was not a success. The conditions for the failure of Dunlap's play which I have discussed – the subject matter too close to the actual event, the attempt to make a hero of a former enemy and a spy as well, the weakness of the production on the opening night – separately might not have brought on disaster; together they created a great hazard. What effectively and finally ruined the chances of the play were its political aspects, something which Dunlap could not foresee.

His intention was to write a patriotic American drama, transcending party strife, but it was almost impossible for him to do so, given the turmoil of the times. In 1798 America was in the midst of one of the most emotional periods in its history. Faction and dissension were everywhere between the leading parties, Federalist and Anti-Federalist or Republican. Dunlap notes that he attempted to keep a balance, but his own prejudice in favor of Federalism colors the play. More importantly, for the success of *André*, a point of view which gave both sides fairly would have satisfied no one, so intensely partisan was the political climate.

"The Federalist really believed, from 1783 to 1815, that the Repub-

---

[21] *History of the American Theatre*, 223. Dunlap also makes the point both in his history and in his diary that Cooper damned the play publicly as self-defense against his own inadequacies and that Dunlap's friends, annoyed by Cooper's carelessness on the opening night, damned the actor for contributing to the failure of *André*.
[22] *Ibid.*, 222.

licans aimed to destroy property and religion, and to make the United States a satellite to republican or imperial France. The Republicans really believed that the Federalists aimed to subject the country to a Northern plutocracy and, eventually, to a king who would be a satellite to George III."[23]

In 1798, the lines were becoming sharply drawn. The French Revolution and its pervading effect frightened the conservative Federalists while the Republicans saw in it a logical development of the American Revolution, and once more "Liberty" became a challenging cry.

The Federalists under President John Adams and the powerful Alexander Hamilton represented the party of property, chiefly mercantile, and its attitude was one of class-conscious arrogance. Its virtues lay in its recognition that a nation could only become "one from many" if there was order and a steady control over all its members, an ethic of order and control which applied as well to personal behaviour. Opposed to the Federalists and led by Thomas Jefferson were the agrarian forces in society, and also included the property-less, many of whom were impulsive and easily stirred, sometimes to public violence – a "mobocracy" of which the more conservative lived in fear. The Federalists were not aware in 1798 that their time was running out and that they had only two more years before Jefferson was to become President.

In the audience at the Park Theatre when *André* opened, both political factions were present. Dunlap refers to this fact when he mentions the "cockade business",[24] observing that this action "was not, perhaps could not be, understood by a mixed assembly". The cockade incident occurs in the play when Bland is pleading with Washington for the life of André. Washington is patient with the young impulsive soldier but makes it clear that ordering André's death is the only possible course he can take. He ends his explanation by telling Bland that his own merits are not overlooked and that he will be promoted. Whereupon Bland, in blind devotion to André's cause, renounces America, because it has forgotten to "reverence virtue" and tears from his hat the black and white cockade – "what once I proudly thought the badge of virtuous fellowship".[25]

[23]   Samuel Eliot Morison and Henry Steele Commager, *The Growth of the American Republic,* 2 vols, Fifth edition revised (New York, 1962), I, 370.
[24]   *History of the American Theatre*, 223.
[25]   *André*, 33. Officers in the Revolutionary War wore cockades in their hats to indicate their rank. In 1780 the cockade was changed to black with a white relief, indicating the union of the French and American armies. It was a symbol of the Revolution, similar to the flag.

By this action Bland defies both America and Washington, the still living hero of the Revolution. The audience considered the incident an affront to patriotism and an attack on national sensibilities, and there were hisses, the first indication in those days that ugly incidents might occur, leading, if not controlled, to serious altercations, if not to riot.

Although a riot did not take place, and the play was allowed to continue without any more interruption, the outcry against the overt act did not end after the curtain fell on opening night. As Dunlap reports, the argument increased outside the theatre. He was urged not to repeat *André*, even though a second performance had been announced for Monday, April 2. He consulted with his theatre friends, and finding that "general satisfaction was expressed", decided not to withdraw the play, because if he did so, he felt that such a withdrawal would be "an acknowledgement of its insufficiency".[26]

Before the second performance, Dunlap made an alteration in the script in the fifth act, a short sequence between M'Donald and Bland in which the former announces that Bland has been forgiven by Washington and returns to the young officer the cockade. Bland takes it with reverence, calling it the "glorious badge", "the proudest noblest ornament".[27] Although the change in the play was well received on the second night, the damage had been done, as is proven by a public attack on *André*.

In *The Argus*, or *Greenleaf's New Daily Advertiser*, there appeared on April 3 a letter signed "Z". (Dunlap in his diary identified him as "one Conolly an Irishman".) The writer states that *André* is the most insulting piece ever exhibited on the American stage. Dunlap, he says, rather than perpetuating American greatness, depreciates his country and converts Washington into "an unfeeling obdurate monster!" "Z" is horrified at the cockade business: "Bland, in the presence of the general, takes off his cap, plucks therefrom the *American cockade*, dashes it on the floor, and *tramples it underfoot*, vehemently cursing his country and their cause." "Z" then turns to the matter of a spy as hero – "It would seem a spy is to be looked upon as an honorable character! . . . a spy of whatever grade [is] the most detestable character in existence. . . . this man [André], the instrument of so black a deed, is held up a martyr, where every action was counted a virtue."

"Z" then comments upon two important omissions in the play, which by their inclusion would have "elevated" the country: Van Wart, Paul-

²⁶ *Diary*, I, 237.
²⁷ *André*, p. v.

ding and Williams, the captors of André are not present – "the brave and heroic veterans . . . who preferred the sacred cause . . . the liberty of their country – to sordid *Lucre* – that demon to which some of the great men of the present day bow their knee with reverential awe, bartering the liberty of their country, purchased with the blood of patriots, for that accursed dross". The scene of the capture was not included, says "Z", because it would have added too much lustre to the American character. A second serious omission was that of the court martial, the depiction of which would have shown how traitorous André actually was. Worse still, Dunlap's play is colored throughout by admiration for British humanity!

The letter concludes with an attack on the obvious zeal of the actor playing Bland (Cooper) in trampling "the insignia of liberty" underfoot. The inference is clear: an English actor is guilty of insulting an American audience, and, if he repeats his offense, he will be punished.

In the same issue of *The Argus* a reporter indirectly answers "Z" and defends Dunlap by stating that *André* was received with plaudits of the audience as well as the "more uniquivocal tributes to the Author's power by their tears". The report explains the cockade incident, noting that "a part of the audience" disapproved, but argues that Bland's passionate nature allied with his gratitude toward André motivated his action. Bland is strongly criticized in the play by the characters of Washington and others and this criticism clearly represents the playwright's own reaction toward Bland's mad act.

On April 5, Dunlap writes his own answer to "Z" in the third person, addressing his letter "To the crookedest and last letter in the Alphabet, Z". He says that "Z" has accused the author of *André* of perverting the facts in order to degrade his country and Washington. "Z" has attacked the playwright both as a man and as a dramatist. Either the correspondent did not see the whole play or did not understand what he heard, insists Dunlap, demanding that "Z" apologize in *The Argus* for defamation of character. He then proceeds to quote from *André* those passages relating to the greatness of Washington. He also quotes the short reference to the captors of André, in which he praises them for their incorruptibility, thereby answering the accusation of his critic that he entirely omitted the capture. (Dunlap is actually at a disadvantage in his defense, because he can only argue that a fleeting reference proves that attention was paid to the men who apprehended André. If he had dramatized the arrest of the spy, it could have been theatrically effective, underscoring the patriotic quality of the play by showing the rough-hewn American heroes of the capture, as he does in *The Glory of Columbia – Her Yeomanry!*, the revision of *André,* published in 1817.)

Dunlap continues his defense by saying that his play vindicates the execution of André and treats Washington as a hero. He reiterates the argument that Bland acted from unrestrained and misguided passion and suffers the consequences of his rashness; that he did not curse his country or her cause as "Z" asserts. Furthermore, Dunlap notes that Bland's action was a private one, observed only by Washington, and that upon his exit, after his violent speech, Washington, alone, severely castigates him by saying:

> Rash, headstrong, maddening boy!
> Had not this action past [*sic*] without a witness,
> Duty would ask that thou shouldst rue thy folly –
> But, for the motive, be the deed forgotten.

Dunlap then concludes his letter with the statement that, although André is praised, his deed is "reprobated", and the play is in itself strongly patriotic. "Z" has unfortunately "seen everything through the mist of prejudice and error". Dunlap signs his communication, "I".

Two days later, on April 7, "Z" addressing himself to "one I, the straightest letter in the alphabet", refutes the charge of slander and wilful intent to injure the author of *André.* He then proceeds to renew his attack on the play:

> ... the conduct of Bland to his general ... when trampling the national cockade with indignation under foot, because he was refused the life of a *villain*; this is the point which first aroused my indignation, and led me into the investigation of its merits; nor can all your sophisms convince me the author acted right, by introducing a scene of so degrading a tendency; if it were performed in private as you assert, would it have remained there yet, but when brought on a stage, it becomes a transaction of public notoriety, and therefore ceases to be a private deed, or taking it literally in your own words its a libel on the general, by insinuating he ever talked in private, what in public would meet his severest censure.

"Z" continues to argue that the capture of André should have been presented in order to extol patriotism and those who saved their country by taking the British spy. Finally, he states that Dunlap has been equivocal, praising André but not his deed, a deed "at the recital of which humanity shudders, a deed that contemplated nothing less than butchering in cold blood our brave citizen soldiers, and subjecting this fair tract ... to the galling yoke of British tyranny; if such actions as these draw praise he [André] has merited it in an eminent degree".[28]

Neither "Z" nor Dunlap comment upon one aspect of the cockade scene, enough to rouse the ire of the heady patriots in the audience. The violence to the cockade was accompanied by extremely provocative lines. Bland declares that he will keep his sword, proclaiming:

> Would, André, thou hadst never put thine off.
> Then hadst thou through opposers' hearts made way
> To liberty, or bravely pierc'd thine own.

Bland is romantically overwrought, and it is understandable that he would feel bitterly that injustice was being done to André, yet he is actually saying that André's "opposers", his captors, the highly honored patriots, Van Wart, Paulding and Williams, the salt of the earth and true democrats – should have been killed, thus giving the betrayer of America, one of the officer class as well, his freedom, or, at least, a fair chance to die honorably.

The letters end after April 7, there being no further production of *André*, and thus the paper war was discontinued. Dunlap, however, disappointed in what he hoped would be a successful venture and conscious that he had stirred more than a hornet's nest in a period of intense partisanship, continued his defense in the published edition of *André*.

The apology to the friends of André which Dunlap makes in his preface would seem to curry favor with the elite classes. All who knew André, he says, were his friends. Consequently, he has "adorned the poetical character of André with every virtue; he has made him his hero; to do which he was under necessity of making him condemn his own conduct in the one dreadfully unfortunate action of his life".[29] This statement was hardly conducive to appeal to the ardent patriot of 1798, when there were portents that the hard core of Federalists in the government, led by Hamilton, might make overtures to England in order to avoid further alignments with France. Those Republicans who saw or read *André* would not have forgotten that one of the principal defenders of the spy was Hamilton.

The preface is also illuminating for the defense Dunlap makes of Bland, who, in his defiance of Washington, has appeared to be almost pro-British. With somewhat obscure logic, Dunlap explains his interpretation of Bland. Instead of arguing that Bland acts as he does be-

---

[28]   *The Argus*, June 3, 5, 7, 1798.
[29]   *Preface*, iv.

cause he was under the malign influence of André, Dunlap writes:

To shew the effects which Major André's excellent qualities had upon the minds of men, the Author has drawn a generous and amiable youth, so blinded by his love for the accomplished Briton, as to consider his country, and the great commander of her armies as in the commission of such horrid injustice, that he, in the anguish of his soul, disclaims the service.[30]

Once again the emphasis is on the excellence of André, which is so pervasive that it can make men act against their judgment and side with an implacable enemy! Dunlap appears to realize that he may be straining his argument, because he reemphasizes the motivation for Bland's loyalty to André. This reason for Bland's devotion should, Dunlap explains, cause the audience "to mingle with their disapprobation a sentiment of pity". Unfortunately for Dunlap, pity would not outweigh the anger of the Republicans in the audience over what they could rightly assume was a sentimental justification of the relationship between an American soldier and one of the enemy. Dunlap in his diary on March 31, the day after the opening, confides as much. "Our warm and ignorant people look upon Bland's action as an insult to the Country" and on April 2, he notes, "I am told that the people are so offended at the Cockade business as to threaten to hiss off the play tonight". (It was performed, but the audience was sparse because a violent storm raged over the city; the applause, however, was "constant".)[31]

In his introduction to *André*, Professor Allan Halline calls attention to the reflection of Federalistic currents of the time in the play and to the prevailing conservative regard for the discipline of man's weak and impulsive nature by enlightened judgment and reason, and in contrast, the libertarian concept of man's freedom of choice and action.[32]

Washington, Melville, M'Donald, the chief American officers, represent the former point of view, while Bland is the violent apostle of heroic romanticism. By emphasizing this weakness in Bland, Dunlap draws the moral that rashness cannot be condoned in a well-ordered state, that man can live in harmony in society only if he respects the regulations imposed for the good of all. Bland's praise of the American soldier has a similar vein to that of Washington, but there is an obvious difference which demonstrates two points of view.

[30] *Ibid.*
[31] *Diary*, I, 237-238.
[32] *American Plays* (New York, American Book Company, 1935), 47-49.

BLAND

Brave spirits, rous'd by glory, throng our camp;

. . . .

To labour firmly under scorching skies,
And bear, unshrinking, winter's roughest blast.
This, and that heaven-inspir'd enthusiasm
Which ever animates the patriot's breast,
Shall far outweigh the lack of discipline.[33]

In the next scene, Washington comments:

'Tis well. Each sentinel upon his post
Stands firm, and meets me at the bayonet's point;

. . . .

SEWARD

They know to whom they owe their present safety.

GENERAL

I hope they know that to themselves they owe it:
To that good discipline which they observe,
The discipline of men to order train'd,
Who know its value, and in whom 'tis virtue:[34]

Bland's impulsiveness runs counter to André, who, in his disavowal of sentimentalism and untempered action, exercises the restraint of the reasonable man, making him similar to the conservative characters. In some respects André is more a Federalist than Washington.

André rings with patriotism and an unabashed love of country, a country, however, secured by union and not fragmented by separation of state against state, an idealized new world where, as M'Donald says, man's mind can be free and unshackled, "A resting spot for man, if he can stand firm in his place, while Europe howls around him." Yet Dunlap's cautionary theme throughout the play is that man is weak, "His tide of passion struggling still with Reason's/Fair and favorable gale, and adverse/Driving his unstable bark upon the/Rocks of error." As in man, so in a nation. The solemn and sober moralizing represents the playwright's honesty and is part of his credo that the first duty of the stage is to raise the standards of society, to make the arts the living embodiment of public and private virtue and to teach by example. The fatal weakness of *André* is that Dunlap's high purpose was imbued with a political didacticism which ran counter to the rising and voci-

[33] *André*, 11.
[34] *André*, 14.

ferous dissension of the common man, who Hamilton, the Federalist, once called "a great beast". *André* might have been successful if it had been produced in the triumph of Washington's first administration; in 1798, it had no chance of survival.

CHARLES H. SHATTUCK

PLAYHOUSE POLITICS: WILLIAM WOODFALL AND THE HAYMARKET THEATRE, 1777

The golden years of the Haymarket Theatre in the eighteenth century were those when the elder George Colman managed it (*pace* Samuel Foote!), and the goldenest year was the summer of 1777, Colman's first.[1] Colman had learned the business of management in association with Garrick at Drury Lane, had practised management with distinction for seven years at Covent Garden, then in 1774 had withdrawn to private life. After three years of rest – gentlemanizing, scribbling, publishing his *Dramatic Works* – he was ready once more to serve the public. Not, however, at either of the unmanageably expensive major houses, but at the only licensed summer house, the Little Theatre in the Hay.

When Colman took over the Haymarket from Samuel Foote, he was determined (but he kept his plans to himself) to fill it with a program which would rival the best that Covent Garden and Drury Lane could offer. The program which Foote had conducted, brilliant in its way, had been extremely limited, a one-man operation. He wrote his own plays – satires on contemporary topics and personages – and was his own principal actor. His supporting players were expected to behave like nobodies (anyone who dared to outshine Foote would find himself out of an engagement); stage management and rehearsal were minimal; scenery was drawn from the barest stock, shabby from overuse; costume was everyday wear, or if special dresses were needed, Foote rented them by the night from a nearby shop.[2] The attraction of Foote's theatre lay in Foote alone – his mimicry, effrontery, and wit.

Colman intended to reform this altogether. He would keep the house open six nights a week (Foote had played on alternate nights only), offering a program of comedies old and new, tragedies (especially

---

[1] The fullest history of the Haymarket is W. Macqueen Pope, *Haymarket: Theatre of Perfection* (London, 1948). Macqueen Pope disdains documentation, but is in the main reliable. For Colman, see Eugene R. Page, *George Colman the Elder* (New York, 1935).

[2] George Colman the Younger, *Random Records* (London, 1830), I, 231.

Shakespeare), musical plays, farces, burlesques – even Foote's own satires, which he hired Foote to perform. To sustain this ambitious program he engaged over forty actors and actresses, plus half a dozen child actors and a troupe of child dancers, capable among them of every kind of entertainment.[3] He brought into town to lead his company four players whose names had grown great in the country (and would grow greater in London hereafter): John Henderson, Elizabeth Farren, John Edwin, and West Digges. He would mount and dress every production to the limits of his resources, and stage manage them meticulously. His program would revolve with ceaseless novelty: no play, however attractive, would be allowed a run, but after one or two repetitions would give way to the next.

Such was Colman's bold plan – or so, from hindsight, it appears to have been. He did not publish it; he did not even, it appears, explain it to Foote at the time they sealed agreements for the transfer of the property. Foote, whose ideas about the Haymarket were fixed in the mold he had created, had declared that no one but a blockhead would dare attempt to conduct "so peculiar a theatrical concern as mine"; and as Colman's innovative program unfolded before him he betrayed his annoyance in sour comments upon it.[4]

Yet Colman confided in one influential figure, his young friend William Woodfall, the editor and theatre critic of the *Morning Chronicle*.[5]

Woodfall, who in later years won the nickname of "Memory Woodfall" for his astonishing feats of parliamentary reporting, in the 1770's took the lead among newspaper men in developing theatrical journalism toward something like its modern dimensions. He not only provided exhaustive descriptions of new plays (according to time-honored custom), but was singularly generous in writing up revivals of old plays, in heralding new actors and analyzing their work, in criticizing stage management and production, and in printing news of the backstage world. Other writers of the time followed his lead, to be sure, but Woodfall is conspicuous among them for his intimate knowledge of the theatre and his devotion to its welfare. His reporting was personal and

[3] The company list is given by Colman the Younger, I, 238.
[4] Colman the Younger, I, 232, 252.
[5] For the best account of Woodfall's work, see Charles Harold Gray, *Theatrical Criticism in London to 1795* (New York, 1931), pp. 220-226, 265-278. The sobriety of Woodfall's writing, together with anecdotes about his seriousness of manner, makes it difficult to remember that at this time he was not an *old* man. In 1777, he was 31. Colman was 45. John Henderson was 30.

lively, his judgements interested but for the most part impartial. Having grown up in the age of Garrick, he measured performances and players by high standards; yet, having himself dabbled briefly in the acting profession, he knew something of its practical difficulties, and could therefore bend his standards, if need be, for the accommodation and encouragement of newcomers. By 1777, Garrick had retired, and the London theatre was supposed to be sinking into hopeless decline, but Woodfall was committed to its resuscitation. Thus, when Colman, the wisest old hand in the business, was ready to take up management again, Woodfall was eager to support him. From the opening of Colman's season, the *Morning Chronicle* issued a steady flow of "theatrical intelligence" from the Haymarket, and the new productions were reviewed, re-reviewed, and paragraphed in generous measure.[6] Furthermore, according to the reminiscences of the playwright Samuel Arnold, it was Woodfall's custom "to send a private letter, on the morning following the production of any new piece at the Haymarket Theatre, to Mr. Colman, criticizing, with friendly zeal, the composition and the performance, and recommending such alterations, as none but a studious observer and sincere and experienced lover of the drama could have suggested".[7]

Colman's license allowed him to play from May 15 to September 15, and on May 15 he put on a show. But the odds were unexpectedly against him. Exactly a week before that date *The School for Scandal* had begun its triumphant career at Drury Lane. This drew the crowds away, and two or three of the actors Colman had engaged, being members of *The School for Scandal* company, were prevented from joining him. It rained too, torrentially, on May 15, so that although the carriage trade filled the Haymarket boxes respectably, the pit and gallery were nearly empty. Colman closed his operation at once, and trusting that Drury Lane would finish its season by the end of the month, announced a second opening for May 28.

Woodfall enthusiastically wrote up the May 15 performance as if it were a major event, filling twenty-three column inches on May 16, and on the following day adding several paragraphs more. He described

[6] By rough estimate, the *Morning Chronicle* devoted three or four times as much space to theatricals during this summer as did the *Morning Post*, and many times as much as did the *Gazetteer*.

[7] Richard Brinsley Peake, *Memoirs of the Colman Family* (London, 1841), II, 246. Arnold is not reporting the 1777 season, for he was then a toddler, but a somewhat later one when as a very young boy he accompanied his musician father to Haymarket rehearsals.

Colman's special Prologue,[8] which was an exercise in modesty, fun, and managerial cunning; it said almost nothing about future plans, for the moment had not come, in the game as Colman played it, to reveal what the summer would have in store. The Prologue led off with playful simile: the vast winter theatres, like great warehouses, for eight months dispense huge bales of merchandise; now with the coming of summer the little shopkeeper of the Haymarket, "the smallest haberdasher of small wares",[9] would bring out his "slight goods" for the summer trade – "his Taffata and lutestring plays". A summer theatre is a foolhardy venture, perhaps, like the Laputan scheme to draw sunbeams out of cucumbers, for the citizenry has small need of plays in summer weather. See fat citizen Inkle and his fatter wife turning their backs on the Haymarket and climbing Highgate Hill, where, unbuttoned, they stuff their bellies with "fish, flesh, fowl, pastry, custard, jelly" from their picnic basket and enjoy the evening air. Only in the final section of the Prologue is there any reference to the entertainments that lay ahead, confirming what was already generally known, that Samuel Foote, "your good old hay-maker, long here employed", would be on hand

> ev'n in the hottest day,
> And kindly help us to get in our hay.

The main piece of the evening, Colman's own ten-year-old comedy of *The English Merchant*, offered little for critical comment, but Woodfall praised the "regularity and propriety" of its production "which spoke the care and attention of the manager", noticed the actors, objected to one inappropriate costume, and acknowledged two new scenes, a Saloon and a Library, painted by Mr. Canter. The farce gave him more to write about. It too was an old piece – Garrick's *Lilliput* – but it had been freshed up for the occasion. Garrick contributed a new song about the "Ton, the dear Ton". Colman satirized the current passion for gambling with a procession of figures dressed as playing cards, and added to the procession a couple of figures to spoof current absurdities in female dress: one woman wore a monstrously tall wig and a huge cork rump, another rode an ostrich whose backside had been plucked bare to provide the plumage she wore on her head. The

[8] *Morning Chronicle* (May 16 and 17, 1777). The Prologue was printed in the *Gazetteer* (June 16, 1777), and published by Colman in *Prose on Several Occasions* (London, 1787), III, 217.
[9] Colman, who like Garrick and Henderson was very short, was commonly referred to as "Tiny Coley" and the "Little Manager".

cast of *Lilliput* consisted mainly of child actors and the dancing pupils from the school of Monsieur Georgi. It occurred to Woodfall that the professional elders of these children might take lessons from their unaffected playing:

Admiral Flimnap would teach them a natural mode of expressing humour; which consists of the art of exciting laughter in the audience without the actor's once grinning himself. His foppish brother would shew that a comedian may exhibit the character of a coxcomb, without appearing to assume an unnatural appearance.

For his second opening two weeks later Colman still had to mark time, for *The School for Scandal* was still running strong at Drury Lane and would continue until June 7. Taking his cue from a current labor strike by the Journeymen Tailors of London, he revived another old piece, a burlesque called *The Tailors, A Tragedy for Warm Weather.* Of this Woodfall could find little distinctive to say beyond congratulating the manager for his attempt to laugh the Knights of the Thimble out of their absurd revolt and back into "industry, good meals, and good wages".[10]

As the season proper got under way, Woodfall called the attention of his readers to one after another of Colman's managerial accomplishments. On June 5, for instance, he noted that Colman had put together a company which would satisfy every playgoer's appetite. For wit and humor he had engaged old Foote (already seen in *The Nabob*). For music there was a troupe of songsters headed by the well-known Mr. Dubellamy. Monsieur Georgi's children would be on hand to play the fairies in *A Midsummer Night's Dream* or for "some other two-foot-and-a-half capacity". Next to be seen, as Kate Hardcastle in *She Stoops to Conquer*, was a "very, very young Lady" from Liverpool and Birmingham, Miss Elizabeth Farren: Woodfall urged the Town to give her a friendly reception. Beyond these attractions (and unheard of in the summer time) "the lovers of the roast beef of the drama" should know that Colman has "given direction that some of the best cuts of that English ox, Shakespeare, may be cooked according to the Bath fashion, and served up by the King of the Western kitchen, Mr. Henderson".

In his review of *She Stoops to Conquer* and *Midas* (June 10), Woodfall praised the new order of stage management. Whereas under Foote's direction "a relaxation of discipline has been fallen into at the Haymarket Theatre, and the town have long since given up every expecta-

10 *Morning Chronicle* (May 28 and 29, 1777).

tion of a correct representation there", we are now both surprised and pleased by "the very regular manner in which the Comedy and the Burletta were exhibited. All the business of the stage perfect, all the little parts smoothly given, and the whole rather superior than inferior to a performance at either of the Winter Theatres!" Again after Henderson's first appearance in *The Merchant of Venice,* Woodfall wrote in the same flattering tone (June 12):

If the exhibitions at the Haymarket playhouse ... continue to be equally respectable with those of yesterday and Monday, it will seem as if Mr. Colman meant to satyrize the conduct of the Winter Managers, by not only representing their stock plays as well as they have done, but in producing to the Town such actors and actresses as give the lie to the general exclamation, "That the stage is rapidly on the decline, and that there are not any good performers to be obtained."

In mid-June when Foote's scheduled performances were interrupted by his sudden illness, Woodfall commiserated with Colman on this disruption of his arrangements – but, "the little man possesses a great soul, and faces danger boldly" (June 19). When Colman produced John Gay's *Polly,* Woodfall praised the cuts and revisions by which Colman gave the loosely written piece "dramatic rotundity and completeness" (June 20). He was delighted with the dressing and scenery of *Richard III,* especially with the staging of the Tent scene, "judiciously managed with regard to the lighting it withinside the tent only" (August 8). After the appearance of West Digges, he congratulated Colman for having put on exhibition, in the persons of Henderson and Digges, the finest representatives of the "new school" and the "old school" of tragic acting (August 16). At the end of the season (September 16) he publicized Colman's generosity in awarding benefits, including the fact that Henderson was given the total receipts of this night, without a shilling's deduction for house expense. Finally he reminded his readers that although at the beginning of the summer Colman had introduced himself as no more than a retailer of "lutestrings and taffaties", he had in fact served up a program of extraordinary richness and variety.

May the encouragement he has received stimulate the managers of our winter Theatres, to exert themselves in the same manner, by which means the publick will have a perpetual round of rational entertainment, as superior to mere shew, pageantry, and pantomime, as sense is superior to absurdity!

Yet as that summer passed all was not puffs and roses. Woodfall was no sycophant, and as monitor of public opinion he had to maintain his reputation for impartiality. When singers warbled out of tune or actors misinterpreted their roles he called them to account – in kindly fashion if it appeared a matter of first-night nervousness, but sharply if he thought them dead wrong. When a pair of careless actors once spoiled a scene of Miss Farren's by not knowing their lines, he rebuked them. Although he admired the comedian John Edwin, he had to scold him once for reading his part from the book, again for overacting Justice Woodcock, again for underacting Autolycus. Let an actress, out of vanity, disdain to dress and perform a low comedy role as it was written, and she and Colman and all London would hear of it. On June 20 he read a lesson in this matter to Mrs. Davies, who had got up the old bawd Diana Trapes in *Polly* as a fine lady:

> She appeared to throw cold water on the character, and played as if she thought her talents trifled with. Surely this Lady did not think herself demeaned by performing a bawd; there never was so ridiculous an idea as that, which some actresses are said to entertain, that whoever takes an immoral character, does herself an injury. There cannot be a more absurd opinion. . . . Let her this evening bring her abilities fairly forward, let her face resemble old age, and let her dress like Diana Trapes; she last night looked more like one of the beauties just imported . . . than the dram-drinking procuress, to whom those beauties were consigned.

His criticism was attended to. Thereafter Mrs. Davies dressed Trapes in character, and played it "with that proper degree of humour and spirit, which marks her acting in general".

When Colman presented West Digges in Addison's *Cato*, he was courting danger. Digges, the Roscius of the North, being an actor of the "old school", his style, like that of the play itself, was formal, statuesque, oratorical, "classic" – reminiscent (for those with long memories) of the style of Barton Booth and James Quin. The "natural" acting of Garrick and Macklin, and now John Henderson, had long since persuaded London that the "old school" was intolerably obsolete. Yet Colman dared to test whether such a museum piece could still please. He took great pains to mount the play very much as it had looked sixty-five years earlier: arranging a grand funeral procession, dressing the actors in the "Roman style", with full-bottomed periwigs, as in bygone days.[11] On the whole, he got away with it. Digges' authority was sufficient to carry the role. But the playing of the supporting actors was wretchedly out of keeping, and Woodfall put the blame squarely on Colman's shoulders.[12]

---

[11]   Colman the Younger, I, 253.
[12]   *Morning Chronicle* (August 15, 1777).

The Tragedy of last night was presented in such a manner as sufficiently shewed the Manager was out of town, or rather not at rehearsal, while it was getting up; we do not mean by this to censure the Manager, we hope he was better employed for the publick in the composition of some new piece, and only hint at it, because most of the actors slurred over their parts without sufficiently enforcing the beauties, and discriminating those particular varieties, which may escape even good actors, but which a Manager is not only presumed to be capable or seeing, but which it is strictly his duty to teach the performers.

Because the actors had not been taught their business, the characters of Portius and Marcus were undistinguishable, the fiery Marcus being played as cold as ice; Marcia and Lucia, too, "both spoke in the same key"; Mr. Blisset failed to bring power and variety to Syphax, and Mr. Palmer, as Juba, paid no attention to the dramatic situations or the speeches of Syphax, but only spoke in a loud voice, "unmeaningfully threw his eyes into the boxes, or improperly strutted about the stage". As for Digges' performance, Woodfall was delighted with it, professing his "reverence for the old theatre and its peculiarities", comparing his avidity for old school acting to that with which "the Antiquary runs to see an ancient coin", likening the actor to "a book full of truth and logic, printed in the old black letter, – disagreeable and crabbed to read at first, but . . . replete with matter worth the searching for even amidst the rust and hardness of antiquity". But the play as a whole had been ruined by bad stage management, and the manager's feelings were no bar to Woodfall's making his displeasure known.

The most exacting critical problem for Woodfall that summer was what to do about the prize lion of Colman's company, the young *débutant* from Bath, John Henderson.[13] Henderson was bidding for London recognition; Colman, though he had other strings to his bow, was staking the success of his season upon the success of Henderson. The Town was divided. Half the public, hankering after novelty, proclaimed Henderson heir-apparent to Garrick:

> Though dead to the Town, see a Garrick return!
> And H. like a Phoenix, arise from his urn.[14]

The other half, loyal to Garrick, resented him as a pretender:

[13] Henderson was biographized at the time of his death by John Ireland, *Letters and Poems by the Late Mr. John Henderson, with Anecdotes of His Life* (London, 1786). See also [T. Davies], *A Genuine Narrative of the Life and Theatrical Transactions of Mr. John Henderson, commonly called the Bath Roscius* (London, 1777).
[14] From "An Epigram", in the *Morning Chronicle* (August 18, 1777).

Tho' you deal in magic spell
Hope not Garrick to excel.

You, tis true, do more than well,
But you ne'er can *him* excel.[15]

But everyone flocked to see him, and from court circles to taverns
Henderson was the common topic. Now Woodfall did not like him as
an actor (certainly could not accept him as a second Garrick); yet out
of common fairness, and out of loyalty to Colman, he had to veil his
prejudices. His first notices of Henderson are specimens of cautious
trimming. As the weeks rolled along and the triumph of the management
passed beyond question, he could afford to indulge in plain speaking.
By the end of the summer he had got most of his objections to Henderson into print.

There was, of course, much about Henderson to be admired. He was
highly intelligent, well educated, skilled in languages, modestly gifted
as a painter and poet, well versed in the classics of English literature,
devoted to Shakespeare. In society he behaved like a gentleman, and
professionally he was mannerly and unassuming – at least until the
autumn of 1777, after the close of his Haymarket engagement, when
as we shall see he became involved in a tactless, unbecoming piece of
self-promotion. The story of his career attracted sympathy too. When
he had earlier sought entrée to the London theatre, three of the great
moguls of the establishment – Garrick, Colman, and Foote – had
snubbed him. Banished, as it were, to the provinces (Garrick, to be
sure, had helped him secure an engagement at Bath – but spiteful
whispers went the rounds that Garrick, fearing rivalry, would do anything to keep him out of London), he quite by his own efforts achieved
the status of leading actor, became known as The Bath Roscius, won a
reputation which reverberated throughout the kingdom.

Woodfall may have admired all this. But private virtues are not
actorship, and success in Bath might or might not presage success in
London. In September of 1776 (Race Week), Woodfall went down to
Bath to see for himself. He found what he probably expected, and came
home half pleased, half disappointed.

His mixed report appeared in the *Morning Chronicle* of September
26, 1776, oddly disguised as a letter from an anonymous correspondent.
Undoubtedly Woodfall wrote this letter, which is addressed to himself

[15] Refrain lines from a long poem addressed to Henderson, in the *Morning
Chronicle* (August 20, 1777).

and signed "A London Rider". In the opinion of this fictitious "informant", Henderson lacked the figure, features, or voice to be a good actor, and won applause solely because he had "good sense enough to conceive what he says" – i.e., because of the intelligence of his reading. The "informant" saw him in four roles. First as Sciolto in *The Fair Penitent*: "I never received a worse impression of a performer in my life. From scene the first to scene the last it was a palpable mimickry of Garrick's voice, without that great accompaniment, Garrick's eye and expressive countenance." Particularly offensive was his imitation of the "unwelcome guttural harshness" which afflicted Garrick toward the end of his career. Next as Lorenzo in *The Spanish Friar*: though easy and vivacious enough, he totally lacked the figure to impersonate an attractive rake. As Comus, on the other hand, he was surprisingly excellent – "delivering the silvered speeches . . . with a most elegant propriety, equally distant from pedantry and dullness, and the rest of the performers so well, that I not only kept awake, but received as large a share of entertainment as I ever experienced in a theatre." As Falstaff, too, he gave pleasure. He "wanted the speaking eye", be it noted, but his judicious speaking of the language was remarkable. "It was evident from his delivery that he had a clear conception of the character. That he had studied Shakespeare with a very inquiring mind, and that he was perfect master of his meaning." In conclusion, says the "informant", great as are Henderson's merits, highly esteemed as he is at Bath both as a man and as an actor, "I am convinced, that from his deficiency in the external requisites, he would make but a poor figure on either of our London stages. At Bath he passes for current coin; in town he might possibly be deemed a counterfeit."

Henderson was fully aware of Woodfall's visit, and knew him to be the author of the damning letter. During his negotiations with Colman in March of 1777, he alluded to Woodfall's advice "to stay where I am, cultivate my private character, and resign all hopes of fame and fortune to those who are better qualified by nature to contend for them".[16] He confessed his fear of being rough-handled by Woodfall when he entered on his London engagement. Obviously he was unaware of the close alliance between Woodfall and Colman – a cabal which would work in his favor.

Colman managed Henderson's début with superb finesse. The two

---

[16] Peake, I, 424, and Ireland, 189. See also Ireland, 186, for a letter from Henderson to a friend on November 7, 1776, in which he identifies "A London Rider" with Woodfall.

faults which would most seriously endanger Henderson before a London audience were these: his awkward figure and his resemblance to (tendency to imitate?) Garrick. Therefore Colman decreed that he should open in Shylock – a role not in Garrick's repertory, and one in which his figure would be concealed under the Jewish gaberdine.[17] Henderson objected strenuously: Shylock belonged to Charles Macklin, as everybody knew, and to play it, he thought – especially to open in it – would stir up invidious comparisons. He wanted no contest with other actors, nor with the "public spirit". Indeed, he preferred to avoid heavy and serious drama altogether during his first London engagement, and to creep humbly into public favor with such comic roles as Valentine, Oakley, and Leon: "I do not think myself ripe enough in the high tragic line; and . . . tragedy will never be followed in the dog-days except some extraordinary planet of attraction appears." But Colman talked him down, assuring him that his acting style was so remote from Macklin's that his Shylock would seem wholly new, would provoke not comparison but healthy controversy. "He added also, that to make people talk and argue, and dispute, was what he aimed at, and seemed to be certain, that if he could do that, my reputation would be established by it." [18] Colman's strategy was dangerous, but the event proved him right. Most of the critics of the June 11 opening inevitably *did* refer to Macklin's Shylock, but rather as a topic for consideration than as a club to beat down Henderson.[19] And the Town did begin to talk.

In his own review, as if by agreement, Woodfall did not mention Macklin once. He flattered Henderson generally and generously. "His scene with Tubal, was equal to any piece of acting we remember to have been witness of." He said that Henderson completely understands the poet's meaning; he is perfectly free from any charge of imitation; he has a "dramatic mind". He deserved all the applause he received, and if he keeps up to this measure in his future roles, the town will soon agree with us that he is "not only a good but a great actor". Into this praise of Henderson Woodfall threaded as much praise of Colman; after that he praised the supporting actors. At the very end he remembered to find fault with one costume, but apart from that little touch his review was an unadulterated puff.[20] Shylock succeeded so well that during the next week Henderson played it four times.

[17]   Colman the Younger, I, 248.
[18]   Letters from Henderson to John Ireland, January 8, and February 12, 1777. See Ireland, 189-192.
[19]   For example, the *Morning Post* and the *Gazetteer*, June 12, 1777.
[20]   *Morning Chronicle* (June 12, 1777).

On June 19 Woodfall paragraphed a teasing bit of news from behind the scenes. A debate had been in progress there over which character Henderson ought to play next. One party, led by the "real Roscius" (i.e., Garrick), insisted that having now painted a "dark" character, he should next exhibit his comic skill in Don John of *The Chances*. Colman, however, decided otherwise. Since tragedy is the "nobler theme", the second role would be Hamlet, and the tragedy of that name has gone into rehearsal.

The reasons for Colman's decision were much more complicated than this which Woodfall advertised. He knew that a second success was absolutely necessary to cap the success of Shylock, and Don John was emphatically not the role in which to seek it. The Don John of David Garrick had been one of his most celebrated pieces of comic acting, a miracle of gaiety and grace. If Henderson played it he would imitate, or seem to imitate, Garrick and be damned for his pains; if he took care to avoid imitation he would be damned anyway by comparisons. Moreover, Don John was an "undisguised" role – that is, it was then played as a contemporary London rake, dressed in the height of fashion – and undeniably Henderson "wanted figure". According to Colman the Younger, his father counted on Hamlet's "inky cloak" and "solemn suit of black" to divert attention from Henderson's awkwardly made body.[21] The choice was right. When *Hamlet* played on June 26 and 27, it was hugely successful.

At this point Woodfall apparently concluded that the moment of danger had passed – that Henderson had won popular acceptance and Colman's venture was justified. His tone sharpened; he permitted himself to "criticize". His review congratulates Henderson for his success, of course, and congratulates the public for having found a new favorite, who "now stands in the publick opinion as an actor of infinite merit". But at once it points out that Henderson's Hamlet is "clearly built on Mr. Garrick's model". Not, to be sure, that Henderson has servilely copied Garrick, but that like Garrick he allies himself to "nature" and exhibits a "thinking mind". Woodfall would not *compare* the two – yet he makes plain that Garrick's Hamlet is the better. He grants Henderson that no one has ever given the advice to the Players more effectively, for here Henderson lays aside the actor and in an "easy gentleman-like manner" gives the good sense of the author fair play. Yet there are passages in which he is "below par". In the opening scenes he sinks too deeply under sorrow, and adopts a "womanish expression". In the

[21]   Colman the Younger, I, 248.

Closet scene, he is pathetic rather than indignant in comparing his uncle and his father. In challenging Laertes in the Grave scene he speaks too sensibly: there he ought to "rant" a bit as a sign that his judgement is drowned in passion. There is too much pantomine in his dying scene. If he will but remedy these small defects he can easily render his much commended performance altogether perfect.[22]

After Hamlet, Colman was willing to risk his prize actor in what we should call a "straight" part. This was the noble Leon, in *Rule a Wife and Have a Wife,* which opened on July 15. As Leon, Henderson had to stand forth as an undisguised gentleman-comedian-hero. At once, almost forseeably, the critics from all sides began to snap at him. According to the *Gazetteer,* for instance, "he labors so much at being correct, that he destroys the passion, and presents the mere actor to the view".[23] The *Morning Post* objected, in terms which echo the judgement of "A London Rider" nine months earlier, that he has little to commend him beyond close study of the author and sensible recitation:

This however will go but a little way toward constituting the real *actor.* Voice, – person, – features, – dignity and grace, – passions of the finest texture, with a thousand inexpressible, though necessary *minutiae* must all unite their first-rate qualities, and center in one man, to stamp him the genuine hero of the *sock* and *buskin.* How far the gentleman in review comes within the scope of this description, let his too zealous panegyrists declare.[24]

On this occasion Woodfall seems almost to have lost heart for his subject. His review is brief. He can praise the humor of the early passages in which Leon plays the "natural", and can mention the "firm and feeling" delivery of those lines in which Leon asserts command over his wife. Yet, he says, Henderson does not quite bring off the scenes in which the dignity of the character rises; and on the whole this performance is inferior to either his Shylock or his Hamlet.[25]

If Henderson's Leon justified the hostile prophecies of "A London Rider", his Falstaff (July 24) struck Woodfall as even worse. If Colman was relieved at getting his actor hidden once more under costume, no amount of padding concealed from Woodfall what he *now* took to be Henderson's inadequacy for this difficult role.[26] He began by admitting that the audience laughed a great deal, but what audience ever

[22] *Morning Chronicle* (June 27 and 28, 1777).
[23] *Gazetteer* (July 16, 1777).
[24] *Morning Post* (July 17, 1777).
[25] *Morning Chronicle* (July 16, 1777).
[26] *Morning Chronicle* (July 25, 1777).

failed to laugh when the fat Knight was on the stage? In the present instance it is the poet, not the performer that excites pleasure.

Mr. Henderson is denied by Nature two great requisites for a successful personifier of Falstaff; his figure is too *petite*, and his voice too limited, in point of power and variety. In consequence of the first defect, he looked more like a descendant of the Knight, when the race of Falstaff had degenerated in size, than the Knight himself; and, in consequence of the latter, he sounded as if the race had also degenerated in the power of expressing the family humour.

Having thus, as it were, thrown Henderson's Falstaff out of court, Woodfall softens his blame with faint acknowledgments of worth. Henderson is as good a Falstaff as in the present state of the stage we can expect. He has conceived the part better than he can express it. In most of the scenes of the first three acts he was "very near the standard of excellence". In the fourth act he described his tattered regiment in a manner "exceedingly happy". But the phrase "exceedingly happy" suddenly turns on itself, pun-like, and means "*too* happy": Henderson "played too long on the same key, and finding that the house felt the humour of his beginning the description, pursued it monotonously to the finish of it". What this means Woodfall would spell out more clearly a few months later, when Henderson repeated Falstaff at Drury Lane: "He puzzles the hearer by chuckling in the middle of a period, and laughing at his own joke, as it were, before it is born." [27] In the catechism of honor, says Woodfall, he "failed egregiously", expressing the negatives in a manner "ridiculous and disgusting" (evidently Henderson chose to bellow every repetition of the word "No!").[28] He did not give force enough to the line, "If thou embowel me today, I'll give you leave to powder me and eat me too tomorrow." His humor throughout was not sufficiently "luxuriant and rich", and most of the time he quite forgot the "age and unwieldiness" of the character. Woodfall concludes his attack with the conventional apology: last night the actor was applauded by fifteen out of every score of the audience; if he will mend the faults here mentioned (Query: get born again as unlike himself as possible, as Shaw would sometime advise Beerbohm Tree?) he will be applauded by all twenty.

Henderson's fifth role (August 7) was Richard III, and, happily for all concerned, Woodfall was again able to eulogize.[29]

---

[27] *Morning Chronicle* (October 22, 1777). See also "Quin's Ghost" in the *Gazetteer* (August 19, 1777), and "Clio" in the *Morning Post* (October 25, 1777).
[28] See "An Admirer of Genius" in the *Morning Chronicle* (July 26, 1777).
[29] *Morning Chronicle* (August 8 and 9, 1777).

Mr. Henderson's merit has so firmly fixed him a favourite with the Publick, that whenever he performs a new character, he is sure to be both brilliantly and numerously attended. The audience last night did themselves honour by the encouragement they gave to genius, and the loud applause they bestowed upon the able representative of Richard.

This, he believed, was Henderson's very best role, "a perfect and complete specimen of great acting".

In the early part of the play his manner was finely adapted to deceive common observers; in the scenes with Buckingham, he refined upon that manner, so as to defy the detection of even those who look closer; and after the death of the Princes, the mask was evidently thrown aside, and nature spoke her sentiments without disguise; in fact he gave the simulation, dissimulation, and naked feelings of the character, with a nicety and a force of discrimination, which spoke at once the man of genius, and the actor of ability.

Woodfall was delighted by certain restorations Henderson had made to the Cibber text, proving his close study of Shakespeare; by his handling of the "side speeches", treating them seriously, as Garrick did, and not tossing them out as mere jests for the amusement of the galleries; by his delivery of the soliloquies; by his exhibition of the tortures of conscience after the Dream scene; by his sustainment of the dignity of Richard in the last acts. There were corrections to offer, of course ("we are not blindly bent on crying him up as a miracle of perfection"), but not censoriously. His appearance is perhaps too youthful ("a certain round juvenility of face"); and in the Wooing scene he adopts too whining a manner. In a second notice, a day later, Woodfall spelled out an objection of wider application:

We would also advise Mr. Henderson to be somewhat less deliberate in his delivery; he appears occasionally, rather, as it were, to labour at emphasis, which not only takes from the spirit of the author, but is an ill compliment to the judgment of the audience, and warrants an inference that they could not readily comprehend, if the poet's meaning was not rammed into them.

This is an astute recognition of a certain schoolmasterly attitude which sometimes affected Henderson's playing – the condescension of an "intellectual" actor to an audience which he thinks cannot grasp the idea unless he "rams" it home. On the whole, however, Woodfall's reviews of *Richard III* are a flattering endorsement of Henderson. He even congratulates the management of Drury Lane for having by now engaged him for the ensuing winter: "He will certainly be a brilliant ornament in their crown, and ought not any longer to continue set in lead among foil-stones, and pieces of cut glass."

We need not follow closely Woodfall's opinions of Henderson's final three roles of the season, for they add little to what he had already expressed. August 19 brought at last the trial of Don John in *The Chances*. It won little credit from Woodfall. Although he found it "pleasing" and noted the satisfaction of the audience, yet "all his master-strokes ... are direct and close imitations of Mr. Garrick's voice, gesture, action, and deportment".[30] Thus Colman's earlier decision to withhold Don John until Henderson had fixed his London reputation was vindicated. Bayes in *The Rehearsal* (August 25) ought to have garnered unique laurels, for it was customary in that role to parody the style of well known actors, and Henderson was a gifted mimic. But whether from modesty or from fear of reprisals, Henderson declined to play that game. According to the *Morning Post* he introduced *compliments* to Garrick and a satiric reference to newspaper critics, but otherwise confined himself to the letter of the text. Woodfall, in a notice of unusual brevity, claims to have seen "a more laughable Bayes, but we do not remember any performer who stuck more closely to the dramatic nature of the character".[31] On September 3 *The Merry Wives of Windsor* was got up for the benefit of Mr. Jewell, the Haymarket treasurer, and Henderson played the lesser Falstaff. Woodfall compliments him briefly (though finding him "a little under par"), acknowledges the wide range of characters he has performed during the summer, and ends on a curious note of admonishment:

He is entitled to general encouragement, and although he is yet much short of perfection as an actor, he cannot fail of improving rapidly, if his too zealous friends do not intoxicate him with false praise, and entice him to form a premature opinion of his own merit, and shut his ears against instruction.[32]

Similar warnings against pride and the dangers of flattery had appeared in other papers during the summer, which one would take as no more than the customary advice to rising actors. The "zealous friends" that Woodfall refers to were probably specific persons. Two months later one of them (evidently Tom Davies) published a book about Henderson which seriously damaged his reputation. Entitled *A Genuine Narrative of The Life and Theatrical Transactions of Mr. John Henderson, commonly called The Bath Roscius*, it "bespattered" Henderson with "fulsome flattery" and was "nauseously contemptible" (so the *Morning Post* put it), and it savagely attacked the critics and various men in the

[30] *Morning Chronicle* (August 20, 1777).
[31] *Morning Post* (August 26, 1777); *Morning Chronicle* (August 26, 1777).
[32] *Morning Chronicle* (September 4, 1777).

profession who were supposed to have hindered Henderson's advance-
ment. From its contents, including private letters, everyone could see
that Henderson had been a party to the compiling of it. Although he
printed a feeble disclaimer, no one believed him, and the reviewers of
his work at Drury Lane, including Woodfall, grew increasingly acerb.[33]

It has not been my purpose in this essay to assess George Colman's
whole accomplishment in that remarkable first summer at the Haymarket, but only to bring to light certain strategies of his managerial
technique. The partial view of John Henderson which emerges here
nowise represents his actorship as it ultimately developed. To appreciate Henderson one would have to study his career in its entirety,
taking into account the testimony of the Kembles and Boadens of the
following generation, who remembered him worshipfully as a master
player.[34] In the summer of 1777, whatever his histrionic abilities may
have been, he was an innocent in playhouse politics, a pawn in the
hands of a cunning manager. In that summer, luckily but almost un-
wittingly, he had greatness thrust upon him.

The figure who comes through most vividly from these events is the
critic William Woodfall. The actor's art is half lost in shadow, the
manager's ingenuity is a matter of hearsay. But Woodfall's very words
– his instant responses to the events – are preserved in the files of his
newspaper exactly as he wrote them. His news and reviews of the
Haymarket that summer, if hardly "great criticism", are the lively, warm
effusions of a generous partisan. At times they are rambling, garrulous,
repetitious, as if he believed that the more inches he wrote the better
he would serve the cause. From week to week his opinions are not
perfectly consistent – indeed, one might say, not always quite "honest",
for in his secret commitment to the politics of management he sometimes had to temporize. At the beginning of the season, for instance, he
praised Henderson more than he "honestly" should have done, because
to a degree Colman's success depended upon Henderson's success, and
he preferred to muffle his distaste for Henderson's acting in order to
support the greater cause.[35] When he wrote in this vein, his sentences

---

[33] Denunciations of *A Genuine Narrative* appeared in the *Morning Post* (November 14), and in the *Morning Chronicle* (November 12 and 14, 1777). Henderson's
disclaimer is in the *Morning Chronicle* (November 13).
[34] For a balanced account of Henderson, see Bertram Joseph, *The Tragic Actor*
(London, 1959), 177-186.
[35] John Ireland doubtless had Woodfall in mind when he said that some of the
daily critics praised Henderson "for merit he did not profess" and that their motive
in this was to serve Colman. See Ireland, 201.

repeat themselves and stumble into platitudes and evasions in a manner which betrays his private discontent. Later on, when Henderson's drawing power was established beyond doubt, he could write more incisively, denouncing his "bad" Falstaff or dismissing his Don John and Bayes as the second-rate work he held them to be. Toward the end of the summer he could acknowledge without strain (yet again without committing himself on the actor's *quality*) that Henderson had performed the most ambitious repertory ever seen at the Haymarket, had pleased the Town, and had really earned the forthcoming Drury Lane engagement which would rescue him from the "foil-stone and cut glass" surroundings of the provincial theatre.

His wobbling attitude toward Henderson is not altogether blameworthy. Although it produced some specious writing, the motivation of it was generosity. The overall effect of Woodfall's summer's work is encouragement, gratulation, and rejoicing. Seeking nothing for himself, he watched, praised, criticized, and advertized in every way that could sustain the grand plan to make the Haymarket a playhouse of first-rate importance: a worthy investment of journalism for the public good.

RICHARD MOODY

AMERICAN ACTORS AND AMERICAN PLAYS ON THE LONDON STAGE IN THE NINETEENTH CENTURY

Every theatre season produces a lively interchange between London's West End and New York's Broadway. Plays, performers, and entire productions move in both directions. During the past twenty-five years London's Drury Lane Theatre has been occupied almost constantly by American musical theatre troupes, from *Oklahoma* to *My Fair Lady* to *Mame*; and as we all know the past few seasons on Broadway would have been exceedingly bare without London's *The Hostage, A Man For All Seasons, The Caretaker, Oliver, Beyond The Fringe, The Knack, Oh What a Lovely War, The Killing of Sister George,* and *The Man in the Glass Booth.* This is not a complete list. Most of us are also aware of our early theatre's dependence on the mother country. Most of the plays performed here in the late eighteenth and early nineteenth centuries were British plays, and those of local origin, more often than not, were based on English models. Throughout the nineteenth century every English actor of any consequence sought a substantial part of his fortune in the new country: Edmund Kean, William Macready, Henry Irving and Ellen Terry, to mention two of the early invaders and two from late in the century. Less familiar is the record of the performers, plays, and miscellaneous theatrical exhibitions that made the eastbound journey across the Atlantic during the nineteenth century. The record of that American invasion of the English theatre will be explored in the following pages.

The first American who made any substantial impression in England was, of course, John Howard Payne, although there were a few other early actors whose names are now little known. On October, 13, 1802, a Mr. Hardinge, advertised as "from the Theatre, Philadelphia" appeared at Drury Lane in a play called *The West Indian.* He was playing the part of a Major O'Flaherty and evidently was ill-prepared to handle the Irish brogue, at least the audience held that opinion. A Mr. Bibby played at Covent Garden in April and May, 1816, as Shylock and as

Sir Pertinax MacSycophant in *The Man of the World*. Again there were a few hisses, and only mild applause. One critic wrote that there was nothing of feeling or originality in his Shylock to suggest that he had encountered the inconveniences of study and thought. Mrs. Young, from America, made a single appearance as Desdemona at Drury Lane in June, 1823. Although she was cordially received, no one thought that she could outstrip the established favorites in the part. These three were identified as from America; they were probably English actors who had tested the new country and were now returning home.

Payne's initial impact was not much greater than any of these. His staying-powers were, however, stronger. His first performance of young Norval in Home's *Douglas,* the standard debut role for young actors, at Drury Lane in June, 1813, was favorably, if not enthusiastically received. One writer advised him that if he intended to make the stage his profession, he should possess himself of some principal action. Flexibility alone was not enough. "It is not merely bending his arms and legs, which ever way they can be made to turn, that will give grace, dignity, or effect to a fine speech." Another found him "quaint, effeminate and monotonous". After his initial engagement, he toured the provinces, came back to London, and being unable to find a place, went to Paris to study French declamation. In Paris he was cordially received by all the theatre managers and made friends with Talma. After he had returned to England, Talma wrote him a long letter on the art of acting. "My dear friend," he advised, "the first rule of acting is to be deeply impressed. Impregnated with the character and the situation of your personage, let your imagination be exalted, your nerves agitated, the rest will follow. Your arms and legs will properly do their business. The graces of a dancer are not requisite for tragedy. Choose rather to have a noble elegance in your gait, and something historical in your demeanor."

Even with Talma's advice, Payne never got a firm footing in the London theatre. He was much more successful in Dublin and in the provinces. Although he appeared occasionally at Drury Lane and Covent Garden, the London managers were not disposed kindly toward him as an actor. When his play *Brutus* was first performed at Drury Lane in November, 1819, the *Theatrical Inquisitor* noted: "We cannot depart from our consideration of this performance, without adverting to the obstinate fatality which has excluded Mr. Payne from a place in this theatre; in Liverpool, Dublin and Bath we have seen him elicit many touches of the most electrical nature." If Payne, as an actor, was not favored by the managers, he had many friends among the literati of the day. In 1822, Charles Lamb invited Payne to come and stay with him: "I have a room for you," he wrote, "and you shall order your own dinner three days in the week. I must retain my authority for the rest."

Payne put a permanent mark on the century with his plays. In total number of performances in England, no other American playwright comes even within striking distance. His *Brutus, Clari,* and *Charles The Second* were on the boards regularly during the first half of the century, and at fairly regular intervals thereafter; and all of the other plays received a warm reception at their first showings: *Accusation* (1816), *Brutus* (1818), *Thérèse* (1821), *Ali Pacha* (1822), *Clari* (1823), *Charles The Second* (1824), *The Spanish Husband* (1830), although it is interesting to note that not a single program gives any credit to Payne.

Payne was American born and did his first acting and writing in America, but there was little that was strongly American in his plays. A half year before the first performance of *Brutus,* a somewhat more peculiarly American phenomenon occurred at the English Opera House in the Strand. In June, 1819, a group of "Native American Indian Warriors" exhibited an Indian dance extravaganza in which they filled the theatre with their war whoops and enacted an invasion on the territories of the Wyandotts by a Seneca party. Apparently there was some skepticism about the authenticity of the exhibition. On the programs for June 22, 23, 25, 1818, the manager wrote: "Injurious doubts having been expressed whether the Indians are really natives of the America, the publick are respectfully informed that every evening, they will make their appearance in the Great Saloon, after their performance, in order to satisfy publick curiosity, and to remove all suspicion of the nature alluded to." This close up view may have been a mistake. One reviewer found them "a sorry spectacle of human nature, uncouth, rugged, pitiable. Their dress is disorderly and unseemly; their visages are so mutilated and disguised as to be truly horrid."

Indian exhibitions never really caught on, though they recurred during the first half of the century. An Indian "flying rope vaulter" was at Astley's in 1822. In 1835, an Indian Spectacle featuring a native American Indian festive dance with real Indian warriors, giving a complete picture of Indian life, was on at the Victoria. In 1840, Catlin, dressed in the costume of a "Crow", showed his paintings at the Egyptian Hall and lectured on the honesty and moral conduct of the Indians. In 1844, nine Ojibbeway Indians and their squaws appeared at the Egyptian Hall and gave a special performance for the royal family.

One reviewer wondered "if their intercourse with polished life will have wrought any change in the manners of the Driving Cloud, the Moonlight Night, the Boy Chief, and other members of the company".

Indian plays did not appear in any great profusion. The "new American drama", *Pocahontas* by James Nelson Barker with J. B. Booth and Thomas A. Cooper was on at Drury Lane in December, 1820, and although December 19, the third night, was listed as the author's night, Barker's name never appeared on the programs. The *Morning Post* noted that it had "some poetical passages which would stand as unrivalled ornaments to some of our modern tragedies". The *Morning Advertiser* was disturbed by the language. "Americans are not satisfied with their 'mother English', they are too fond of coining words. The names of the Indians are not only hard but 'lengthy' to borrow an Americanism, and the actors didn't help with the pronunciation. They addressed each other simply as 'my daughter', 'my comrade', etc."

The other Indian plays deserve only brief mention. *Omala: or, Settlers In America* (1825), a burletta spectacle which depended mostly on its scenic displays: an American Forest by Moonlight, and the Falls of Niagara. *The Cherokee Chief* (1840) which featured a "dreadful encounter of the Indians with the two fierce dogs, Hector and Bruin". Forrest's prize piece, *Metamora* (1845), met with little approval. *Indian Girl! or Pocahontas, the Delaware's Daughter* (1860) was called "a drama of great and powerful interest". And in 1861 the program at Covent Garden commenced with an *Indian Legend*; *The Song of Hiawatha*. Words by Longfellow and music by Robert Stoepel, read by Miss Matilda Heron (the composer's wife), "the principal tragedienne of the United States". One reporter noted that she recited "with beauty and feeling, but the interest is too gloomy and dismal to be attractive".

If the Indians made little impression in England, the Yankees caught on almost immediately and held the stage for some fifty years. The first was James Hackett. He appeared in an interlude called *Sylvester Daggerwood* at Covent Garden on April 5, 1827. Of course, the audience was already familiar with the Yankee character through the impersonations of the English actor Charles Mathews, particularly in his "Annual Lecture on the Peculiarities, Character and Manners, founded on observations and adventures during his late trip to America". In his "at Home", as he called these exhibitions, on April 1, 1824, he took the audience on a trip to America in which he introduced them to various characters, including a real Yankee, called Jonathan W. Doubikin. During the evening he also impersonated a Kentucky shoemaker, a runaway Negro, a French emigrant tailor, a Dutch heiress, and a Mr. O'Cullivin, an improver of his fortune. (Not unlike the exhibitions of Sid Caesar and Bert Lahr!) In September, 1824, Mathews formalized this entertainment into a play called *Jonathan In England*.

James Hackett's first appearance – it seems to have been for a single night – was not a resounding success. Most of the audience seemed to be mainly interested in comparing him with Mathews. One reviewer happily noted that Hackett "out-Herods Mathews – certainly the transatlantic brethren can not now complain about Mathews". Although Hackett's specimens of American boors were probably delineated with fidelity, the jokes and stories were pointless, some of them not understood, and most of them much too long. He was greeted with an uproar of "Off! Off!" Had he not been possessed of "stern republician nerves", one critic noted, he would have retired to the wings. However, when he shifted his ground, he brought strong applause. He concluded his program with an imitation of Kean as Richard III and Macready as Virginius. Curious that the London audience would permit this kind of imitation of their stage heroes, but they did.

Hackett's second visit, six years later, lasted longer and created a greater stir. In March, 1833, again at Covent Garden, he appeared as Colonel Nimrod Wildfire in *The Kentuckian*; *or A Trip to New York*. Hackett boasted that Nimrod was half horse, half alligator, with a touch of the 'arthquake and a sprinkling of the steam-boat. His peculiarities and whimsicalities delighted the house. They roared with laughter when he boasted that the Kentucky soil was so fertile that if you plant an iron bar overnight, in the morning it would sprout ten penny nails, or when he bragged that he could dive deeper and come up drier than any man. Although the audience delighted in his rough manners and incredible claims, the *Court Journal* thought Nimrod was the most obnoxious sample of American manners, proving the veracity of Mrs. Trollope's writings. Another reporter prayed that "if this be a true representation, Lord preserve us from coming in contact with the original".

Hackett was back in London in 1838, this time including *Rip Van Winkle* in his repertoire. In 1839, he enlisted the services of T. D. Rice to appear on the same program with him; and in 1844, he alternated between playing Nimrod, Rip, and Sir John Falstaff in *Henry IV*.

After Hackett's success with the uncouth Kentuckian, the Yankee actors began their forays. The first significant entry was G. H. Hill in 1836, though a John Reeve had appeared as Jonathan W. Doubkins in

Jonathan In England in 1831. Hill first appeared at Drury Lane in November as Hiram Dodge in *The Yankee Pedlar: or Old Times In Virginia.* (He was on the same program with Edwin Forrest.) The audience took to Hill and his Yankee. They found him not unlike their own "canny Yorkshire lads", and his dialect "not wholly unlike that of our own eastern counties". They enjoyed his sleek, plausible cunning, his great industry, and his scanty and pliant honesty. They delighted in his pitch for his pedlar's wares: "Lookin glasses that you can see a mile deep in; Boston clocks which go all the days except Sunday and razors so keen that if you only 'ile 'em well, and put them under your pillow at night, you'll get up in the morning clean shaved."

Hill returned to London again in 1846, two years after the second Yankee actor had made his entry. Dan Marble appeared at the Strand in October, 1844, in *The Vermont Wool-Dealer,* continued through the fall and spring, and according to one report the "Strand was filled nightly with merry folks, laughing until their sides were sore".

During the fifties and sixties, three other Yankee actors took over: Josh Silsbee in 1851 and 1853; J. H. McVicker in 1855; and John E. Owens in 1865. McVicker made the least impression. Silsbee specialized in Jonathan in *The Forest Rose* and Owens in Solon Shingle in *The People's Lawyer.* Some of the audience seemed to be unable to understand Shingle's jokes and many were disgusted with his stage business of taking a wad of tobacco out his mouth and putting it on the side of the witness box.

The Yankee actors made a strong impression. "Jonathans", as they were called, were printed regularly in the newspapers. Two samples will suffice:

"A painter painted a bottle of spruce beer so naturally that the cork flew out before he could paint the spring to fasten it."

"There is an old maid up in Sullivan Street who can look so all fired sour, that she goes out by the day to make pickles. It saves a heap of vinegar."

Another group of entertainers belong with the Yankees, though they did not confine themselves to the Jonathan character. These were the duo acts of Mr. and Mrs. W. J. Florence and Mr. and Mrs. Barney Williams.

The Florences appeared at Drury Lane in April, 1857, in *The Yankee Housekeeper.* She played Peg Ann Mehitable Higginfluter, a Yankee girl from Maine, and he an Irish servant, Barney O'Connor. The audience was apparently captivated by her singing of "Bobbing Around".

One reviewer remarked that the true Yankee style in which she 'bobs' about and sidles up to the various parties she desires to cajole is altogether so outre and extravagant that the humour is irresistible. In May, she appeared in a series of parts in *Mischievous Annie*; *or A Lesson For Husbands*. She played Annie Tottle, a young actress; Madame Ankilto Wilhelmina, a French opera singer; Mlle Julie, a Danseuse with a grand Spanish dance; Hezekiah Slocum, a Yankee Boy; Molly Leaf, a child of nature; Frau Sligiterskypipesfunderknickelpopplesox, with her great Dutch organ song; and Tom Taffrail, a sailor boy.

The Williamses appeared during the same spring, 1857, at the Adelphi in *Barney The Baron* and in *Yankee Courtship*. The critics were a bit hard on some of the exhibitions but not the public. Of *Barney The Baron,* one reporter insisted that he had never seen more "wretched, insufferable twaddle. How painful to admit that all was favorably received by an enlightened British Public." In *Yankee Courtship* they demonstrated all items of Yankee courtship: how to fill the pockets with gingerbread; how to munch apples together; how to be distantly shy; and how to be gradually 'hitching on'. One reviewer had speculated that Mrs. Florence's songs and dances might well become as popular as "Jim Crow". There was little chance of this. Nothing could match "Jim Crow".

T. D. Rice made his first appearance in London on July 9, 1836, at the Surrey. This was three years after Hackett had made his big hit and just three months before Edwin Forrest's debut. He began with "an entirely novel and original Native Black Operatic Extravaganza" called *Bone Squash Diablo.* "Although not perfectly understood by some," one reporter noted, "it was relished by all. His song of Jim Crow did not quite bear out its American reputation, though its fits and starts, its odd grimaces and grotesque twitchings, and all but impracticable freaks, now and then, were quite convulsive." At least part of the interest seemed to derive from the fact that he was presumably "delineating African manners and peculiarites as actually existing in America". Rice caught on immediately and continued throughout the season, though not without a few detractors. On July 15, 1837, a year after his opening, one disgruntled customer observed: "We saw this 'apology for a man', a few evenings since, and not withstanding our disgust, could not forbear laughing at the fellow's impudence. We rejoice to hear that his days in this country are numbered." Others complained about his overwhelming success at the box office: "This disgusting buffoon carries away seventy pounds per week, while many of our charming and lovely young actresses, cannot, by unwearied assiduity, earn more than from twenty-five to thirty. What gross injustice. What an indelible disgrace to our country." The public, however, did not object. They continued to fill the theatres. When Rice appeared with Hackett in 1839, the *Times* observed: "The presence of this gentleman on the stage is enough to shake the sides of the company with laughter, and his acting last night was more than sufficient to make them sore with mirth."

The success of the Negro minstrels in London was not surprising. The public's taste for negro melodies and dances had already been indicated in their applause for Rice. However, the most optimistic enthusiast could not have predicted their phenomenal history. As one reporter noted in 1881, after seeing the 7,805th consecutive performance of the Moore and Burgess Minstrels: "dynasties have fallen, whole empires have been upset, but the Moore and Burgess Minstrels go on forever."

The first group was that of Messrs. Emmett & Pelham, the Sable Minstrels from the Park Theatre, at Davidge's Royal Surrey Theatre on September 4, 1843. The first full minstrel group, the Ethiopian Serenaders, appeared first at the Hanover Square Rooms on February 7, 1846, and then at the St. James's Theatre. The minstrels took the town immediately; and the following year there were at least ten troupes operating in the metropolis. "Although not publicly known," one reporter noted, "we well know that many of them are English with their faces made black or copper colour. . . . What a state of affairs when our own talent is obliged to represent a foreigner to produce a living. Our readers will scarcely believe that Macready is about taking a tour through the provinces, and announcing himself as the great Ohio tragedian." The *Theatrical Journal* reported on June 19, 1847: "There never was and, let us hope, never will be again such a rage. . . . Everyone wanted to be an Ethiopian; every theatrical manager hunted among his own company for a band of 'original Ethiopians' and forthwith announced an arrival from Africa, New York."

For the next decade minstrel troupes were everywhere: singing their sentimental plantation melodies, shaking their bones, strumming their banjos, interspersing their merry meetings with a bundle of not-so-new conundrums, and concluding the program with their imitation of a railroad engine racing off into the distance. Toward the end of the fifties some reviewers seemed to think the "African melodists" were going out of fashion. The public did not subscribe to this notion, and after a brief period of consolidation, the Christy's and the Moore and Burgess troupes continued well into the twentieth century. In 1880, Haverly's

Original Mastodon Minstrels 40-count-em-40 (one reporter said he counted 42) invaded London and found plenty of eager customers. Apparently the Haverly's depended less on sentimental ballads and more on the eccentric routines; one heard less of "the shutters being put up because little Willie's dead", as one reporter put it.

No other American-style entertainment caught on so quickly in England and endured so long. The only other American importation that came close to matching the minstrel record was *Uncle Tom's Cabin*.

The first performances of *Uncle Tom's Cabin* on our side of the Atlantic were in August, 1852, in New York, and in September, 1852, in Troy. In September, 1852, there were two *Uncle Tom* productions in London: one at the Standard, another at the Olympic. In October, three more were added: at the Strand, Surrey and the Pavilion. In November two more joined up: *Slave Life; or Uncle Tom's Cabin* at the Adelphi and an "equestrian drama on the subject", at Astley's. On boxing night (December 26), Drury Lane presented a pantomine version with Henry Wallack playing Uncle Tom. For the following three years England was blanketed with Uncle Toms. I have not canvassed them all, but enough to convince me that by 1855 there was probably not a single theatre in London or in the smallest provincial town that had not had at least one production of the Tom play. Even after this first great rage, Mrs. Stowe's slavery document did not disappear. In January, 1857, the Howard family, with little Cordelia as Eva, appeared at the Marylebone Theatre and later at the Soho and Sadler's Wells. In 1878, Jarrett & Palmer's new dramatic version was on at the Royal Aquarium in the afternoons and at the Princess's at night. This production, which seems to have run for four hours, was filled with "hymns, choruses, breakdowns, a plantation festival, a mimic steamboat race, and rivers of floating ice, and featured 100 real American freed slaves and Sarah Washington, 'the celebrated camp leader and shouter'." In 1882, Jay Rial's American company brought over a similar Tom extravaganza to Her Majesty's.

During the middle years of the century, London was treated to other American subjects, and other entertainers. Plays about the gold rush and the Bloomer rage were common during the decade of the fifties.

In 1849, the adventures of the gold rush were elaborately explored in such plays as *A Trip To California; or, The True Test Of Gold* and *The Gold Friend of California; or, The Victim of Wealth*.

In 1851, the Bloomer rage took over. The bills for the Strand addressed themselves to "Wives, Mothers, and Daughters", exhorting them to come see the Petticoat revolution in *Bloomer Costume*: *or, A Figure Of Fun.* At the Adelphi, in the course of *Bloomerism*: *or, The Follies Of The Day*, the company introduced "A grand vegetarian banquet", followed by a lecture on Bloomerism resulting in the Bloomer polka with twelve pretty bloomers all in a row. At least a half dozen other Bloomer plays were on the boards during the year.

In 1844, Tom Thumb, "The American dwarf, twenty-five inches high and weighing but fifteen pounds, imitated ancient statues at the Princess's, and with his guardian, Mr. Barnum, appeared at Buckingham Palace, where his quick replies to the various questions put to him by the Queen elicited great astonishment. Although the public, particularly the ladies, seem to have been impressed by the little man, he had his share of detractors. One reporter commented that the production of this little monster afforded another melancholy proof of the low state of the legitimate drama. An offended husband deplored the way in which he had taken over: "His song finished, the little monkey was furnished with books and prints of himself which he proceeded to sell at a shilling, giving to each lady purchaser a kiss, being what he called a 'stamped receipt'. What a great humbug about a little individual."

Thus far we have touched only the eccentric American importations. There were, of course, many actors who crossed the Atlantic to appear in the standard repertory at the London theatres.

Discounting the early actors already alluded to, the first of these was an actress, so I have chosen to deal with the female contingent first. Josephine Clifton, the brawny amazon, who was later to become Forrest's companion, appeared at Covent Garden in October, 1834, and later in the season at Drury Lane, two years before Forrest made his debut at Drury Lane. Miss Clifton, billed as "from the Theatre Royal, New York", played Belvidera in *Venice Preserved,* and Lady Macbeth. She did not capture the town. As one reporter noted: "As so many of our performers have been admired and cherished by our transatlantic brethren we are sorry not to be able to speak in terms of praise of the fair debutante. She possesses many personal qualifications, but from the specimen we had, we much fear she lacks mental qualifications."

Charlotte Cushman was more generously endowed. The audiences at the Princess's recognized her talent immediately. Her first engagement began on February 13, 1845, and continued until July 15, somewhat to the distress of her compatriot Forrest, who appeared with her during this first engagement but who was forced to retire from the Princess's in April. The press did not hesitate to acclaim her immediately. One reporter insisted that there had been no such debut since Kean; another wrote: "Genius is of no country or clime. Although she has been unsupported by any clique or national advantage, she has plucked the best laurels from the brows of those who for some time past have occupied our tragic boards. If she is too masculine, the fault is on the right side, for the milk-and-water school of acting in tragedy is not endurable."

The following spring season, 1846, she appeared at the Haymarket as Romeo to her sister Susan's Juliet for twenty-five successive nights. Now it is difficult to understand the rave notices on her Romeo, yet one cannot ignore the judgement of such a perceptive critic as Sheridan Knowles. He wrote: "I was not prepared for such a triumph of pure genius. There was no simulated passion. The genuine heart-storm was on – on in the wildest fitfulness of fury, and I listened and gazed and held my breath, while my blood ran hot and cold. No thought, no interest, no feeling seems to actuate her, except what might be looked for in Romeo himself."

After a fall season, 1847, with Macready at the Princess's, she did not return to London until 1854. The reporters were then all delighted to observe that the "lightning flashes, the scorching and fierce revelations of terrible seething whirlpools of feelings" were still there. Cushman was certainly the best that America had had to offer.

Anna Cora Mowatt made her debut as an actress in 1848, and as a playwright a year later. During the 1848 spring season at the Princess's, she appeared with E. L. Davenport in *The Hunchback, Romeo, Much Ado,* and *As You Like It.* In contrast to Miss Cushman, Mrs. Mowatt was praised for her gentility, "a pretty woman and a pretty actress. . . . She is a beautiful person with a sweet voice who gives a most delicate representation." Her first play, *Armand,* produced in January, 1849, was not thought to exhibit much power, though it abounded in graceful passages. Her *Fashion,* presented in February, 1850, was more highly regarded. "If comedy should be a picture of men and manners," one reporter wrote, "surely here is one deserving the name." Another critic advised her "to throw aside her timidity and give us something of England and the English; we shall feel proud to claim her as one of us."

Adah Isaacs Menken was, of course, principally known for her wild horse-back ride in *Mazeppa,* "her own person being intriguingly bare". An anonymous versifier wrote:

Of thy broidered floating vest
Covering half thy ivory breast
Which o heavens! I could see
But that cruel destiny
Has placed a golden cuirass there
Keeping secret what is fair.

Before Miss Menken appeared at Astley's on October 3, 1865, Mazeppa had always been played by a man. This was, however, not the only innovation, as the bills carefully pointed out: "In this performance Miss Menken ascends herself the fearful precipices and fights her own combats, not as hitherto done, by deputy. She herself will ride to the top of the theatre bound on the horse. No dummies will be employed as previously." In addition to Miss Menken's daring exploits, the production boasted a cast of 200 soldiers and a grand stud of forty horses. One reporter noted that there were a large number of drivelling old men with opera glasses in the audience.

During the last quarter of the nineteenth century, there was a sizable group of charming American ladies on the London stage: Minnie Palmer, Lillian Russell, Mary Anderson, Jennie Lee, Mrs. Brown Potter, Grace Hawthorne, and Ada Rehan. They deserve more comment than is being given to them.

Most of these American beauties fascinated the London public with their physical attributes and their vivacity rather than with their acting talents. Although Minnie Palmer appeared to belong to that class of young ladies who had been taught to purse their lips by the daily pronunciation of " 'potatoes', 'prunes' and 'prisms', there was something in the kitten-like playfulness of this saucy, fascinating fay that made her irresistibly droll and entertaining".

When Lillian Russell made her first appearance, one reporter noted that the "mashers and others assembled in strong force to discover whether the reports concerning her good looks had been exaggerated".

Many thought that Mary Anderson was the most beautiful actress who had ever appeared on the London stage. Her beauty compensated for her "general restlessness of limb", as one critic described her, and for her American pronunciations. She may have pronounced "cups" as though it referred to coverings for the head of her grandmother, and "yonder" as though it should rhyme with the male goose; "but was this more shocking and offensive than the use of the slippery 'H' and the obtrusive 'R' offered by some of our English beauties."

Jennie Lee delighted the audiences with her hoydenish vivacity rather than with her beauty. "She sat on the table, she winked and grimaced at the audience, she mauled cold meat and pretended to devour it, she drank from a bottle and pretended to be what she called 'muzzy.'" As one critic remarked, "The unskillful laughed at all this, but the judicious had cause to grieve."

Mrs. James Brown Potter was a society beauty who had come to London to enter the social world rather than the theatrical world. When she yielded to the temptations of the stage, she found that she could command the audience with her emotional power as well as with her beauty. As one observer remarked, she understood emotion and could speak from the heart. "When she says 'I love you' she means what she says."

Grace Hawthorne did double duty, as actress and manageress, first at the Olympic and then at the Princess's. As an actress she was praised for her spontaneity and naturalness. Her productions were said to have been always "gorgeously dressed and lavishly mounted", and in both capacities she always demonstrated "great good taste".

The real American sensation was Ada Rehan. For the dozen years following her first appearance at Toole's Theatre in 1884, she was the favorite. As one critic remarked, "There is but one actress who could approach Miss Rehan; that actress, of course, is Ellen Terry." In the column after column devoted to her in the London newspapers and magazines, I have not encountered a single unfavorable notice. Whether as Katherine in *Taming Of The Shrew,* Rosalind, Viola, Lady Teazle, or as a pixieish hoyden in one of Daly's plays, she thrilled the audience with her high-strung nervous energy.

It is difficult to select among the glowing tributes. These words of William Archer must suffice. He wrote in *The Sketch* on June 28, 1893: "Her features can express to perfection every conceivable emotion of feminine humanity, from rage and scorn to the most melting tenderness, from dignified melancholy to hoydenish playfulness. Her eyes are 'passionate as an April day' – they can now blaze with anger, now sparkle with merriment, now languish with love. . . . In her utterance, as in her movements, she can venture with impunity upon effects which in a woman of ordinary endowment would seem merely grotesque."

Before commenting briefly on the male actors, a few words on Ada Rehan's mentor and manager, Augustin Daly, are in order. His company and his managerial prowess were highly praised. (He was not, of course, the first American manager in London. That honor belongs to Stephen Price, who became manager of Drury Lane in 1826. However, Price, along with Simpson, his partner in America, was principally concerned with recruiting British actors for the American stage.) Daly brought his entire American company to London and presented them in a series of notable Shakespearean productions as well as in his own plays. His actors were invariably praised for their remarkable ensemble playing – one critic thought that in this regard they surpassed the Meiningen company. Again, it is difficult to select the passages that will best indicate their quality and the nature of their reception.

One critic described them as a "compact little army in which drill, neatness, unison and close touch of each other is instinctive to each player. . . . I wish we had a comedy company of wits that could stick together . . . we have nothing like these delightful folk from over the sea." For eight seasons, beginning in 1888, Daly and his company were welcomed as old friends when they began their London engagements. In the course of the years there were occasional mild complaints: their scenery was too gaudy and flashy in its colour, their furniture too obtruisively rich. One critic noted that the characters used the device of the cross and alteration of stage position with extraordinary frequency: "Sometimes they flit across the scene from one door to another as though fearful that we might forget all about them in their absence." Again and again the critics pointed out their superiority over any English group. "They bring every word of text home to every listener in the house. They are never afraid to speak out. Sadly, I must admit, it is not always so with us." Three notable American actors, in addition to Miss Rehan, achieved particular notice for their contributions to Daly's company: James Lewis, John Drew, and Otis Skinner.

Daly was the first and only American in the century to build his own theatre in London. Located on Cranbourne Street, just off Leicester Square, it was begun in 1891 and opened on June 27, 1893.

The story of American actors in England who devoted themselves to the standard repertory really begins with Edwin Forrest. Well in advance of his first appearance, in the fall of 1836, the public was advised by an elaborate publicity build-up that they were to see a true-blue son-of-liberty, the embodiment of American physical and spiritual vigor brought to the stage. During this first season the London audiences were fascinated by his fearful animal-like power. Many compared him favorably with their own Edmund Kean. When he returned for a second season in 1845, some critics worked up a storm of opposition to his rant, roar, and muscular posturing. Forrest, convinced that these anti-American sentiments had been engineered by his strongest English competitor, William Macready, sought revenge by "hissing" Macready's Hamlet in Edinburgh. This episode led to a long series of vitriolic "notices" posted by the principals and their adherents, both in the American and British press, and finally precipitated the incredible Astor Place theatre riot when Macready appeared in New York in 1849.

None of the American tragedians who invaded London after Forrest created as much stir. J. H. Kirby, John R. Scott, McKean Buchanan, James Murdoch, and James Roberts were all in a way second-rate imitators of Forrest. These "fine, burly iron-lunged representatives" managed respectable engagements, though most critics thought their personations of tragedy "belonged more to the wilds of Connomara, in the far West, or way down South", than they did to the stages of Drury Lane or the Olympic.

Two actors stand out in the period of the sixties: Joseph Jefferson and Edwin Booth, although Booth did not really achieve a marked success until his appearance with Irving in 1881. Jefferson, on the other hand, was immediately labeled as the "most original and finished actor seen on any stage". His Rip Van Winkle, which had 172 performances in 1865 and was done regularly thereafter, was called "a treat such as has rarely been placed within the reach of the playgoers of our time".

Booth's first engagement of five weeks at the Haymarket in the fall of 1861 could not be called a success. Of his *Richard III* one critic wrote: "There are long intervals of level and rapid (too rapid) speaking between the more energetic passages; some wilful missing of opportunities, and the dropping of words and phrases that ought to be rendered emphatic. A feeling of dissatisfaction pervaded the audience." Regularly the reporters were generous with pointers that would improve his renderings of Shylock and Richelieu.

Even during his triumphant engagement in 1881-82 – when J. Palgrave Simpson remarked that he was a very great actor, full of fine scholarly intelligence and matured execution in his art – many critics thought that he was too cold, correct, and formal, and too prone to exhibit the whites of his eyes.

While Booth was alternating with Irving between Iago and Othello, McCullough was doing the same with Hermann Vezin at Drury Lane. One reviewer noted: "The existing conjunction of theatrical stars in the constellation of Othello is all the more remarkable, since out of eight leading artists engaged in the performance of Shakespearean tragedy at the Lyceum and Drury Lane respectively, four, McCullough, Booth, Vezin, and Miss Bella Pateman are Americans."

During the last quarter of the century several dozen actors made their mark on the London theatre, most notably among them John McCullough, Lawrence Barrett, and J. T. Raymond, in addition to Daly's trio, James Lewis, John Drew and Otis Skinner. McCullough was described as an actor of the people, though some thought he belonged more to the Far West than to a small London stage. Lawrence Barrett was an imitator of Booth, though "wanting in the grave and tender qualities" of his mentor. J. T. Raymond fared better with the critics than Mark Twain when he appeared as Colonel Sellers in *The Gilded Age*. "It is in five acts;" one wrote, "but it would be better in one; and it would be much better in none. How a writer with Mr. Clemens's keen sense of humor could pen such a farrago of nonsense passes comprehension ... happily the play was saved from utter condemnation by the admirable acting of John T. Raymond."

The last quarter of the century was a lively period for Americans in London. Although I have chosen to speak principally of the actors, I must mention the American playwrights who invaded the London theatre: William Gillette, Clyde Fitch, Henry James, Charles Hoyt, Langdon Mitchell, Brander Matthews, Bartley Campbell, Bret Harte, Mark Twain, Joaquin Miller, David Belasco, and Bronson Howard.

To attempt some brief generalizations on these playwrights and their plays is hazardous, and, of course, cannot give the full flavor of the impact they had on the London audience. Often praise and condemnation was centered on the same qualities. Audiences were fascinated with the documentary exploration of American scenes, American characters, and American language. For example, *The Henrietta* (Bronson Howard) presented a "vivid picture of the feverish acquisition of wealth in New York". *Held By The Enemy* (Gillette) offered "striking situations from the war years". *The Danites* (Miller) depicted "a true and romantic picture of life in the far west a la Bret Harte". "Purely American, American to the backbone", and similar descriptions appeared regularly. "American Scenes! American Homes!! American Characters!!!" became standard promotion copy. Often the interest in documentary detail was very specific: *In Old Kentucky* (Dazey): "race track, paddock, and other scenes of surpassing beauty in Kentucky"; *Arrah Na Pogue* (Boucicault): "The latest American fire appliances and life saving apparatus." At the same time, many reporters found the American slang "wearisome and objectionable", "the western types not sufficiently familiar", "the jokes driven home as with a sledge hammer", and, of course, one of the favorite comments was: "It becomes eminently clear that a less refined popular taste exists in America than in England." However, the plays were generally popular and held the stage for extended periods, particularly those of Augustin Daly, William Gillette, and Bronson Howard. For example, Howard's *Brighton* (the British label for *Saratoga*) had engagements at various times in six different London theatres.

One of the most fascinating stories of Americans in England is that of Colonel Hezekiah Linthicum Bateman and his family.

On August 25, 1851, the St. James's Theatre bills carried the following announcement: "Under the direction of Mr. Barnum of New York, the inimitable youthful artistes, Kate and Ellen Bateman, only eight and six years of age (from the United States of America) in *The Young Couple* and *The Spoiled Child,* plus the Fifth Act of *Richard III.*" Ellen played Richard and Kate, Richmond. On September 13, they performed part of *Macbeth,* and on October 6, Portia and Shylock in the trial scene. After a full season in London and the provinces, they sailed for home on August 9, 1852. For their year in England, Barnum was reported to have paid them $20,000 in addition to their expenses.

These child prodigies, although they were only eight and six respectively, had already had four years experience. They had been carried on in Baltimore, had played in Louisville, in Indiana, in Boston, and in 1849 at the Broadway Theatre in New York. However, not until they arrived in London in 1851, did they get the attention that they apparently deserved. The *Theatrical Journal* wrote on August 27, "It is not saying too much when we state that there are few artists who have arrived at a more mature age who are capable of producing so great an effect as these two children. They must have undergone rigorous tuition, but they must also have powerful intellect to have arrived at so great a pitch of excellence, particularly when we are informed that they are devoid of education."

When Colonel Bateman and his family returned to London in 1863, they had left one child behind – Ellen had retired from the stage and married – but they had two more young ones coming along: Isabel and Virginia.

Kate Bateman first appeared as a mature actress at the Adelphi Theatre on October 1, 1863, in the part of Leah, a part with which she was to be identified for the rest of her life. The play was a translation and adaptation by Augustin Daly of Mosenthal's *Deborah.* One critic noted that she had "an extremely good figure, a fine intelligent eye and a face of remarkable beauty". Another reported that she was "an actress capable of the most intense and forcible, yet most graceful, exhibition of pathetic situations and emotions".

Late in the fall they toured the provinces, and Bateman had a look at a young English actor who was in the Manchester company and who was assigned the part of Joseph in *Leah*. This first meeting led to a series of letters between Bateman and the young Henry Irving. On January 20, 1864, Bateman wrote to Irving: "I cannot encourage you in the prospect of a speedy opening here now. If you should have an opportunity of appearing in a principal juvenile character, I might come down to Manchester and see you. Next season Miss Bateman will require a young gentleman to support her in the juveniles and it's quite possible you might receive an offer, should all things prove compatible. Evidently, things did not prove compatible. Irving was not hired. Kate continued to play Leah with occasional performances of *Fazio, The Hunchback* and a new play, *Geraldine,* said to have been written by Mrs. Bateman.

On December 22, 1865, the program at Her Majesty's announced that Kate would take her farewell, prior to her departure for New York and her retirement from the stage. On this final night she played Juliet and her two little sisters, Virginia and Isabel, made their first appearance in the afterpiece, *Little Daisy*. Kate did not marry, and on October 19, 1868, was greeted with "tumultuous applause" when she reappeared as Leah at the Haymarket. Again after a full season, she returned to New York; but when she came back to London in 1870, she came to stay.

The following year was the big year for the Batemans. The Colonel had taken over the management of the Lyceum, and on September 11, 1871, opened the theatre with *Fanchette*. Isabel made her debut as a mature actress supported by the coming star, Henry Irving, whom Bateman had spotted in Manchester seven years earlier. The venture got off to a good start. If there were any doubts about the eventual success of the new combination, they were dispelled on November 25, when Irving appeared for the first time as Mathias in *The Bells* — "The whole produced under the immediate direction of Mr. H. L. Bateman." *The Bells* ran for 151 nights.

Bateman was an astute manager and showman. He alternated Irving and Kate; she appeared alone in her roles and Irving in his with Isabel in support of him. It was a happy family operation; for Irving had been taken into the Bateman household after he had stepped out of his wife's carriage in Hyde Park, vowing never to see her again. He never did.

The culmination of Bateman's management came in 1874 when he announced that he was going to present Irving as Hamlet. Although Irving's reputation was now established, there were some who doubted that he was ready for Shakespeare. *The Englishman* commented: "We trust that for the sake of the bard, and for his, he will not make this rash experiment."

Hamlet opened on October 31, 1874 with Isabel as Ophelia. Bateman had been right. Irving was ready. In a way, it was the managerial coup of the century. On November 7, 1874, the *Illustrated London News* wrote: "There be managers of theatres and managers. Some blindly follow what they consider the public opinion, to discover that the receding idea is but a shadow, and so soon arrive at failure. Others follow diverse caprices ... Mr. H. L. Bateman pursued a different course altogether. Trusting to the self-determination of his own mind, he formed a conception of management that should proceed in accordance with the loftiest ideals that he could command. ... Among the rising actors of the day he selected Mr. Henry Irving, and most carefully placed him on the path of success. He was not disappointed."

It was a spectacular run. In February they passed the one-hundreth consecutive night. In mid-April the run was interrupted for a week, a melancholy interruption. Colonel Bateman had died. The family council decided that the play should continue and Mrs. Bateman should assume the management. The *Hamlet* run extended until June 29, 1875. After the curtain closed on the final performance, Irving addressed the audience. He reported that he had never believed it possible for *Hamlet* to continue for 200 nights, yet the record must be regarded sadly: "For in my pride and pleasure at your approval I cannot but remember the friend whose faith in me was firm – the friend to whom my triumphs were as dear, ay dearer, I believe – than had they been his own." Before he concluded he announced that plans were already under way for the next season. Kate (who was now Mrs. George Crowe) would appear with him in *Macbeth*, and Mrs. Bateman was going to present *Queen Mary,* a new play which was being written by Alfred Tennyson, with him and Kate.

Although Bateman's efforts at the Lyceum were well rewarded during his life-time, the full measure of his contribution to the English theatre was not assessed until after his death. Of the many eulogies, I have selected one by an unidentified contributor: "The Americans have always stood high as Shakespearean scholars; and if that desired reform – greater interest in Shakespeare – takes place, it will be in a great measure due to the American gentleman who ruled the Lyceum and gave Irving the opportunity of which he made so noble a use."

Mrs. Bateman continued with the theatre until 1878, when she relinquished the management to Irving. During this period she presented *Macbeth* and *Othello* with Irving, Kate, and Isabel in the principal roles. In 1879 she took over the lease on the Sadler's Wells Theatre. The Bateman girls were the chief attraction. After her death in January, 1881, Isabel assumed the managerial post until the end of the season. Thereafter the girls followed independent careers, with only occasional appearances together. In 1892 Kate established a school of acting. In 1899 Isabel deserted the theatre for the church, joining the Anglican Community of St. Mary the Virgin, at Wantage. In 1920 she became Mother General of the Order. Phyllis Hartnoll attended the school operated by this order and well remembers Isabel's great interest in nurturing the theatrical talents of the students. After her mother's death, Virginia joined the Edward Compton Company and almost immediately signified her permanent allegiance to this group by becoming Mrs. Edward Compton. She is now best remembered as the mother of Fay Compton and Compton MacKenzie.

Even this sketchy story of the Batemans is enough to demonstrate that the Colonel from Baltimore and Louisville contributed remarkably to the glory of the English stage during the last three decades of the century.

American actors may not have had any profound effect on the course of the English theatre, but clearly they supplied an extraordinary share of the entertainment available to the English public. In the nineteenth, as in the twentieth century, London audiences have been fascinated by American theatrical manners and have given our players a warm welcome.

WALTER J. MESERVE

BARNEY WILLIAMS: A GENUINE
AMERICAN PADDY

The stage Irishman came to America long before "Ireland's chief export", fleeing the potato famine at home, began to affect the politics of Boston, the folk humor of the nation, and the various branches of the American Temperance Society. By the middle of the nineteenth century he had modified his character and thrown in his lot with such individuals as the Yankee, the Indian, the Backwoodsman, the Dutchman, the Negro, and the New York Fire B'hoy to become a peculiarity of American theatre. Hack playwrights turned out Irish plays by the hundreds, and numerous actors made their fortunes or tried to in Irish parts. Among those who had the greatest following were Tyrone Power, John Collins, John Brougham, and Barney Williams. All played their characters differently, or slightly so, but for many nineteenth century critics and audiences Barney Williams frequently had the edge on his brogue-speaking colleagues.

During his life upon the stage Barney Williams attracted attention by his great energies and his experimentation. He was a hard working actor who rose slowly over the years to become recognized as a star, then outlived the popularity of the Irish character on stage. And there are those unkind critics who suggest that much of his success came from the superior talent of his wife, with whom he acted after their marriage. For a man of his theatrical fame and fortune, however, much too little is known.

From one of the early accounts of Barney Williams (*Spirit of the Times* of May 20, 1854) through the latest histories of the American theatre, historians have been rather careless in dating the actor's progress through life. He did not, as a matter of fact, start life as Barney Williams, but rather as Bernard Flaherty in Cork, Ireland, August 20, 1823. While he was still a young boy, his family came to America, where Barney worked as an errand boy for a New York printing company. Story has it that when he was in his mid-teens he first appeared on the stage as a supernumerary at the Franklyn Theatre in New York. One evening an actor named Alonzo Williams became ill, and Barney took his place for that performance and his name for the rest of his life. That was the beginning, but he did not have a particularly exciting career for several years. Not until the mid-1840's did he begin to achieve some popularity, having tried a variety of approaches to the stage. In 1849 his marriage to a fine actress helped him considerably as their matched character parts made them one of the most popular acting couples in nineteenth century American theatre. Then within the next eight years they reached the heights of their success throughout America and England. When he died on April 25, 1876, his fortune was assessed at about half a million dollars — no small achievement for a man of Williams' talents. One of the "richest actors of his day" was the way Oral Coad described him.

Barney Williams' star rose slowly, without great distinction, and in a manner similar to the track of a faulty skyrocket which gyrates haphazardly before bursting into spectacular splendor. His experiences at the Franklyn obviously provided him with a direction in life, and his name began to appear on the list of supernumeraries at the National Theatre and Bowery Ampitheatre as well as the Franklyn. By 1841, however, although still in his teens, he began to perform as a singer of Negro songs and as a dancer. In February of that year he was advertised along with Billy Whitlock in a variety of Negro songs and specialty acts at the Bowery Ampitheatre. The association soon blossomed, and Williams' first career in the theatre, if it may be so designated, was as a Negro minstrel.

Frequently with Whitlock, who is generally identified with Dan Emmett, another Negro minstrel, Barney Williams was a member of several Negro minstrel groups during the next several years, performing as a blackface singer and dancer as well as a "wench" impersonator with frilled panties and huge shoes showing beneath his gaily colored skirts. At the Chatham Theatre in September of 1843, for example, he performed with Whitlock, H. Mestayer, and T. G. Booth. On that occasion they called themselves the Virginia Minstrels. By January, 1844, the Virginia Minstrels had disappeared, and Williams along with Booth, Whitlock, and a man named Donaldson were back at the Chatham as the New York Minstrels. The next month they played at the Olympic Theatre as the Kentucky Minstrels, moved in March, under the same billing, to Barnum's Museum, played at the Knickerbocker Theatre in May and returned to Barnum's in August. In the

fall of the next year Williams was still playing Negro minstrels, although his teammates frequently changed. At the Castle Garden Theatre in September, 1845, the Four Minstrels were featured: Barney
Williams, Billy Whitlock, Charles White, and Dan Gardener. During
the summer they had played at the Vauxhall Gardens which Williams
was then managing, yet only for a brief time. Although during the first
half of the decade of the Forties Barney Williams was also trying on
several other theatre roles, his work with the Negro minstrels obviously
involved a noteworthy part of his theatric energies.

Evidently Barney Williams simply loved to perform. What his
various parts as a super were it is impossible to determine, but as early
as 1840, if one is to believe Lawrence Hutton (*Curiosities of the
American Stage*), he made a "palpable hit" in the character of Pat
Rooney in *The Omnibus* at the Franklyn Theatre. Perhaps this was
the beginning of his interest in Irish parts. Within a couple of years at
any rate he seems to have been playing as many Irish parts as he did
minstrels. At the Chatham at New York on September 16, 1843, for
example, he played Jerry Murphy in *Bumpology* and O'Smirk in *The
Dumb Belle*. Later that month he played Corporal Corney in H. P.
Grattan's *The Rebel Chief* and then began to forge slowly ahead. By
December he was playing Paddy O'Rafferty, the part Tyrone Power
gave distinction to in *Born to Good Luck*, and Terry O'Rourke in *The
Irish Tutor*. As the reviewers observed, Williams was becoming a
"delineator" of Irish characters, and in between the acts of the plays
or between two Irish one-act plays, he would dance an Irish jig, sing
a song, or deliver an Irish narration. During these years encompassing
the first half of the 1840's, however, he was simply a hard working actor,
trying to get ahead. One night he was a minstrel, the next an Irishman;
one night he danced an Irish jig, and the next evening it might be a
Cotton Plantation jig.

By the middle of the 1840's, however, he was more Irishman than
minstrel. Perhaps a week in May of 1845 at the New York Olympic
will illustrate his new emphasis. On the 12th he played O'Rafferty in
Born to Good Luck; for the 14th he performed Pat Rooney in *The
Omnibus*; on the 16th he appeared as O'Rourke in *The Irish Tutor*
and the next night as Murphy in *Bumpology*. His career was now
assuming a definite direction, although he still appeared as a minstrel
in 1845. In 1846 he played more and more Irish parts. The great Irish
character actor, Tyrone Power, had died five years previously, and
audiences craved a successor. There was John Collins and, of course,

John Brougham, but there was also Barney Williams trying desperately to fill those Irish shoes and obviously making up in vigor and vitality what he lacked in finesse and finish. A week in February, 1846, shows his efforts as he acted on successive nights *Born to Good Luck, The Irish Tutor, The Happy Man, Paddy's Trip to America, The Irish Lion,* Ragged Pat in *The Emerald Isles,* and Terry Madigan in *The Card Drawer.* These were the usual plays in the repertoire of the Irish specialty actor, and by this date Barney Williams was being mentioned whenever Irish parts were played.

It is difficult to determine exactly when a nineteenth-century actor became a star because reviewers sometimes handled the term rather freely, and there was a certain amount of self-determination in advertising and theatre bills. But there was also a progression of terms in theatre reviewing. Barney went through them all – slowly. In fact, in one of his references to the Irish character actor Odell noted that for a man of Williams' ability he certainly advanced slowly and tardily. Barney, however, worked hard at this career and in spite of what must have been rather discouraging moments eventually made it to the top. En route, critics commented on his progress, and by 1847 declared that he had reached the level of "rising into eminence". The critic of the *Albion,* May 8, 1847, had this to say: "This very talented young man is gradually rising into eminence as a delineator of Irish character. He has a rich brogue, although it, perhaps, would be difficult to establish what particular county of Ireland could lay claim to its paternity. His style is dashing and rolicking, as becomes a true son of Erin; he rattles off a song with humorous effect, and he is withal natural and unaffected. These are all great qualifications for his line of characters. Experience and practice are giving finish to his acting, and he bids fair to lay claim to a portion of that ubiquitous mantle of 'poor Power', that has been divided into so many shreds since the death of the original possessor."

Although Barney generally stayed close to New York during his early years in the theatre, he did tour. Philadelphia seems to be the first city he entertained after his beginning in New York, but to be a star he had to be recognized in a wider circle. "Star fashion up to the hat" (*Spirit of the Times,* "Barney Williams and his Wife", May 20, 1854), Barney won notable success in Baltimore, Washington, Cincinnati, Louisville, St. Louis, Lancaster, Little Rock, Natchez, New Orleans, and numerous other towns and cities. Throughout, he played his Irish repertoire such as *The Irish Tutor* which Tyrone Power had made popular. In this farce the father of Charles, the hero who is in love with Rosa, wants to hire a tutor to add a "polish" to his son. He sends for a Dr. O'Toole, but this gentleman is ill and his servant Terry O'Rourke (played by Barney Williams) accepts the position, posing as his master. When O'Rourke is recognized by Rosa's maid as her lover, Charles and Rosa agree to keep his secret if he will let them go to a village dance that night. This he does, explaining his action to Charles' father in a scene of hilarious double talk concerning his "system". But at the dance he is talked into doing a jig, is caught by the father, defended by Charles, and eventually ends the play with the certain future of marriage to the maid and a job of butler in the household. It was good farce throughout, and Terry O'Rourke was typical of the rolicking Irishman that Williams did so well.

Soon the critics declared Williams a "rising" or "recognized star", but his repertoire changed very little. To the plays previously listed he added *Irish Post, Teddy the Toiler, The Bashful Irishman, Sprigs of Ireland, Kate Kearney, The Irish Ambassador,* and *The Limerick Boy.* He acted in other plays, too – even tried the part of Mose in Baker's very successful *A Glance at New York* (January 26, 1849, at the Olympic), but the Irish plays brought him his greatest popularity. Seemingly the audience never tired of the same old plays. Critics did get a bit bored, however, and began to refer to Barney's "hackneyed repertoire" at the same time that they called him a "recognized star". By 1849 he was one of America's better known actors, and at this date, too, he increased his reputation by a rather fortunate union.

Charles Mestayer was a comic actor who played in the same theatres that engaged Barney Williams. Barney knew him well and knew his talented wife, the former Maria Prey. Then in the spring of 1849, Mrs. Mestayer became a widow, and the following November she and Barney Williams were married. For Barney this event signalled the beginning of a new phase of his career which brought him his greatest fame upon the stage. As a husband and wife team of Irish and Yankee roles, they almost immediately achieved a remarkable popularity. Previously Barney had been a fair singer and a good dancer whose brashness and vitality had brought him some success in the theatre. He had fought his way to stardom alone. Now, however, he had a partner who not only shared his success but obviously helped him achieve it.

There is no doubt that Barney Williams' marriage was an advantage to his career. *The National Cyclopedia of American Biography,* 1894, bluntly stated that "she shared in all of her husband's successes, and her beauty and talent had much to do with making him famous". Odell credited her with more talent than her husband. The daughter of Samuel Prey, Maria was on the stage by her mid-teens and had had some success of her own by 1849. It was while she was married to Mestayer that she had become interested in Yankee characters and had played in *The Forest Rose* with Josh Silsbee. Once married to Williams she capitalized on this talent extensively and seemed always to be a favorite with the critics.

By early 1850 Mr. and Mrs. Barney Williams were starting a career together in Philadelphia and New York which would reach its height by mid-decade just before they embarked on their extended foreign tour. It is significant that their appearance this year at the National Theatre in New York was in *The Irish Boy and Yankee Girl*, the division of talent and success which they shared until Williams' death a quarter of a century later. Mrs. Williams had been a past favorite of the patrons of the National, and their two week engagement beginning the end of April brought them a lot of good publicity. On May 2nd she performed the part of Caroline in *Our Gal*, and a week later the critics were still commenting on the "nightly crowds", the versatility and vitality of the new Mrs. Williams, and Barney's Irish amusements. Through the summer of 1850 and into September the Williamses were engaged around New York, establishing a repertoire both individually and as an acting couple. Mrs. Williams repeated her popular roles successfully, particularly in *Our Gal* and as Diamond in *The Female Forty Thieves*. Barney Williams stayed with his Irish character in such plays as *Born to Good Luck* or *Limerick Boy,* generally playing with his wife in *Ireland As It Is, In and Out of Place,* and *The Irish Lion,* to name a few. During these months they seem to have appeared in the expected places such as the National, Niblo's Garden, the Bowery, and Brooklyn Athenaeum. It was only fitting that they return to the National, and they closed out that theatre's season (August 26, 1850 – September 7, 1850) with what was termed a "popular engagement".

After having begun to establish a popular repertoire and themselves as a starring team, they started to tour. From this point until their extremely successful tour to California four years later they were quite constantly in demand. In October, 1850, the "Gossip from Boston" reported in the *Spirit of the Times* that they were doing a "strong business at the National". Early the next month, they were back in

New York where at the National on November 6 they brought out Jones Pilgrim's *Paddy, the Piper* with Barney playing the lead and Mrs. Williams as Kathleen. They continued with other favorites there before going to Philadelphia for a week's engagement at the Arch Street Theatre, where they played their usual repertoire, which also included such plays as *Paddy's Trip to America, Brian O'Linn, Irish Tiger, Irish Farmer,* and *Irish Post.* They then returned to New York but were back in Philadelphia early in February, 1851, for another long engagement. Among their plays then were *Ireland and America, Alive and Kicking, The Custom of the Country, Irish Genius,* and *Irish Assurance and Yankee Modesty.* A complete list of Irish plays would be of considerable length. Let it suffice to say that Barney and his wife probably tried out most of them. In Philadelphia as in New York they enjoyed tremendous popularity. Their benefits, wrote the critics, were "perfect *jams*".

It was during their Philadelphia engagement that Barney introduced a new play by James Pilgrim called *Shandy McGuire; or The Bould Boy of the Mountains* which became a vehicle for him and suggests the kind of play written for him by such farce writers as Pilgrim and Samuel Johnson, whose *Brian O'Linn* Barney also used considerably throughout his career. The two-act farce-melodrama of *Shandy McGuire* takes its scene from Northern Ireland and shows the conflict between a country boy, Shandy, and the English villains who control his country. In the play, Shandy is a hard-fighting, witty boy who uses tricks and disguises to woo his sweetheart from the clutches of the English villain. He is a symbol of all that is right and just in Ireland – a rogue who is tough with the villain and tender with women. Including Irish songs and dances to entertain the audience, Pilgrim also exploited the sentiment of Ireland toward America: "we will shake off our oppressors yet! There are hearts across the big waters, in the New World, that have stretched forth a helping hand to poor Ireland, and will do it again!" Brian O'Linn, in the play by that title, was another country boy with a weakness for girls, so much so that he got engaged to three of them and escaped to marry the one he really loved only by feigning death and giving himself, with some prearrangement, to the girl who would assume his funeral expenses. He was a delight on the stage, no question. "There is no lie in it," one character says, "when I say he is the merriest and gayest boy in the whole country. For a dance or a song, give me Brian before any chap in the parish." With such plays as these and with the help of a very talented and amusing wife, Barney

Williams was steadily accumulating both fame and fortune on the mid-nineteenth-century American stage.

These years of the early 1850's must have been most satisfying for Mr. and Mrs. Barney Williams, as critics found many opportunities to praise their efforts. The couple were a practical guarantee for full houses, as Barney's "quaint humor, rich brogue, and ready wit" kept the audiences in "a complete roar of laughter from beginning to end". According to a reviewer in the *Spirit of the Times* (June 26, 1852) who saw them at the Broadway in New York, Barney excelled as a rustic peasant and was undoubtedly the best Irish actor in America, singing "with taste and expression the songs of Ould Ireland" and dancing "capitally". More recent critics might probably suggest that they "took the counting by storm"; it seemed, at any rate, a "remarkable popularity", as Odell described it.

At the end of 1852 they enjoyed a "truly astonishing" success in New Orleans, particularly in *Ireland As It Is* and *Shandy McGuire*. Here again it was the "rolicking humor of the Irish peasant" and Barney's quick changes of dress which pleased the crowd. Back in New York the *Spirit* critic commented on their immediate popularity at Burton's Theatre (May 28, 1853): "Barney, as representative of the low-comedy Irishman, has no equal; he has a rich brogue, and his voice, though not powerful, is as sweet as cream. What shall we say of Mrs. Williams: That she is the only Yankee girl on the stage, would be superfluous. She is, in fact, the Mrs. Fitzwilliams of the American stage: in Irish, German, French, Yankee, it is all one to her – at home in all; we do not wonder at the signal success of these performers, for they are worthy of all the support they receive." And then the critic suggested something of the result of success in the theatre. "We have been informed, and from a responsible source, that Mr. Williams purchased a house in Nineteenth-street, which, with its contents, cost over $17,000, which he presented to his aged mother. They are still at Burton's playing that very successful drama of *Uncle Pat's Cabin*."

Because of "lines of business" nineteenth-century actors spent a lot of time imitating the more successful mannerisms of their predecessors. At the same time critics had difficulty avoiding the temptation to compare an actor to someone in the past who had played the same part. At this stage of his career Barney Williams was frequently compared to the great Irish character actor, Tyrone Power, who had died at the time that Barney was just getting started on the stage. Both actors were extremely popular with American audiences, and Barney, like any

Irish character actor, performed in many of the plays that Power had made popular. Comparison was a fairly obvious ploy for a theatre reviewer.

Suggesting the popularity of "the Irish Drama", the *Spirit of the Times* published an essay on the subject on January 14, 1853. Tyrone Power (1795-1841) had introduced the Irishman as a distinct character part. "Possessed of good person, a jolly, laughing face, rolicking manner, a musical voice, and a great variety of brogue", he became, in both of his visits to America, the "pet of the public". In each of the three classes of Irish acting which the critic distinguished – the genteel, the eccentric, and the low Irish schools – Power was superior. His success in acting a single character, a career which began in the mid-1820's, clearly stimulated other actors to look for regional peculiarities to emphasize. Although Charles Mathews the Elder was an initiating force in the popular creation of Yankee character parts, it is probable that Power's success upon the stage was a considerable factor in the production of the innumerable Yankee plays, Irish plays, Dutch plays, and "Mose" plays that inundated the American theatre at mid-century. Among the Irish actors that the *Spirit* critic found significant, John Brougham and Barney Williams were the best then on the stage. He enjoyed Brougham's dashing, off-hand manner, his good humored face, gentlemanly brogue, and native wit. Brougham's acting he found both delicate and refined, with a polish which Barney Williams lacked. Most critics agreed upon this point, for Williams' success came with the low Irish comedian, the Irish peasant. Although critics seemed to feel that Williams lacked the versatility of Power, he played more of Power's plays than any of his peers and played them better. He was certainly the one who stood "nearest to the place vacated by Power's death of all the actors who have ventured upon the same field" (*Spirit of the Times,* May 6, 1854).

A year after the *Spirit*'s essay on "The Irish Drama" it published a piece on "Barney Williams and His Wife" (*Spirit of the Times,* May 20, 1854). Mainly it is an essay of praise, and it may very well have been written on order from Williams himself. In between phrases concerning the "acknowledged chief and king of Irish characters", "his amiable and brilliant wife", and the fact that "their performances are invariably by crowded and enthusiastic audiences", the writer told of an offer of $7,000 which the Williamses had received and refused from the manager of the Marylebone Theatre in London. He also noted that the couple would soon be going to San Francisco, where the manager of the Metropolitan Theatre, Mrs. Catherine N. Sinclair, was to pay them $500 a night with benefits once a week. This figure, the critic assured his readers, worked out at a rate of $150,000 a year. In terms of audience popularity, newspaper space, and financial reward, there is little doubt that Barney Williams and his wife were now among the top attractions on the American stage.

On September 25, 1854, Mr. and Mrs. Barney Williams made their first appearance in California at San Francisco's Metropolitan Theatre. If one believes the critics, the audience was the largest and most enthusiastic ever assembled in that theatre. The people also paid a generous $3,300 for their evening's amusement, and that was only the beginning. This engagement lasted twenty-one nights and netted the Williamses over $16,000. For the remainder of their tour in California they played in Sacramento, Marysville, Stockton, and the mining towns in the north before returning to San Francisco and a final side tour into the southern part of the state. Critical reactions were generally favorable, particularly to Mrs. Williams; Barney lacked versatility, some discriminating reviewers said, but he made up for this problem with his quite completely winning personality. The couple consistently attracted great crowds as they played more than forty of their Irish farces. The California correspondent for the *Spirit of the Times* (November 18, 1854) predicted with confidence that "they will do well, and make at least $60,000, in *round dollars*, during the present season".

Their success on the California stage as well as any other stage in America depended not only upon their individual acting talents but their joint efforts in a single play. They were a team, a successful team, and they required a certain kind of play. James Pilgrim's *Irish Assurance and Yankee Modesty* is a good example; so is John Brougham's *The Irish Yankee*. In Pilgrim's farce the hero is Pat, a manservant to Mr. Buffer, who hires Pat to make love to his old maid sister. But in the Buffer household Pat meets a Yankee named Nancy, and together they solve the romantic problems of Buffer's daughter before the "tigress Yankee girl" agrees to become Mrs. Pat. As Nancy, the tempestuous and independent Yankee, Mrs. Williams might be described as a national favorite, her success was so constant. "I guess I'm spunky right up and down, like a yard of pump water. No two ways about Nancy. I am a screamer." In *Irish Yankee* Barney took the role of Ebenezer O'Donahoo while Mrs. Williams played Lyddy Jinks. Both plays capitalize on strong nationalism and patriotism in the Yankee parts and the spirit of Irish-American friendship throughout, but this was only part of the appeal. The Irishman was a romantic rogue, performing heroic tasks and delighting his audience with a charming brogue. Together the roles provided an unbeatable combination.

Since he had achieved stardom, Barney Williams' repertoire had been enlarged by plays written especially for him, such as *Ireland in America* by James Pilgrim, who wrote several Irish plays. Although in the very nature of things audiences demanded that Barney play the character that they loved and that he do extremely well, they also wanted to see their Irish character in different situations. One might also assume that Williams himself might have wanted some variety. Because the numerous Irish farces were brief, slight, and rather ephemeral pieces (although some of them held the stage for years), an actor such as Barney Williams needed a large repertoire of plays. The same was true, of course, for all of the Yankee actors or Frank Chanfrau of "Mose" fame. Even the repertoire of over forty plays that the Williamses took to California was not more than enough. And they had other problems with plays. During these years actors established priorities with plays either by paying for a play or by introducing it upon the stage. If another actor "stole" a play, there seemed to be some loss of prestige for the original actor. Every actor, therefore, tried to build a repertoire of *his* plays and expand it whenever possible.

In terms of their developing careers in America, Mr. and Mrs. Williams' tour of California provided a significant climax as well as a revealing experience. Although on their return to New York their popularity continued on a very rewarding scale, they were aware of a plateau. Having new plays was one way to help solve their problem. Even in California one "Solitaire" had written an original farce for them entitled *The Miner on a Spree; or, Wearing the Breeches,* a play that took advantage of Mrs. Williams talents in "breeches" roles as well as Barney's character part. Soon after their return from California in the spring of 1855, therefore, the Williamses advertised for original plays with the requirement "that the principal male and female characters should be, the former an 'Irishman', and the latter a 'Yankee Girl'." Barney proposed $500 for the best five-act comedy, $250 for the best three-act comedy, and $150 for the best farce, but the results of his efforts were not rewarding. *The Spirit of the Times* (September 1, 1855) reported that not one play from among the many submitted was "at all calculated for successful representation". The committee finally waived one of the requirements, however, that of the Yankee girl, and recommended that Williams accept a one-act Irish farce for which he subsequently paid "the highest premium yet given for a one-act farce". It is not clear which play this was in the Williamses' repertoire, but most probably it was *Modern Mephistopheles; or, Lucifer Matches* by Henry Plunkett, which they brought out at the Broadway in New York on November 2, 1855, with Barney as Phelim O'Bogerty and his wife as Comfort Cullen.

It is interesting that the author of this prize-winning farce was the same man, Harry or Henry Plunkett, who had provided the Williamses with a quite successful play, *The Fairy Circle*, which they had opened at the Broadway in late July of 1855. A drama of Irish legend involving a charm for hunting gold, the play had spectacular staging as well as good parts for Barney (Con O'Carrolan) and his wife (Molshee O'Carrolan). In this instance Barney, as did many actors, bought the play outright in an attempt to control the acting of it. In any event Plunkett's name should be placed with that of Pilgrim and Johnson as a successful hack writer of Irish farce.

In another attempt to maintain their popularity, the Williamses became involved in what the *Spirit* described (Dec. 8, 1855) as "the fastest move ever made by managerial tact". This was the advertisement that appeared in the newspaper:

National Theatre – Carnival of Thespis and Dramatic Festival. Centennial Anniversary of the establishment of the Drama in America. Mr. and Mrs. Barney Williams, the leading American stars, will appear in two different cities on the same night. In order to render the occasion signally great, Mr. C. Bass, Mr. J. M. Dawson, Mr. J. Jefferson, and Mr. Charles Howard, will appear in Washington in the great comedy of the "Heir in Law". In the Baltimore Museum, Mr. and Mrs. Williams will appear at seven o'clock in the "Irish Lion", at the conclusion of which a special train will start for Washington, where they (the Williamses) will appear in the "Happy Man" and the great protean production of "In and Out of Place". A limited number of guests will accompany the party. Certificates, admitting them to the Museum, furnishing carriage hire both ways, fare to Washington and back, admitting holders to the National Theatre, are but two dollars.[1]

During the winter of 1856 Mr. and Mrs. Barney Williams toured

---

[1]   This reference to a "Centennial Anniversary of the establishment of the Drama in America" is interesting. Hunter's *Androborus* was written considerably before 1755. The celebration, however, might have had something to do with the building of a New York theatre. A *Spirit* essay on January 12, 1855, had commented in some length on the "first building erected for a theatre in New York . . . in Nassau – st., east side, between Fulton and John sts. where the *sasaparilla* depot is." That was in 1753, however, a little early for a centennial in 1855. *The Masque of Alfred* was produced at the College of Philadelphia in 1756, too late for a 100th celebration.

outside of the New York area a final time before their departure for England and were, as usual, well appreciated. Louisville met them, for example, with "the most enthusiastic greeting . . . ever witnessed within the walls of the theatre". By April they were back in New York attracting crowds at the Broadway. It was a long engagement, one of fifty nights, ending with a farewell benefit on May 31, 1856. Early in May, Henry Plunkett had again provided a vehicle for Mrs. Williams with a dramatization from Frances M. Witcher's *Widow Bedott Papers.* It became a fair season for the Broadway mainly because of the Williams' popularity, which stimulated even more attention as they prepared for the English audiences. From the reviewers' standpoint, the Williamses were going to England for more than one reason. They had attained a tremendous popularity in America which pride clearly demanded that they test in England. It was also noted that the lack of copyright laws to control acting rights in America irritated Barney Williams. Other actors, wrote the *Spirit of the Times,* May 31, 1856, who "stole" his parts not only "brought contempt on the authors" of the plays but have "created a prejudice against the peculiar style of the performance their great talent has rendered so popular". That their visit involved something more than a test of their acting is clearly suggested by the length of their stay abroad. A number of Americans had transferred their theatrical talents to England, and the Williamses may have had some thoughts in this direction.

Their first engagement in London (June, 1856) was at the Adelphi, to which their success at the box office caused them to return repeatedly during their extended tour. There they performed many of the plays that had brought them success in America and received both polite and enthusiastic reviews. At first the critic for the *Athenaeum* (July 5, 1856) was more impressed with Mrs. Williams than with Barney, who was immediately compared with Tyrone Power and shown to suffer in his interpretations. Barney was considered too loud and vehement, although unmistakably Celtic. It took a little time for the English to appreciate his "remarkable vivacity of temperament" and his breed of Irish peasant, but they soon accepted him with delight. At the Adelphi the Williamses performed *The Custom of the Country, Born to Good Luck, The Irish Lion, Irish Assurance and Yankee Modesty,* and *Ireland As It Is,* among several others. Throughout the summer they received good reviews and generally enjoyed enthusiastic audiences. And upon their return engagement to the Adelphi in February, 1857, critics and audiences alike found great pleasure in the "best Irishman that has appeared on the English stage" since Tyrone Power (*Athenaeum*, February 21, 1857).

Interestingly enough for audiences accustomed to the work of Buckstone, Jerrold, Fitzball, Bayle Bernard, and Sterling Coyne, the English critics complained about the lack of literary merit in the farces in which the Williamses performed. "They have been permitted to pass muster for the sake of the singular artistes they introduced to our acquaintance", wrote the reviewer for the *Athenaeum*, October 4, 1856; "those clever artistes should learn that their pieces are not accepted on their merits, but purely as vehicles". With a mixture of snobbery and truth, the *Times* of August 13, 1856, managed to equate *Irish Assurance and Yankee Modesty* with the mainstream of American drama – "one of those indescribable works that now seem peculiar to the other side of the ocean". And the *Observer* (August 17, 1856) condemned the play while praising the acting. Only occasionally, however, did the low quality of the plays destroy the evening and cause the curtain to descend "with ominous silence". Generally the audiences got into the spirit of the Williamses' performances and enjoyed themselves thoroughly. J. Sterling Coyne even wrote a play for the visitors entitled *Latest from New York*, which involved a characteristic repeat of the Yankee Gal and the Hibernian lover. The Williamses brought it out at the Adelphi early in July of 1857.

The audiences of London treated the American visitors very genially. Clapp and Edgett, in *Players of the Present*, reported that Barney and his wife had the honor of appearing before the Royal family more than once – on June 24, 1856, February 19, 1857, and again on March 18, 1857, at which time the Queen requested *Ireland As It Is*. The actors also toured the provinces and beyond. After leaving London, they played in Birmingham, Manchester, Liverpool, Glasgow, and Edinburgh, before going on to Belfast, Cork, and Dublin. It was in Dublin that they were reported so well appreciated that after one evening's performance the idolizers of their acting unhitched the horses from their carriage and began to pull the carriage through the streets to their hotel. At this point Barney became a bit unhinged himself and, with his wife, proceeded on foot. Their visit to Ireland also elicited a letter to the "Editor of the Dublin Freeman" from William Carleton which was reprinted in the *Spirit of the Times*, January 1, 1858. Carleton's thesis was a comparison of Williams and Power, and his conclusion was "that the tenth part of a feather would turn the scales". He emphasized Barney's ability to bring laughter without speaking, to create "that illusion which makes us forget" that he is acting at all. Barney, "as an Irish actor, and Mrs. Williams as an exponent of American life, stand without rivals upon the stage".

Henry Morley, author of *The Journal of a London Playgoer*, saw Mr. and Mrs. Williams and made what is probably a fair assessment of their reception in London. "Their sphere is farce", he wrote; "Mr. Barney Williams shines most as an American notion of an Irishman, and Mrs. Barney Williams delights London with the humors of the Yankee Girl . . . . In farces suited to their humor these artists excel, and they have the rare merit of a complete absence of vulgarity. They know how to act broad farce with refinement. Of the two actors, the lady, as it is fit, appears to be the better artist, and her whimsical songs, which are of a kind that any lady might sing who had but enough power of ludicrous expression, have already found their way into the London streets." From this comment and the comments of others one could conclude that Barney Williams and his wife were well appreciated for what they could do. And the fact that they were able to play for a considerable length of time is also a comment on their success.

In September of 1859, after an absence of more than three years, the Williamses returned to America and soon started an engagement at Niblo's Garden in New York, performing old favorites such as *Born to Good Luck* as well as the farce written for them in England, *Latest from New York*. For the next half dozen years the Williamses performed mainly in the larger cities on the East coast from Washington to Boston. They did not, however, enjoy the same adoration which marked the years from their marriage until they left for England, although they were still popular. One difference was competition. With Mr. and Mrs. W. J. Florence now firmly upon the scene, they were not the only popular acting couple in America. Interestingly enough, Mrs. Florence was Mrs. Barney Williams' sister, and they both performed Yankee girl parts with their husbands' Irish characters. Although the Florences' joint acting in such parts had begun only in mid-1853, they had anticipated the Williamses by touring England from April through August of 1856 and introducing there the characters with whom Mr. and Mrs. Williams had generally greater success. Back in America during the absence of Barney and his wife, Mr. and Mrs. Florence usurped some of the enthusiasm once reserved for Mr. and Mrs. Williams.

Barney and his wife, however, continued to play their popular roles in *Custom of the Country, In and Out of Place, The Irish Lion,* and *Barney the Baron.* They also continued to try out new pieces in an attempt to gain appeal with audiences. As popular as an actor might be, the fickle nineteenth century audiences (like all audiences) demanded something new occasionally. At the Winter Garden in New York in September 10, 1860, the couple brought out two novelties. Barney's *Phelim O'Donnell and the Leprahaun* failed, but his wife fared better in *The Magic Joke; or, Prince Doloroso.* The following July at the Academy of Music they tried to provide something for everyone by joining forces with the Florences: Mrs. Williams starring in *The Custom of the Country,* Mrs. Florence in *A Lesson for Husbands,* Barney in *The Irish Tiger,* and Mr. Florence in *The Irish Lion.* This quartet had its appeal, and each couple occasionally appeared for the other's benefits. During these years one can follow Barney and his wife here and there in New York with some of the same old pieces – *Ireland As It Was, The Happy Man, The Irish Tutor, Latest from New York* – at the usual places, Winter Garden, Academy of Music, the New Bowery, Niblo's Garden, the Broadway.

Perhaps to add another dimension to his theatre work, Barney secured a two years' lease on the Broadway Theatre in March of 1867. This was not his first excursion into theatre management. In 1845 he had managed Vauxhall's Gardens in the Bowery for a very brief period. During his two years at the Broadway, however, he managed appearances by such notables as Edwin Forrest, John E. Owens, and Lotta Crabtee, and productions of Augustin Daly's new *Under the Gaslight* and John Brougham's *The Emerald Ring,* which starred Mr. and Mrs. Williams. But his was not a particularly exciting management, and two years seemed to satisfy him.

During the next couple of years Mr. and Mrs. Williams appeared in New York and in various cities in the eastern United States. Critical reaction was distinctly diminished from what it had been ten years previously, although they were involved in what were termed "star engagements", and still retained some of their popularity both in and out of New York. In September, 1869, for example, they played a month in Boston and returned the next fall for a three week engagement. But critical enthusiasm was not now as exuberant. Perhaps it was an attempt to infuse some excitement into their audiences or perhaps a return to former success that influenced them in the spring of 1871 to embark on another tour of England, where they played Liverpool, Manchester, Birmingham, and Dublin. But poor health forced

Barney to cancel his engagement at the Theatre Royal Adelphi in
London. Their return to America was more precipitous than they had
planned as Barney's health became a factor in their performing
schedule.

From this time until Barney's death their engagements became more
sporadic, probably for several reasons. It is perhaps most significant
to remember that certain trends in American acting and American
plays were changing. The great popularity of the Yankee actor, the
Irish actor, the "Mose" actor, or the "Dutch" actor was on the way
out by the 1860's. The Civil War had been a tremendous shock to the
American people, whose changes of attitude were being reflected in the
theatre. Many events – Darwin's work, Comte's writings, the ideas of
Herbert Spencer, territorial expansion, industrial problems, scandals in
the government – were forcing man to look at life more realistically.
Local color fiction and drama stressed an interest in realism, and the
works of Howells, James, and Mark Twain were becoming popular.
The Yankee of George Handel Hill, John E. Owens, and Dan Marble
was changing to the local color Yankee of Denman Thompson as
Joshua Whitcomb. In the early 1870's American theatre audiences
were in the midst of changing their preferences, and Barney Williams
would not be part of the new popularity. It should also be pointed out
that part of Barney's success had always been recognized in his vigor
and vitality, and he was now approaching fifty and not in the best of
health. He also did not need to act if he didn't want to: he had plenty
of money.

Barney and his wife still performed with some frequency, however,
– a week at the Booth Theatre in New York in October of 1874, two
weeks in Boston the next month – but there were longer periods of
relaxation. Barney was also forced to recognize that his style of acting
was not as popular as it had been. During the fall of 1874 he had
been fulfilling an engagement at the Providence (Rhode Island) Opera
House, when he reached what must have been a most painful conclusion. At the end of the third night of his engagement he told the
manager that it was no use to go on: the public did not want him, and
he was reluctant to have the manager lose money on his account.
Although he continued afterwards to play in New York and to tour,
he must have lost some of his enthusiasm. After a week's engagement
at the Arch Street Theatre in Philadelphia, Mr. and Mrs. Williams
appeared for the last time together on January 29, 1876. Barney died
the following April 25th of what was termed paralysis of the brain.

Considering the popularity that Barney Williams and his wife enjoyed in mid-nineteenth century America, the enthusiasm of many contemporary reviewers, and the fortune that he made, it might be thought surprising that American theatre historians have never paid much attention to him. There are, however, probably good reasons for this lack of interest. In the first place there have been few historians who have treated seriously this brief mid-century period in American theatre which could boast so few first-rate actors. From 1849 until 1856 Barney Williams was an extraordinarily popular actor, but one would never claim him as either a major or a first-rate actor in the American theatre. Only as one kind of specialist actor was he superior, but for this talent in that small area of the Irish peasant character he deserves to be remembered.

There are probably other reasons, too, why his name has been neglected by theatre historians beyond the fact that the full history of American theatre has yet to be written. He had a rather slow start in the theatre as he tried the minstrels before emphasizing the Irish peasant, and even in the latter role did not immediately catch the public favor. Yet he did succeed as a single actor. While it is true that his "charming and accomplished" wife added immeasurably to his career, Barney enjoyed billing as a recognized star a full two years before his marriage. Historians are in error to give her most of the credit for their success. Certainly the numerous comparisons of Barney with Power suggest his individual talent. The two of them, however, man and wife, were a novelty, particularly with a Yankee girl in a period of nationalism. And here is perhaps another reason for Barney's slighted accomplishments. He acted Irish parts, not Yankee parts, and therefore suffered as critics and historians tended to emphasize the Yankee specialist. Williams also had a reasonably brief career, which he interrupted at its height with a foreign tour which lasted for over three years. Never again did he and his wife quite attain the popularity of those early years of their married life. It is also a factor in his reputation that he did not act in long or significant plays or take a role in any of the better remembered melodramas.

Yet within the limitations that his Irish character defined, Barney Williams was at the top of his profession for a brief period. Before he was out of his teens he was a man of the theatre and as one critic put it, "familiar with every rope of the ship theatrical". He was evidently a man of small build and sufficiently agile and graceful in his carriage to be considered a good dancer. Although not all reviewers considered him a superior singer, he knew how to handle a song with the taste and expression that pleased many. It was the low comedy character that he seemed to do to perfection, the rather loud and vehement yet witty Irish peasant. He was a rustic character, but if one is to believe the reviewers, Barney played him in a way that could never be considered vulgar. To enhance his portrayal, Barney mastered a marvelous brogue that always seemed to please, and he used effective changes of costume. Within the limits of this character Williams was obviously a talented actor with an excellent sense of timing and a mastery of the body movement, gestures, and general business that brought instant laughter. With "the richest of brogues, a roguish eye, a merry face, a well modulated voice, and a lively and taking manner" (*Spirit of the Times,* January 14, 1853), he was a genuine Paddy, and he successfully supplied audiences with a character they enjoyed.

In the history of American theatre Barney Williams occupies a rather minor but noteworthy position. Among the specialist actors, who were themselves a significant aspect of mid-nineteenth century American and English acting, Barney was generally considered the best in his area. Several playwrights thought well enough of his work to supply him with plays, and for a span of years his appearance in a theatre meant a remunerative engagement for the management. If he outlived his popularity, it was not his acting that was at fault, but the fact that the theatre must mirror the tastes and demands of the changing society. And there were many changes that came as the consequence of numerous events surrounding the period of the Civil War. For a brief time, however, his career, with his talented and charming wife, reflected, successfully and meaningfully, both the life and theatre that was America.

HORST FRENZ

ALEXANDER TAIROV AND THE 1930 WORLD TOUR OF THE KAMERNY THEATER

Alexander Tairov, one of the most outstanding Russian theater directors, founded the Kamerny – Chamber/or Intimate – Theater in Moscow in 1914. He was opposed to the naturalistic presentation of life on the stage and, at the same time, rejected the conventionalized symbolic theater; he found the photographic recording of everyday events as inadequate as the emphasis on the painted scenery and the color schemes so characteristic of the "stylized" stage. Tairov considered all these approaches as static, effete, and uncreative; he felt that they had a negative effect on the theater, primarily because they made the function of the actor a subordinate one. Tairov had in mind a revival of the Italian *Commedia dell'arte* which he considered the highest development of the emancipated theater, freed from the tradition of literary expression as the dominant force in a stage production. He ascribed to the actor not the place of interpreter of ideas and life, but that of an artist who conveys exquisite feelings by creating on the stage an "unreal" life out of "the magic realms of fancy".[1] In this futurist, cubist, or post-impressionistic theater, as it has been variously labelled, Tairov sought an aesthetic harmony of various theatrical forms. To achieve this harmony the actor had not only to act; he had to be a dancer, a singer, and an acrobat at the same time. His body, in the words of Nicolai A. Gorchakov, had to "sing and resound 'like a magic Stradivarius'".

In Tairov's concept of the theater, music is one of the important sister arts. While he thinks of the stage as a "keyboard" which helps the actor to create a meaningful scenic action, he believes that the task of the director is "to sense the rhythmic beat of the play, locate its sound, its harmony, and then, as it were, orchestrate it."[2] Also the

---

[1] René Fülöp-Miller and Joseph Gregor, *The Russian Theatre* (London, 1930), 55-58.

[2] Nicolai A. Gorchakov, *The Theatre in Soviet Russia* (New York, 1957), 225. Cf. Alexander Tairov's chapter on "Music in the Theatre" in *Notes of a Director*, translated by William Kuhlke (Coral Gables, Florida, 1969), 103-105.

designers – prominent among them the brothers G. and V. Stenberg – contributed to this symphonic synthesis of Tairov's theater productions. The result was the extreme theatralization of the theater. The dramatist's function was minimized, the actor held the center of attention, and such theater arts as lighting, costuming, and stage setting were always employed in such a way as to underline the artistic efforts of the actor. As Tairov saw it, the essence of the theater is always action sustained by the actor – action which reveals the dynamics of life.[3]

Three times audiences outside of Russia had the opportunity to get acquainted with the artistic aims of the Kamerny Theater. In 1923, Tairov played in Paris and various German cities such as Berlin, Frankfurt, and Dresden; in 1925, he went again to Germany and also performed in Vienna. Tairov's third foreign tour in 1930 was his most ambitious undertaking. While the extensive trip allegedly enabled him to have his Moscow playhouse remodeled, it also gave him valuable time to consider the best way to adjust his conception of the theater to the demands of the Soviet ideology. In an interview with the drama critic of the *Neue Zürcher Zeitung,* Tairov expressed the opinion that the inner core, the very essence of his theater, had to be altered so that it would stay in line with the transformations that had been going on in the social life of Russia since the revolution, and that a new style appropriate to the times had to be found: "By necessity the theater has to keep pace with the development of society. We must work for a new meaning of the theater and with a new dramatic theory which will express the change in outlook and the transformation of man. The new dramatic theory must correspond to the demands of the new masses. This can only be done through new dramatic contents and through a reform of the stage. Our main task is the search for new forms capable of reflecting the tremendous developments which are now taking place in society."[4]

What Tairov did not tell in this interview, however, was that he had been under constant pressure from the Soviet authorities to change his primarily aesthetic concept of the theater and to take greater cognizance of the Revolution and its effects on life in Russia. Neither did he say that, a few years earlier, he had begun to realize his precarious position in Soviet Russia and decided to make an attempt at presenting

---

[3]   Quotes in *La Stampa* (Turin) of April 19, 1930, where a reference is made to the lucid exposition of Tairov's ideas in Gino Gori's book, *Scenografia.*
[4]   *Neue Zürcher Zeitung* (May 12, 1930).

social problems in a form that was still basically theatrical. The American playwright Eugene O'Neill seemed to him ideal for this purpose, and Tairov turned to him and to a few other Western dramatists to give a new direction to the work of the Kamerny Theater. When Tairov returned to Moscow after this last tour, he tried to conform more and more to the dictates of Soviet standards of art, added a number of Soviet playwrights to his repertoire, and adopted – although reluctantly – social realism as the guiding principle for several of his dramatic productions. However, Tairov never succeeded in pleasing the authorities completely and, after numerous difficulties, the Kamerny Theater was finally closed in 1950, the year of Tairov's death.

For a number of reasons, Tairov's tour in 1930 takes on a special significance. It was the last time that the West was able to view the artistic work and the international repertoire of the Russian director. Also, it was the only time that European and South American audiences had the opportunity to see plays by O'Neill as interpreted by distinguished Russian artists. The tour lasted for almost six months. It started in the Schauspielhaus of Leipzig, Germany, where the Russian company gave seven performances between March 28 and April 1. After three nights in each of the following three playhouses – Deutsches Theater of Prague, the Neues Wiener Schauspielhaus of Vienna, and the Gärtnerplatz-Theater of Munich – Tairov and his group went to Italy and played in Turin at the Teatro di Torino, four nights in Rome at the Valle, and five nights in Milan at the Filodrammatici.[5] After two appearances in Zurich (May 12 and 13), the company traveled to Paris and gave seventeen performances at the Pigalle between May 20 and June 1. Then the members of the troupe attended the International Theater Congress in Hamburg and gave two performances there on June 17 and 18, after which they embarked for South America. They played at the Odeon in Buenos Aires for about six weeks (July 23 to September 7) and ended their tour in Montevideo, where they made eight appearances at the Solis between September 10 and September 17. Altogether, they covered six Euro-

---

[5] According to an essay on Tairov and the visit of the Kamerny Theater in *La Stampa* of April 19, 1930, the company was scheduled at the "Teatro di Torino" for the five nights from April 22 to 26 and supposed to play *Storm*, the two operettas by Lecocq, and the two O'Neill plays. However, it has been impossible to ascertain whether or not a performance was given on April 24. If the Kamerny Theater played that night, it must have been a production of O'Neill's *Desire Under the Elms*. The nine performances in Prague, Vienna, and Munich were given between April 4 and 13, the Italian productions between April 22 and May 10.

pean and two South American countries and played in eleven major cities.

The repertoire consisted of one Russian pre-revolutionary play, Alexander Ostrovsky's *Storm*, Oscar Wilde's tragedy *Salome*, Eugène Scribe's melodrama *Adrienne Lecouvreur*, three musical comedies – *Giroflé-Girofla* and *Day and Night* by Charles Lecocq and *The Three Penny Opera* by Bertold Brecht and Kurt Weill –, and two serious plays by Eugene O'Neill, *All God's Chillun Got Wings* and *Desire Under the Elms*. The eight plays, all performed in Russian, represent substantially the kind of work Tairov had been doing in the Kamerny Theater from 1914 to 1930, except that the plays he took on tour were restricted to those written in the last hundred years. Three of the plays – *Salome, Adrienne Lecouvreur*, and *The Three Penny Opera* – and three special evenings of dances and variety shows were presented only in South America. Since Tairov stayed in Buenos Aires longer than in any other city, he offered his most varied program there.

The tour turned out to be a great success, and critics everywhere admired the artistry of Tairov's productions. They commented on the range that he covered – from farce to tragedy, from the epic to the portrayal of everyday life; from the somber plays of Eugene O'Neill to the Lecocq operettas, where "everything is whirling about in gay circles".[6] They watched with pleasure an ensemble of actors and actresses who could dance, sing, and clown; who could master any type of play and act in comic as well as in serious plays, in operetta and pantomime. The spirit of the ensemble was ever-present, and several of the foreign critics were amazed that those who held the major roles in one production might turn up in mob or chorus scenes in the next. Often this fact was attributed, probably incorrectly, to the impact of the Russian Revolution – to the idea of "collective" ensemble – while in reality it was simply consistent with Tairov's concept of the actor's theater. W. A. Cunningham, who attended the performance of *Day and Night* and *The Negro* (Tairov's title for *All God's Chillun Got Wings*) in Vienna, made this comment on the "star-less" ensemble: "But what a blow it must have been to the directors of the Burgtheater and other noted Viennese stages to see Alexandrov, Ganschin, and Tschaplygin, the wonderful trio of chief actors in *The Negro* listed here as chorus men. Not only listed, but actually and unrecognizably subordinate in the ensemble. And to see Nathalie Efron, who the evening before was a bitter, sinister Hattie Harris, fluttering about the

[6] Josef Chapiro, *Neue Freie Presse* (Vienna, April 8, 1930).

stage in a secondary part, while Eugenie Tolubeeva, a girl from the mob scene, had the leading role. Such casting proved better than all his assertions that Tairov practises what he preaches, achieving his results by an ensemble that is really star-less." [7] Likewise, the critic of one of the Viennese newspapers commented on the fact that Ivan Alexandrov, who the night before had played the part of Jim in *All God's Chillun Got Wings*, appeared in the chorus of *Day and Night*. He, like most of the other actors, submitted "to the greater cause" of a true ensemble. [8]

O'Neill's *All God's Chillun Got Wings* was probably the most imaginative and most powerful production in Tairov's repertoire. The careful attention to details, the originality of the stage design, the inspired use of the cinematographic technique, [9] the ever-changing application of lights, and above all the impressive interpretation of the protagonists justified the opinion that the audiences were watching a masterpiece. Again and again, the great artistry of the actors was evident. The critics pointed out that Alice Koonen was able, with few external means, to portray suffering and despair; [10] in "the 'active' role of struggle, concession, rebellion, protest", as the white woman, the idol, she showed "a spirit, a strength, and a tone which we have rarely seen in a dramatic actress" and sustained difficult situations such as "the long moment of madness with an expressive sobriety in her words, looks, and gestures which consecrate her as an exceptional actress." [11] Ivan Alexandrov played the "passive role of suffering . . . and resignation" [12] and communicated "with furious passion" the frustrations and the deep pain of the Negro protagonist, the tortured complexity of his character. [13] "Even the three-dimensional theater proves through these two actors that the theater is unchangeable and that the human element

---

[7]   *Boston Transcript* (May 16, 1930).
[8]   D. B., *Arbeiter-Zeitung* (Vienna, April 10, 1930).
[9]   For instance, F. B., in *La Stampa* of April 27, 1930, refers to the "artistic importance and the influences and suggestions which cinematography can provoke" in Tairov's production of *All God's Chillun Got Wings*. Likewise, the critic of the Milan newspaper *Corriere della Sera* of May 11 and Gérard d'Houville in *Le Figaro* (Paris) of June 2 discuss the "cinematographic" devices in the Russian performances of O'Neill's *Desire Under the Elms*.
[10] For example, L. Hfd. in *Neue Freie Presse* (April 9, 1930).
[11] *La Nacion* (Buenos Aires, September 3, 1930).
[12] Ibid.
[13] *Neue Freie Presse* (April 9, 1930). Fritz Rosenfeld, in *Arbeiter-Zeitung* of April 10, 1930, characterized Alexandrov as "ein Schauspieler von grösster Eindringlichkeit der Gebärde und des Bewegungsspiels, von ergreifender Schlichtheit des sprachlichen Ausdrucks".

is its only true dimension."[14] Gabriel Boissy, in *Comoedia*, stressed the expressive and convincing acting of each Kamerny player and, in particular, the sincerity, simplicity, grace, and subtlety of Alice Koonen. He was especially impressed by her acting in the role of Abbie Putnam in *Desire Under the Elms*: "We would like to study her movements in each scene and follow with fascination each detail of its composition. Every image she draws stands on a high level of excellence even in the boldest scenes where her acting borders on the completely emotional. At one moment she is full of fire, at the next cold as ice. Her whole being thrills with passion."[15]

Other critics fully concurred with this opinion. The French critic Gérard d'Houville maintained that Alice Koonen played the part of Abbie "with remarkable vehemence, brutality, naturalness, and violence" and that the whole company showed great talent, expressed ardent passions, and displayed harsh realism. He found the scenery skillful, conveying a "sordid" picture of society and representing "with fitting irony a house so deeply coveted".[16] According to the critic of the Argentine newspaper *La Nacion,* the outstanding acting of Alice Koonen, "aflame with a passion that burns without exploding", and of the two main male roles, played by Nicolas Tschaplygin and Leon Fenin – as the young lover Eben and the old husband Ephraim Cabot, respectively – with strong determination and explosive feelings, augmented the powerful suggestiveness of the drama and left a deep impression on the public, "the kind of impression which remains after a quake that makes everything vibrate with its strength . . .".[17] Particularly interesting is this critic's remark that Tairov's version of *Desire Under the Elms* contains characters who are "archetypes rather than persons",[18] who encounter experiences which belong "to all epochs and all places."[19] Reluctant to judge "this very extravagant melodrama" in terms of language (twice removed from his own tongue), d'Houville was especially impressed by the celebration scene in which Cabot and the guests dance, laugh, and shout to the sound of shrill music, for it was "directed with this feeling for ensembles which is particularly Russian . . .".[20] Here again was the kind of scene Tairov

[14]   *Neue Freie Presse* (April 9, 1930).
[15]   Quoted in *The Moscow Kamerny Theatre* (Moscow, 1936), 13.
[16]   *Le Figaro* (June 2, 1930).
[17]   *La Nacion* (August 2, 1930).
[18]   Ibid.
[19]   Ibid. (August 6, 1930).
[20]   *Le Figaro* (June 2, 1930).

could handle most effectively, which was not so much Russian as most characteristic of Tairov's idea of a "total" theater.

In Paris, André Antoine admitted that, after having seen Tairov's production of *All God's Chillun Got Wings,* he left the theater "with the impression of having seen something truly unusual". Antoine, who expressed a certain uneasiness about the monumental setting of *Storm,* the constant movement of the actors, and the fanciful costumes in the production of Lecocq's *Giroflé-Girofla,* was moved by the intensity and the pathos of O'Neill's play and felt that Tairov had succeeded in bringing out "the novelty, the quality, and the magnificent ambition of the work".[21] Others reacted similarly to the display of "sweeping soul-kindling emotion, a continuous development of plot and action as intense as the progress of a great symphony superbly played." [22] According to the Italian critic F.B., racial struggle, a frightening lack of understanding, physical horror and disgust predominate in O'Neill's *All God's Chillun Got Wings.* He considered the introductory children's scene a delightful masterpiece and reported that Alice Koonen as Ella and Ivan Alexandrov as Jim played a little girl and a boy "of such truth, grace, and imagination that they aroused, in a few strokes, an enchanting emotion".[23] It should be added here that not all critics agreed with this evaluation of the early scenes; at least one of them objected to the portrayal of children by grownups and found it ridiculous.[24] Of special interest is F.B.'s evaluation of the scene in the second act, in which Jim and another Negro spiritually test each other, confide the pains, suspicions, and anger they feel about the cruel fate of their race, and are "finally reconciled in the great pity of their common destiny". Here was a tragedy of the spirit, a tragedy of the

[21]   *Le Théâtre,* II (Paris, 1932), 471. In 1923, André Antoine wrote about the Kamerny Theatre: "Everything in their performance, their scenery, their costumes, their style of acting, aims at the destruction of our dramatic traditions. These Russian players, who are here to make converts, will be less surprised by the coldness of our reception when they consider that we have never failed to draw attention to the originality of many of their ideas and the interest attaching to their aim; at the same time we are not prepared to acquiesce in our complete annihilation." Quoted in René Fülöp-Miller and Joseph Gregor, *The Russian Theatre,* 55-58.
[22]   *Boston Transcript* (May 16, 1930).
[23]   *La Stampa* (April 27, 1930). Cf. the comments by the critic of *Corriere della Sera* of May 9: "The gaiety of the childhood games of the first scene; the awareness of the metropolis noisily rendered by echoes, crashes, and commotion across a small street corner; the lights and shadows of the love scene; the tragic solemnity of the wedding scene with which the first act closes – all these are realized by Tairov with a marvelous poetic and theatrical truth."
[24]   Peter Fleming, *Spectator,* CL (June 20, 1933), 939-940.

races which, according to the Italian critic, brought home to the audience both "the most refined and the most barbaric things", always presented "in a magic style".[25]

It is interesting to note that Tairov made certain changes and technical innovations in the productions of O'Neill's *The Hairy Ape*, which he did not take on tour, as well as in *Desire Under the Elms* and *All God's Chillun Got Wings*, which were performed in most of the countries visited.[26] For instance, in *Desire Under the Elms* Tairov had followed O'Neill's division of the house into four parts, but the elms had become the beams of the home, and this converted the whole scene into an architectural unit. One of the Italian critics actually gave Tairov undeserved credit for the division of the house and the simultaneous acting in different parts of it.[27] Likewise, the device of making the walls of Jim's home expand and contract was O'Neill's idea and not the "ingenious" invention of the Stenberg brothers,[28] although their execution may have differed greatly from the original American production. More serious was Tairov's implied attack on Western civilization through the medium of this play. Instead of presenting a study of greed, jealousy, and love, he used *Desire Under the Elms* to expose the capitalistic world and to insinuate the degeneration and the downfall of Western or more specifically American civilization.[29]

That some other changes had been made in *All God's Chillun Got Wings* may be gathered from the "director's notes" which Tairov prepared for his audiences, native and foreign, and which throw a great deal of light on the Russian director's approach to the work of the

[25] *La Stampa* (April 27, 1930).
[26] Altogether, on this tour Tairov presented *All God's Chillun Got Wings* thirteen times and *Desire Under the Elms* at least eight times. Prague, Munich, and Montevideo were the only cities in which he did not stage an O'Neill play.
[27] *Corriere della Sera* (May 11, 1930).
[28] "The climax and suspense of the mad scene in *All God's Chillun Got Wings* was greatly helped by an ingenious device ... by which the harsh red walls of Jim's parents' home were made to expand and contract like the beating of a pulse and gradually to hem in Ella, who, finally unable to stand the strain, seizes the knife and stabs the negro mask, which, together with a portrait of a Black Admiral and an ebony table, two chairs set mid-stage, make up the sole furnishings." Derek Hill, "Stage Design in Modern Russia", *New Writing and Daylight* (London, 1942), 80-81.
[29] Peter Fleming, *Spectator*, CL (June 30, 1930), 939-940. A Soviet critic, Konstantin Derzhavin, concluded his discussion of Tairov's interest in Eugene O'Neill by maintaining that "the Kamerny Theater perceived – and perceived correctly – this remarkable playwright as an ally of our ideological and socio-ethic strivings" and used three of his main works "as an indictment against bourgeois civilization". *The Book about the Kamerny Theater* (Leningrad, 1934), 174.

American playwright.[30] Tairov maintains that he selected this particular play for presentation because O'Neill had made a serious attempt to deal with the racial problem, "one of the most painful and ugly problems given birth by the capitalistic system". He points out that O'Neill hates the social structure of the West and does not expect a solution of its problems "within bourgeois society". Therefore some of his plays are significant and valuable to the Russians, and Tairov feels justified to make use of O'Neill's powerful attacks on his society. Also, Tairov finds the play interesting and original because of its dramatic structure – two parts (with 4 and 3 scenes respectively) quite different from each other, the first giving fragments from the various age periods of the main characters, the second unfolding the complex picture of the psychological existence of the protagonists.

The first scene seems important from an ideological as well as a dramatic viewpoint – the realization "that racial antagonism is not unavoidable and does not belong to the nexus of instincts with which a man is born" and the necessity for the director to impress upon the audience, through appropriate staging and directing, the complete absence of racial prejudice among the children as a basis for the play's development, in contrast to subsequent changes in race relations under the influence of the environment. It is evident throughout the second scene that Jim is not only a loner but also the object of resistance and ridicule. Tairov therefore feels that in the production the external hostility against Jim must be emphasized appropriately and that, at the same time, the director "must allow the audience to obtain an insight into the characters' emotions which will produce the most favorable reaction toward Jim". In the subsequent scene, he considers it the task of the director to show that, at the base of the union of the white woman and the black man are "the deep feelings of two lost and lonely people for whom life is not a struggle but an escape from it". The problem the director encounters in the staging of the fourth scene is, according to Tairov, to underline the persecution of the two main characters "by the racial and animalistical blindness of the petty bourgeois, middle-class world which knows no mercy and is capable of anything including lynching those 'miscreants' who dare to break their near-sighted morals and the laws they have established."

[30]   Printed as an introduction to the Russian version of O'Neill's *All God's Chillun Got Wings*, published by Modpek, Moscow, 1930. I am grateful to Mariamna Soudakoff of Colorado College for translating the extensive Russian material into English.

In the first scene of the second part (scene 5), Tairov arranges the quartet – Ella, Jim, Hattie, and Jim's mother – and illustrates how impossible it is for Jim and Ella to live in isolation. Next to the unusual treatment of the mask, Tairov finds that the "inner psychological dualism is the most important challenge for both the director and the actress". He speaks here of "two Ellas, the loving one and the hating one, who declare war on one another. For the first time, Ella's duality becomes obvious in the final monologue of the fifth scene which eventually results in schizophrenic insanity." Ella shows in the following scene that in her lucid moments she overcomes her sickness with the help of childhood reminiscences and is capable of being "a tender, loving woman which she would have been had not the conditions of the capitalistic system crippled her entire being".

In the final scene, Tairov points out that the social (capitalistic) order prevents the tragedy of Jim and Ella – the tragedy of the two races – from finding a solution in life, and that "the freedom Ella found only in death represents the death sentence for those social conditions which prevent the discovery of any solution for the living". Tairov concludes with the general remark that in the whole staging of this play he had to make clear to the audience that the entire tragedy of *The Negro* takes place in circumstances foreign to the Russian people and in a completely alien environment, "in this case, the largest center of capitalism, New York".[31]

[31]   At the end of his "director's notes" Tairov makes the interesting remark that he is fairly sure that the play will have social repercussions. To prove it, he adds a review by G. Ignatyev in *Novy Zritel* of April 14, 1929, enntitled "To Eliminate Racial Hatred". In this connection it may be pointed out that at one place in the notes Tairov says that the racism of Hattie, "a racially militant member of the bourgeoisie", is "quite similar to Zionism".

This is the text of the review: "I consider the staging of *The Negro* by the Kamerny Theater a public service. It is to O'Neill's credit that he was able to present vividly to us the other side of the praised American bourgeois culture. O'Neill, as a bourgeois dramatist, could not solve the problem. How can we demand of him that he force Ella to look at Jim through our Soviet eyes? This would have been a lie. Then there would have been no racial problem in the United States and thus no need to write plays. But we know that the racial difference exists, and it exists precisely in such wild and ugly forms as O'Neill portrays it. Is, however, racial hatred eliminated completely here in the Soviet country? And anti-semitism? One cannot close one's eyes to the facts. The play, *The Negro*, is needed for the working class audience, because it creates a feeling of indignation, militant insurrections against the savage distortions 'by the cultural Americans' of the concept of the equality of man regardless of the color of their skin. This play aroused me to the point that I myself want to fight even more viciously by tearing out with my own teeth the tenacious, thorny, thistle-like roots of anti-semitism in our own Soviet land."

From Tairov's notes it becomes clear that this emphasis on class feeling has altered to some extent O'Neill's interpretation of race psychology. While O'Neill has more than once expressed his belief that the causes of prejudice are economic, and his *All God's Chillun Got Wings* bears out this contention, Tairov obviously had an ulterior motive when he made a bourgeois environment and the capitalistic system primarily responsible for the conflict in the play.[32] As to technical matters, Tairov increased the tension of the big city "with jarring rhythm of New York's traffic noises" and, in general, accentuated the devices of expressionism.[33] The heavily burlesqued entrance of the Salvation Army was an alteration in line with Tairov's ideas of a "theatrical" theater, although here, too, the Russian director may have intended to make an ideological point.

Without being aware of the changes in the Russian text, O'Neill approved the architectonic setting, the cinematographic techniques, and the rhythmic staging of his plays and found Tairov's performances of *All God's Chillun Got Wings* and *Desire Under the Elms* very much to his liking. It was the productions of these two plays which O'Neill witnessed in Paris and for which he expressed his feeling of "amazement" and "most profound gratitude", for as he put it, "they rang so true to the spirit of my work". He felt that these productions had been conceived by Tairov "with that rarest of all gifts in a director – creative imagination! They were interpreted by Mme. Koonen and the other extraordinary artists ... with that rarest of all gifts in actors and actresses – creative imagination again!" "A theater of creative imagination," O'Neill continued in his letter of June 2, 1930, "has always been my ideal! To see my plays given by such a theater has always been my dream! The Kamerny Theater has realized this dream for me! ..."[34] In turn, Tairov admired the American playwright as "an artist of large stature", who "shapes the mold of his perishing characters with a natural, deep, human love", who "with a moving ache of

---

[32] Cf. Carol Bird, "Eugene O'Neill – the Inner Man", *Theatre Magazine* (June, 1924), and Louis Kantor, "O'Neill Defends his Play of Negro", *New York Times* (May 11, 1924).
[33] Cf. Peter Fleming, *Spectator*, CL (June 30, 1933), 939-940. Josef Chapiro, in *Neue Freie Presse* of April 8, 1930, writes: "With simple means (wood and iron, bright lights) he gives the impression of the rhythm of a big city."
[34] *New York Herald Tribune* (June 19, 1932). Reprinted in Oscar Cargill, *et al.*, *O'Neill and His Plays* (New York, 1961), 123-124. According to George Jean Nathan, O'Neill considered Tairov's staging of *All God's Chillun Got Wings* "the best production of any of his plays that he had ever seen". Charles Angoff, ed., *The World of George Jean Nathan* (New York, 1952), 33.

his great bloodstained heart accompanies them on their last and fatal journey", and who, "without masking himself . . . unmasks human faces with a rare mastery".[35]

Ostrovsky's *Storm*, well known outside of Russia, had been transformed from a basically realistic portrayal of the predatory, callous, and narrow-minded world of the mercantile class of nineteenth century Russia into a nonrealistic, semi-abstract spectacle. A fusion of the various elements of the theater had been achieved with the help of a "constructivist" setting, austere costumes, and singing speech. However, as André Antoine pointed out, the monumental bridge across the Volga river, which dominated the whole play, made the intimate scenes rather implausible.[36] The same objections were raised by one of the Italian critics who finds it unlikely that the arches, even with changes in color and light, will make the audience think of the diverse places in which Ostrovsky unfolds his drama. He points out the danger a director may run into rather easily by assuming that "a bizarre and incomplete structure, which corresponds to his sensibility and stimulates his imagination, also moves the spectators' fantasy in the direction which he would like". He suggests that he may possibly present "an enigma, pleasing to the eyes, but coldly abtruse for our intellects".[37] The critic F.B. also had certain reservations concerning the setting and felt that the huge stage contraption, suspended across half the stage, was rather cumbersome and uninteresting, just as the stairs used constantly by the actors seemed to him not justified by either artistic or

---

[35] I am grateful to Doris Alexander for the transcript of an essay on O'Neill prepared by Tairov for a brochure Horace Liveright intended to publish in behalf of the American playwright. Here are a few additional excerpts from the English translation to be found among the Saxe Commins papers in the American Literature Collection of Princeton: "O'Neill presents, one after the other, problems of race, of property, of love, of social oppression – conflicts, one stronger and more tragic than the other, which divide embattled humanity with a fiery furrow, and almost invariably those who are potentially the best equipped, the strongest, the most daring, the most deserving claimants to the right to live, his heroes and heroines perish either as physical or psychic victims of the social lie of the European-American social structure . . . . He shows the essence of man and his spiritual likeness in its authentic substance and the inevitable mask, without which his 'normal' life within the confines of the existing order would be unthinkable . . . . There is not a single note of despair, fatigue or apathy in the creations of O'Neill. A tireless creative passion and a great fearlessness mark his path . . . . And there is no doubt that O'Neill will lead his heroes out of the sombre and ominous blind alleys to the free creative realms of a new life by means of his creative fantasy, by the gigantic power of his gifts, which are measureless."

[36] *Le Théâtre*, II, 470.

[37] *Corriere della Sera* (May 8, 1930).

practical exigencies. He admitted that a truly magic and highly theatrical effect was obtained in a few scenes, for instance in the last act
when Katerina throws herself from the high embankment into the void
and immediately afterwards those searching for the girl appear beneath
the arch, "armed with lanterns, dismayed, intent on every noise in the
night". However, he felt convinced that Tairov could have given expression to his artistic intensions without the geometric designs occu-
pying the stage so completely. In every other way F.B. admired the
production of Ostrovsky's play: its moving power and fascinating style;
its sustained, deep, intimate orchestration; the great harmony of the
voices, the characterization, and the action; the perfect coordination of
time and space; the delicate use of pauses and transitions; the gradual
increase in the tension ending in an impressive combination of effects
through light, sounds, choral dancing, and moments of silence.[38] The
consensus of critical opinion was that Tairov had been highly successful in what he himself liked to call a "neo-realistic" and "synthetic"
presentation of *Storm*.

F.B. gave credit to the brilliant acting and fine artistic talents of the
whole cast but singled out for special praise the performance of Alice
Koonen as Katerina, "moving to the point of tears". After having
discussed the wide range and the imaginative power of her interpretation, he selected several scenes for closer analysis and concluded by
speaking of the last scene as showing the actress "at once so sweet and
trembling and imperious that we could desire no better".[39] The theater
critic of the *Frankfurter Zeitung*, Bernhard Dibolt, who had referred
to the expressiveness and extreme simplicity of the production of
Storm, also praised Alice Koonen's interpretation of Katerina and
called it "virtually the incarnation of deepest melancholy in the image
of a marvellous Russian woman".[40]

One of Dibolt's comments is particularly appropriate to the discussion of the only Russian play in the repertoire but applies also to the
other productions. The German critic pointed out that, although he
couldn't understand a word of Russian, he was able to experience
fully the emotion of the actor: "His gestures are Esperanto. His movements are full of an original eloquence. As he bows in Asiatic sub-
mission, or crosses himself to show his piety – here is real acting that

[38]   *La Stampa* (April 24, 1930).
[39]   Ibid.
[40]   Quoted in *The Moscow Kamerny Theatre*, 14.

makes even words we do not understand expressive to us." [41] A similar opinion was expressed by the theater critic of the Argentine newspaper *La Nacion* who wrote that even without understanding the language "all of us were reached (by Tairov's production of *Storm*) not only through its plastic expression, but also through its emotion, warm, tormented, contagious, with the breath of a great creation and the power of a gigantic work of art".[42] Of the audience attending the production of *All God's Chillun Got Wings* in Vienna W. A. Cunningham said that, although only a very small percentage could "understand a word of this unknown play", it "sat spellbound before the unrolling of O'Neill's 'tragedy of the present', half-mesmerized by the mastery of the actors".[43] Likewise, Ludwig Hirschfeld of the *Neue Freie Presse* reported that, although Lecocq's *Day and Night* was presented in a foreign tongue, "the public was kept in roars of laughter and with enthusiasm and admiration expressed the opinion that this was the only real and only possible form of . . . operetta".[44] And the critic of the Argentine *La Republica* maintained that Tairov's interpretation makes the plays "understandable to all".[45] The rhythm of the language, the gestures and the mimicry, and the orchestration of voices certainly made it easy for foreign audiences to overcome the language barrier.

The other light operetta, *Giroflé-Girofla*, which like *Day and Night* belonged to the early work of the Russian director, showed perhaps better than any other production what Tairov meant by the "theatralization of the theater". The play did not deal in any way with social problems. Rather, it was a mixture of vaudeville, cabaret, and revue. Critics spoke of the fairy-dance-scenes and were reminded of the pantomime of the farce and the circus.[46] Not all of them liked the geometrical construction of the stage and the many staircases and platforms obviously designed for the rapid regrouping of actors in a variety of poses and for arranging living tableaux. Nevertheless, colorful costumes, brilliant lighting, continuous rhythmic movements and choral

[41] Ibid.
[42] *La Nacion* (July 24, 1930).
[43] *Boston Transcript* (May 16, 1930). Maurice Rostand writes in *Le Soir* (Paris) of May 21, 1930: ". . . pour ceux qui ne comprendront ni l'anglais ni le russe, il restera tout de même Mlle Alice Coonen et la vie frémissante de son jeu."
[44] Quoted in *The Moscow Kamerny Theatre*, 14.
[45] Ibid. The critic of *La Nacion* of July 20, 1930, agreed that language is not an obstacle to the understanding of Tairov's production: "It is not only the word which intercedes, but also the gesture, the mimicry, the movement."
[46] For instance, Antoine, *Le Théâtre*, II, 470.

singing, together with constantly changing stage settings, made this operetta one of the most popular shows in Tairov's repertoire. As Siegfried Jacobson wrote in *Die Weltbühne*, such a production "can carry us away from everyday trivialities, can free us from ourselves and raise us above ourselves . . . one literally glows from the happiness of being able to participate in such a spectacle".[47] An Argentine critic found that this colorful production of *Giroflé-Girofla*, abounding with ingenuity and good taste, reflected two influences, the Italian "commedia dell'arte" and the "ballet-pantomime". Both of these complemented each other most effectively: "The comically pained expression of the fop whose sweetheart is stolen crystallizes the disillusioned grimace of Pierrot, bathed in a moonbeam. And all the other characters, festively exaggerated in dress and attitude, have also much of the color and intention of the Italian farce. The 'ballet-pantomime' reappears at all times, in the movements, in the dance steps, and in the facial expressions, delicately comical or clownishly festive, depending on whether it is the beautiful Girofla or the impressive Matamoros."[48] *Giroflé-Girofla* became in Tairov's hands a piece of pure theater and an enjoyable and deeply aesthetic experience – an artistic presentation which, according to the French newspaper, *Le Figaro*, deserved to be seen.[49]

There were those who were disappointed by the presentation of such commonplace operettas as *Giroflé-Girofla* and *Day and Night* and felt that they revealed little of Tairov's genius. In the opinion of F.B., the theater had been turned into a circus with acrobatic jumps and capers, duets, choruses, fast music, and all kinds of stage tricks and devices. Even he had to admit, however, that the comic characterization, lighting, the costumes – as compared with the usual treatment of such operettas – were refined with a certain inventive ingenuity; a droll clownish tone gave liveliness to the action. What F.B. missed was the "poetry" in these productions – "grotesque warblings and gaudy dances" were not considered significant enough for a stage director of Tairov's qualifications.[50] His Milan colleague also found a little too much emphasis on circus buffoonery – actors moving like a group of jugglers, jumpers, and acrobats, in the costumes of clowns, constantly entering and leaving the stage at various points, changing from one

[47] Quoted in *The Moscow Kamerny Theatre*, 16.
[48] *La Nacion* (August 23, 1930).
[49] *Le Figaro* (May 22, 1930).
[50] F. B. in *La Stampa* (April 26, 1930).

level to another, running and leaping up and down provisional stairs. Tairov used the operetta as "a spectacle for its own sake", as a "pretext to create a succession of extravagant and bizarre scenes".[51] According to the dramatic critic of *La Nacion*, the production of Lecocq's *Day and Night* lacked strength and distinction, except for the scenic arrangement, the spectacle of color, and the acting. The sense of the caricature, he felt, was less fresh and more exaggerated than in the other two operettas, *Giroflé-Girofla* and *The Three Penny Opera*.[52]

The caricature and the humor – with emphasis on the grotesque and the picturesque – gave substance to the operetta by Brecht and Weill. Everything was presented with a profound and fine sense of the comic; the production was highly original, suggestive, and homogeneous. Particularly interesting is a reviewer's reference to the mime who is "the appropriate medium to transmit and to accentuate the meaning of the play" and who in this production of *The Three Penny Opera* is "marked in characterizations, attitudes, and movements with an elegant clarity of language . . . a mime that stereotypes a smile in the corrosive penetration of the satire".[53]

Quite different yet equally well presented was Wilde's *Salome* with its morbid beauty, its aesthetics of sensualism, and its great erotic force, a performance in which, according to *La Nacion*, even the moon has ceased to be chaste. The august prophet's "egregious sonorousness", Herod's joyfully sinister lasciviousness, Salome's unbridled desire "coiling itself around the cistern of the prophet" and enveloping the whole palace – all of this, together with the scenery, the lights, and the costumes, created a beautiful and original presentation and an extraordinary interpretation of this dramatic work.[54]

[51] *Corriere della Sera* (May 8 and 10, 1930).
[52] *La Nacion* (August 15, 1930).
[53] Ibid. (August 6, 1930). "Tairov's company, as usual, accomplished an impeccable interpretation, with some actors who took part in the first operetta, such as Leon Fenin, who, in a different tone, managed a vigorous, flexible, and picturesque characterization, and Helena Uvarova, also very suited to the character and the situation . . . ."
[54] "Gorgias" in *La Nacion* (August 23, 1930). All actors, among them Nicolas Tschachaplygin, Ivan Arkadin, and particularly Alice Koonen were praised by the reviewer, whose only complaint was Madam Koonen's restraint in the dancing scene.

Alexandra Exter, the designer of the sets and costumes, had interpreted *Salome* "as a magnificent suite of colorful . . . stage forms . . .". She "aimed at speaking in the 'language of correspondences', a cubist dialect, peculiar to her, of the language which the precursor of literary expressionism, Arthur Rimbaud, had erstwhile laid down in his famous sonnet on the colors corresponding to the vowels . . . ." Michael Zelikson, *The Artist of the Kamerny Theater* (Moscow, 1935), 26-27.

Even an antiquated melodrama such as *Adrienne Lecouvreur* – one of the three plays presented only in Buenos Aires – could be brought to life in Tairov's hands and transformed into a harmonious spectacle. There was a feeling, however, that the efforts of the Russian stage director and his company had been wasted on a subject matter which did not lend itself to adaptation and artistic treatment by the Kamerny Theater.[55]

Tairov showed, in his choice of dramatic material, an amazing variety and quality. If we consider his total work, his repertory ranged from Kalidasa to Shaw – if we consider his 1930 world tour, from Lecocq to O'Neill. To what extent did the productions of these plays reflect his theories, particularly his idea that it should be the director's aim to uncover "the naked human substance of the actor"[56] and to make him the subject of an ideal rhythm of movements; in other words, Tairov's contention that it is above all the actor who matters on the stage? Had the Russian director turned these plays into colorful showpieces instead of giving faithful presentations of the original texts? To judge from the critics' reactions in the different countries visited by the Russian company, we may conclude that in many of the Kamerny productions, several essential elements of the theater were combined: a fine or at least an interesting text, inspired direction, and the high artistry of the actors and actresses as well as of the designers brought about the harmony of a brilliant whole. Tairov frequently gave imaginative interpretations of the texts, at times more authentic – at least visually – than those by other producers who would not subscribe to Tairov's theories. This, for instance, would account for O'Neill's favorable reaction to the production of his own plays. Concerning the repertoire of the Kamerny Theater on the 1930 world tour, there is no question that the most successful productions were those of plays by O'Neill and Ostrovsky, in other words, dramas of distinctive "literary" value.[57]

That Tairov was not always consistent in putting his ideas into effect, is evident from the fact that Alice Koonen, Tairov's wife, never appeared in any of the operettas and, as far as I can ascertain, never played in a minor role. Besides, there is no doubt about the paramount importance of the director in the Kamerny productions. As one critic put it succinctly, each member of the company seemed to be "a docile

[55] Ibid. (August 12, 1930).
[56] Silvo d'Amico, "Tairov è morto", *Sipario*, V (Milan, 1950), 14-15.
[57] Wilde's *Salome* was presented only in Buenos Aires.

instrument, an oiled spring in the steady and harmonious hands" of the Russian director.[58] How could it have been otherwise? Alexander Tairov was, after all, a great artist, a true representative of the theater arts, and an original and independent interpreter of the various dramatic forms.

[58] *La Nacion* (August 6, 1930).

O. G. BROCKETT

ANTOINE'S EXPERIMENTS IN STAGING SHAKESPEAREAN AND SEVENTEENTH CENTURY FRENCH DRAMA

Probably no one would question André Antoine's firm place in theatre history, for it is almost impossible to discuss the beginnings of the modern theatre without referring to his work at the Théâtre Libre between 1887 and 1894. But, if the significance of his early career is universally acknowledged, the details of his later career are almost universally ignored. His work at the Théâtre Antoine after 1896 and at the Odéon between 1906 and 1914 usually rates no more than a glance. In history, he has become fixed as the initiator of the independent theatre movement and as the champion of naturalistic staging. Blanchart's view is probably typical:

But the real Antoine, the historical Antoine, remains the emancipator of the heroic years of the Théâtre Libre. . . . After which, prisoner of himself, he exhausted himself in vain attempts at escape, from the first productions of Ibsen at the Théâtre Libre to his classical experiments.[1]

It would be foolish to challenge the view that Antoine's primary importance lies in his work at the Théâtre Libre. Furthermore, the usual treatment of Antoine's career is probably justified in an overview of theatre history. Nevertheless, this attenuated approach fails to do justice to a complex man who continued to experiment throughout his career as a director. Consequently, there is justification for the charge made by his son, André-Paul, that Antoine has never been studied objectively – that historians have confined themselves to repeating such old stories as that about the real carcasses of beef used by Antoine in *The Butchers*.[2] Although it is undoubtedly true that Antoine's sensibilities always led him toward realism, like Stanislavsky he was

---

[1] Paul Blanchart, *Histoire de la mise-en-scène* (Paris, 1948), 75-76.
[2] André-Paul Antoine, "Le Naturalisme d'Antoine: une Legende", *Realisme et Poésie au Théâtre*, ed. Jean Jacquot (Paris, 1960), 233-240. Antoine, according to his son, had intended to use a simple painted drop but having no one to paint it, he, in desperation, hung the beef there at the last moment.

haunted by the need to amend realism, and he experimented often with new approaches. It is the main outlines of these experiments that I will trace here.

In 1906, when he was named director of the Odéon, France's second state dramatic troupe, Antoine was known almost entirely for his work with modern realistic dramas. He deliberately sought the new appointment because he wished to work with a more diversified repertory, especially the classics, for he believed that new approaches to staging older works were necessary to his larger aim of rejuvenating the theatre as a whole. Although the Comédie Française enjoyed greater prestige than did the Odéon, it would have been useless for Antoine to work there, for the actors were too powerful and too conservative to permit him the freedom he wished. Thus, the Odéon was the best platform that Antoine could find for his purposes.

In his eight years as director of the Odéon, Antoine presented 364 plays by authors ranging from Aeschylus to unknown beginners. Many of these were hastily mounted with scenery and costumes taken from stock. On relatively few did Antoine lavish care and expense. Of these few, many were recent plays. Of the older works, Antoine gave major attention to Shakespeare and the French dramatists of the seventeenth century. Since these productions also best illustrate Antoine's experiments, I have chosen to divide my discussion into two parts — one devoted to the production of Shakespeare's plays, and the other to plays by Corneille, Racine, and Molière. In his approaches to both, Antoine was a pioneer, but the nature of his pioneering differed.

Antoine staged five of Shakespeare's plays: *King Lear, Julius Caesar, Coriolanus, Romeo and Juliet,* and *Troilus and Cressida. King Lear,* originally given at the Théâtre Antoine in 1904, was deliberately chosen as a demonstration of Antoine's qualifications for the directorship of the Odéon. When his campaign succeeded, Antoine transferred *King Lear* to the Odéon, with few alterations except in casting.

In many ways, *King Lear* is the most important of Antoine's Shakespearean productions, for it established the general principles which he was to follow thereafter with Shakespearean plays. Antoine's major innovation was the use of an unadapted and almost uncut text, for *King Lear* was the first Shakespearean play to be produced on the French stage in an accurate and full translation.[3] It is typical of Antoine

---

[3] Antoine commissioned a translation of *King Lear* from Pierre Loti and Emile Vedel, since no accurate and full translation then existed in French. Antoine's promptbook for *King Lear* is now in the Bibliothèque des Mises en Scène in Paris.

that he deliberately chose the work considered by the French as the most monstrous of Shakespeare's plays. Thus, Antoine's almost unqualified success is even more significant, for he flew in the face of a long standing belief that Shakespeare's plays were unacceptable to French audiences unless severely adapted.

Although in all his Shakespearean productions, Antoine eliminated a few lines, the cuts were slight. As one critic put it, Antoine was more English than the English,[4] who seldom performed the works in their entirety. Another common motif in the reviews is summed up in a comment on *Romeo and Juliet*: "Thanks to M. Antoine's remarkable production, we now realize that Shakespeare is not so complicated nor his dramatic technique so confused as we had supposed until now."[5]

A major reason for Antoine's success was the staging. He was convinced that the cumulative and rhythmic power of the dramas required uninterrupted playing. For *King Lear*, he permitted two ten-minute intermissions, but managed to perform the uncut text in less than three hours, including these intervals. Except for the intermissions, playing was uninterrupted. This scheme was followed in all of his later Shakespearean productions.

Today, Antoine's scenic solutions do not seem very original when placed in the context of Shakespearean production of the time. Furthermore, unless we examine them carefully, all of the productions seem much alike visually. But in considering them, we should remember two things: first, the solutions were new to the French and greatly impressed critics; and, second, almost all reviewers state that Antoine moved progressively toward greater unity and simplicity. Thus, I think Antoine's scenic arrangements are worth brief consideration.

There appear to be at least three phases in Antoine's experiments with scenery for Shakespeare's plays. The first is illustrated by *King Lear*[6] and *Julius Caesar*, for both of which he used the same basic approach: that is, some scenes were played on the forestage against a neutral background, while more complete settings were being changed behind the curtains. For this arrangement, Antoine acknowledged his

---

Considerable information about Antoine's Shakespearean productions is given in André-Paul Antoine, "Les Mises-en-scène Shakespeariennes d'Antoine", *Etudes Anglaises*, XIII (1960), 159-161; Robert Davril, "Les Pionniers", ibid., 162-171; and Jean Jacquot, *Shakespeare en France* (Paris, 1964).
[4]   Emmanuel Arène, *le Figaro* (December 6, 1904), 4.
[5]   Jean Renouard in *Le Théâtre* (February 1911), 12-17.
[6]   *L'Illustration Théâtrale* (December 17, 1904), 1-36, published nineteen photographs of scenes from Antoine's production.

indebtedness to the director of the Munich state theatres,[7] although the critic for *l'Echo de Paris* credits it to English influence:

We are finally given what the English have had for a long time, a continuous action in a series of settings. The ends of scenes are often played before a curtain to allow changes of scenery. These velour curtains sometimes represent a public place, sometimes a forest, a palace, etc. This, in fact, is nothing, only a device . . . but one must be daring and know how to use it.[8]

The novelty of this approach and the use of neutral curtains as a scenic background impressed the critics.

The approach used with *Julius Caesar* (produced in December 1906) differed little from that of *King Lear*. Curtains were still used as a neutral background for short scenes, but now an architectural framework had been added as well. According to *le Figaro*, the forestage was "decorated on the right and left by two architectural pieces composed of Corinthian columns surmounted by a vault. These . . . remained in place throughout the play, serving successively as a stone frame before the Senate, the Forum, Brutus' tent, and the plains of Philippi."[9] This permanent frame undoubtedly did much to unify the settings.

A second phase began with *Coriolanus* in 1910. Instead of alternating neutral curtains and individualized locales, Antoine now created something not unlike the simultaneous settings used at the Hotel de Bourgogne in the 1630s. Jacques Copeau describes the settings in these words:

At the left, a gate opens onto Rome and near it a passage leads to the country; at right are the ramparts of Corioles. The action's common ground is thus shown. In the center of the stage, M. Antoine has placed a small stairway of three or four steps leading up to a Roman gate. A curtain can be pulled between the columns to mask the perspective or to reveal, at the opportune moment, an interior view of a house which gives the appearance of a new place by a simple backdrop and some practicable pieces which the stage crew put in place while the actors continue to perform in the downstage area.[10]

The visual effect as seen in photographs of the production is rather

---

7 "This innovation I owe to Possart, manager of the royal theatre in Munich", Antoine stated in an interview prior to the opening of the production. *L'Illustration Théâtrale* (December 17, 1904), 37.
8 François de Nion, *l'Echo de Paris* (December 6, 1904), 4.
9 Review by Emmanuel Arène, *le Figaro* (December 5, 1906), 4. *L'Illustration Théâtrale* (December 8, 1906), includes fourteen photographs of this production.
10 *Le Théâtre* (June, 1910), 16-18. Eighteen illustrations of scenes from the production were printed in *Comoedia Illustré* (March 15, 1910), 447-448.

cluttered, and the first impression is that Antoine has succumbed to a desire to represent all locales and to dispense with the neutral curtains used in earlier productions. But it is important to note that through the new arrangement he moved the main action closer to the audience, that much of the action still took place against the neutral curtains of the inner stage, and that realism was further violated by the continuous presence of two widely separated places, Rome and Corioles.

Copeau, never an admirer of Antoine's realism, gave the production his warmest praise. About the scenery, he wrote: "M. Antoine deserves high praise for placing himself, with *Coriolanus*, at the midpoint between two extremes. The twenty-nine scenes unfold in a setting which is unique, essential, and *synthetic*... Thanks to the rapidity of this uninterrupted movement, Shakespeare's tragedy achieves a cohesiveness and grandeur not always felt by those who have not seen it performed in this way." [11] Antoine's son has described the setting as "symbolic", since it represented the two poles between which Coriolanus moves.[12] The reviewer for *Comoedia* labeled the production a landmark in Shakespearean production. He wrote: "In an age which demands the scenic representation of every place, Antoine has led us back to the extraordinary simplicity of earlier times. Hasn't he found the modern equivalent of Shakespeare's theatre?" [13]

Essentially the same solution was used for *Romeo and Juliet* (also staged in 1910). It too had permanent side pieces and a central inner stage for smaller scenes. Yet, the reviewers state that the settings had been simplified further than in earlier productions: there seems to have been more reliance upon painted drops and a few practicable pieces to suggest the smaller settings. For example, one critic states that Friar Lawrence's cell was created with a few touches – a small door, a stainglassed window, a Christ in stone. He adds, "The scenery for *Romeo and Juliet* will remain in its simplicity one of the most beautiful among those which have been seen at the Odeon." [14] Nevertheless, the pictures[15] fail to reveal any marked movement toward simplicity. Perhaps the most significant feature of the staging was the Medieval-like use of space. Except in the intimate scenes, the action spilled onto the

---

[11] *Le Théâtre* (June, 1910), 16-18.
[12] André-Paul Antoine, "Les Mises-en-scène Shakespeariennes d'Antoine", *Etudes Anglaises*, XIII (1960), 160.
[13] Louis Schneider, *Comoedia* (April 22, 1910), 2.
[14] Louis Schneider, *Comoedia* (December 26, 1910), 4.
[15] Six illustrations of scenes were printed in *Comoedia Illustré* (January 15, 1911), 228-231.

forestage. The backgrounds were used to locate the action in the manner of Medieval mansions and the action spread out from them as on the *platea*.

Antoine's final Shakespearean production was *Troilus and Cressida* (in 1912). With it, he seems to have tried still another solution, a less successful one perhaps. Here is the clearest account I have found:

> A curtain is opened sometimes at the left, sometimes at the right, sometimes in the center of the stage. It reveals the interior of a house or an exterior scene, represented most often by a simple backdrop. When the curtain is closed, action continues on the apron and rapid changes are made behind the curtain.[16]

This would seem to indicate that only part of the stage was visible at any time. Although a number of pictures have survived,[17] they do not clarify the stage arrangement, for each merely shows a close-up of a single scene, without depicting the remainder of the stage. Individual settings appear to have been simple, primarily painted drops. One other detail is worth noting: in the scene in which Pandarus and Cressida watch the returning army, they stood on the apron and viewed an imaginary army in the auditorium.[18] Clearly Antoine was not here concerned with preserving the "fourth wall".

Taken all together, Antoine's Shakespearean productions were advanced in one sense and conservative in another. It was Antoine who first made the French aware of the theatrical power of Shakespeare's plays; his were the first unadapted and virtually uncut texts to be seen in France; furthermore, he sought to reveal their strengths through uninterrupted playing. These features were new and forward-looking. Although the settings seem conservative, they grew directly out of Antoine's attempt to serve the text. Visually they represent compromises, since the realistic mode is retained but pushed to the breaking point by the use of some neutral backgrounds and by the simultaneous juxtaposition of widely separated places. It is only one step from Antoine's solutions to the more abstract settings adopted by his successors. Like Antoine, they too desired uninterrupted playing, but they simplified the settings much further than he had. Antoine did not take the final step, but he pointed the way and eased the path by preparing both critics and audiences for the later solutions.

[16]   *Comoedia* (March 22, 1912), 1-2.
[17]   Eight large pictures and several smaller ones were included in *La Petite Illustration* (October 8, 1913), 1-31.
[18]   See review in *Comoedia* (March 22, 1912), 1-2.

In his experiments with seventeenth century French drama, Antoine used quite different methods. He believed that Shakespeare had more universal appeal than did the French classical playwrights. Thus, he argued that, since Shakespeare is essentially ageless, the plays should be costumed and set in the historical periods indicated by the action, for this does not conflict with the spirit of the plays and minimizes anachronisms. On the other hand, he believed that the classical French drama could best be understood as a product of its time; that is, as works firmly grounded in the seventeenth century. He stated: "I would like to restore to our masterpieces the setting which really suits them. For our classical works, any search for local color seems vain to me. I would like to have Corneille and Racine played by actors dressed like the court nobility of their period and in the simplest decor." [19]

This statement, made three years before he became the director of the Odéon, provides the key to all of his early productions of French classical drama. In addition, Antoine's approach to French plays differed from the one he used with Shakespeare because there was no French tradition for staging Shakespearean plays. With Shakespeare, his task was essentially to reveal and popularize dramas with which the audience was unfamiliar. With French works, however, he set out to rejuvenate plays which had been obscured by the accumulation of traditional business and conservatism in staging and acting. Consequently, while Antoine's Shakespearean productions were almost universally praised, his productions of the French classics were always controversial, for Antoine had, in effect, cast himself in the role of schoolmaster to the Comédie Française.

Antoine's aim in staging the French classics was to force audiences to look at them afresh. By approaching the works in new ways, he hoped to make audiences go beyond the expectations and conditioned outlook which had been built up through long tradition. His attempts took many forms, only a few of which can be considered here.

His first important production came in 1907 with Corneille's Le Cid. This is undoubtedly the best known and the most popular of Antoine's experiments, but to me it seems the most misguided, for Antoine here set out to reconstruct the original production of 1636. Corneille's text really became a play-within-a-play as Antoine surrounded it with invented action and characters, in which he utilized his entire acting

[19] Report of a lecture given to the Society of Geography. Unidentified newspaper clipping, dated 17 February 1903, in Rondel Collection, Bibliothèque de l'Arsenal, Paris.

company to recreate the onstage audience at the Théâtre du Marais. An article written some years later described the results:

On the stage, we saw not only the characters of Corneille's tragedy, we were also shown the strange and amusing crowd which formerly mingled on stage with the unfortunate actors: the candle snuffers, the prompter, a tutor and his two pupils, a nobleman disturbing the performance with his noisy entrance in the midst of the play's action, some wits, a musketeer, two fops teasing the actresses, officers, cooks, dressers, stagehands, etc. etc.[20]

In other words, Antoine devoted his major attention to recreating the milieu in which *Le Cid* was performed, rather than to vivifying the text itself. Some of his best actors were cast as spectators. The production was extremely popular and remained in Antoine's repertory thereafter.

A similar experiment was attempted in 1909 with Racine's *Andromaque*, although this time the spectators were subordinated to the play. Antoine's major premise was that Racine's characters are not the rough crew depicted by Homer and that even Pyrrhus speaks in the refined manner of a seventeenth century courtier. To Antoine, the Greek background seemed both irrevelant and misleading. Thus, he set the play in a large drawing room of the seventeenth century, placed a courtier audience at either side, and dressed the actors in the stage costumes of that period – that is, men in the *habit à la romaine* and the women in seventeenth century fashionable garments and plumed headdresses.[21]

It is possible, and perhaps justifiable, to view these two productions as extensions of nineteenth century antiquarianism.[22] But it is important to remember that Antoine's major concern was the illumination of the texts, which he thought had been obscured by producing them in archeologically accurate settings and costumes. Antoine's shortcomings, I believe, stem from too much attention to the seventeenth century *theatrical context* and too little to the *dramatic action*. Perhaps he too came to this conclusion, for his later experiments took a different form.

One of Antoine's most controversial productions was of Racine's *Britannicus*, staged in 1911. Here the storm center was not the decor or stage audience but the casting: Britannicus and Nero were played

---

[20] *Le Théâtre Français* (March 5, 1913), 207. The photographs of this production that have survived are now in the Rondel Collection.

[21] Reviews of this production can be found in *Comoedia* (February 12, 1909), 3, and (February 16), 3; *Comoedia Illustré* (March 15, 1909), 174-175; and *Le Théâtre* (August 1909), 7-10. The last two sources also include illustrations.

[22] They are so viewed by Denis Bablet in his *Le Décor du Théâtre de 1870 à 1914* (Paris, 1965), 135.

by women. Like many Shakespearean directors of our day, Antoine was by this time being accused of concern for novelty rather than for appropriateness. Certainly his intention was to illuminate the text. He conceived, quite rightly I think, that in *Britannicus* the action requires a clear distinction between the adult and the adolescent characters. Antoine cited as authority for his view Racine's own preface in which he states that Britannicus is only fifteen years old and that Nero is at this time still a budding monster. Thus, Antoine saw the young people as dominated by the adults. He believed that the Comédie Française had completely obscured the play by casting practices which permitted Mounet-Sully to play Nero until he was almost seventy years old. Since he did not have trained adolescent boys at his disposal, Antoine argued that he was forced to use women to get the proper effect.[23] Still, it was the use of women that captured attention, and it is doubtful that Antoine's directorial concept was ever given a chance to succeed.

Antoine was much more successful in casting Molière's farces, although his solutions were scarcely less controversial. He believed that the Comédie Française had distorted the farces by cutting them severely and by performing them with actors trained in a style unsuited to them. Antoine viewed these works as descendants of *commedia dell'arte* and French farce of the sixteenth and seventeenth centuries. In an effort to recapture the original spirit, he turned to music hall performers of his own day. Thus, at the beginning of the 1910-11 season, Antoine announced that he was employing two of the best known music hall comedians of his time, Dranem and Vilbert, to perform in Molière's works. The storm which followed can scarcely be imagined. Antoine was bitterly denounced as the desecrator of the classical repertory.[24]

Antoine began his new series in October 1910 with *Monsieur de Pourceaugnac* and went on to *The Doctor in Spite of Himself*, *Le Bourgeois Gentilhomme*, and *The Imaginary Invalid*. All were among the most popular productions ever staged by Antoine. After the first World War, Copeau, Dullin, Cocteau and others were to turn to the

[23] The opening was preceded by a lecture in which Antoine explained his views. For this lecture, see *Comoedia* (October 7, 1911), 2. Other accounts of the production may be found in *Comoedia* (November 17, 1911), 1, (November 20), 3, and (November 23), 2; *L'Illustration* (October 12, 1912), 261; and *Le Théâtre à Paris en 1912*, 8. The last source also reprints an illustration of the production.
[24] Antoine's views about the farces and their acting requirements are set forth in a lecture reprinted in *Comoedia* (October 14, 1910), 3. In it, he also tells of the anonymous and vituperative letters he had received. In the lecture reprinted in *Comoedia* (October 7, 1911), 2, he reiterates his views and his desire to serve, rather than to debase the classics.

music hall and circus as sources of inspiration, but so far as I know Antoine was the first major French director to point the way.

Antoine was not content merely to import new performers, for, as usual, he was insistent upon restoring the texts and playing them in their entirety. He argued that those plays by Molière which had originally included interludes and ceremonies should never be performed without them. As he put it, "It is these which give the plays their character and which reveal their true nature." [25] To all, he restored the original music, and he imported singers and dancers to perform it. His *Le Bourgeois Gentilhomme* was the most complete rendering of that play seen in modern times,[26] with the possible exception of the current one at the Comédie Française which resembles it in many respects.

Probably the best of the productions was *The Imaginary Invalid*, staged in 1912.[27] Two music hall stars, Vilbert and Mlle. Allems, played Orgon and Toinette, while another, Mlle. Marnac, was the principal performer in the interludes. Unlike the Comédie Française, which severely cut the roles of Béralde and Béline and the final ceremony, Antoine performed all of the spoken text and gave an especially elaborate staging to the final ceremony. Thus, his production was said to be the most complete rendering of the play for more than half a century. Costumes for the interludes were based upon designs by Jean Berain. And, in case we still think of Antoine as always observing the fourth wall, it may be worth noting that he had Orgon, Toinette, and Béralde sit in the auditorium to watch the interludes. Above all, Antoine was praised for abandoning the traditional stage business and for clarifying the play with new, more appropriate action.

In these productions of Molière's farces, Antoine was no longer concerned with recreating the original production; now he was seeking to capture the spirit of the works for modern audiences. He moved away from his former concern with the seventeenth century milieu and concentrated upon the more important problem of rendering the dramatic action as effectively as possible. This new direction was further exploited in Antoine's last two major productions – *Esther* and *Psyché*.

With Racine's *Esther*, produced in 1913, Antoine was still intent on faithfulness to text, for he insisted that the play could not be performed

[25]   Lecture, reprinted in *Comoedia* (October 7, 1911), 2.
[26]   See the review by M. Roll in *Comoedia* (October 6, 1911).
[27]   The fullest accounts of this production are those in *Comoedia* (October 3, 1912), 2; (October 4, 1912), 4, and (October 6, 1912), 1-2.

adequately without the music written for it by Jean-Baptiste Moreau, and he employed a chorus and soloists to render the choral passages. More important, however, was Antoine's production concept. He argued that *Esther* has nothing to do with the Biblical milieu; that rather it was written for young girls and was deliberately designed not to shock them.[28] So far this is not drastically different from his view of *Andromaque* or *Le Cid* as works firmly rooted in the seventeenth century. But, this concept was embodied in a way that differed markedly from those earlier productions. According to Antoine, he arrived at his production concept after accidentally coming upon a series of eighteenth century Gobelins tapestries treating the story of Esther. As a result, he decided to present Racine's play as a "living tapestry", in which the action was schematized and idealized in a way analogous to the treatment he had seen in the visual source.[29]

From the seven tapestries in the Gobelins series,[30] Antoine chose the one called "The Swooning of Esther" as the basis of his production, for which he used only one setting, instead of the three indicated by Racine. According to one reviewer, not only did the setting reproduce the visual qualities of the tapestry, but even the bodily attitudes of the actors were based upon it.[31] H. G. Ibels, who designed the costumes, states that he made the garments from coffee sacking and then painted the details on them.[32] One reviewer writes: "The effect is fabulous. Cleverly manipulated lighting sheds a golden atmosphere over all the stage and puts a sort of nimbus or aureole around the characters . . . the ceiling is simulated by a net cloth in order to hide the top of the setting." [33]

So far as I can tell, then, the production had as its unifying principle a visual source. Still, it probably adhered a bit too religiously to the original, for one reviewer states that the entire stage was surrounded by a simulated frame upon which was painted the title of the tapestry.[34] Despite this bit of pedantry, Antoine, with this production, seems to have taken a long step toward stylization, although his effort was little appreciated by audiences, who failed to support it.

[28] See review by Louis Bertin in *Le Théâtre Français* (20 May 1913), 220-222.
[29] Ibid.
[30] The designs for the tapestries, by Jean-François de Troy (1679-1752), were made about 1740.
[31] *Comoedia Illustré* (March 20, 1913), 765. This article also includes an illustration of the production.
[32] Mattei Rousson, *André Antoine* (Paris, 1954), 274.
[33] Louis Bertin, *Le Théâtre Français* (May 20, 1913), 221.
[34] Ibid.

Antoine's final production, and by all accounts his best, was *Psyché*, the collaborative work of Molière, Corneille and Quinault, with music by Lully. Although originally popular, *Psyché* disappeared from the repertory between 1715 and 1862, and was revived only once between 1862 and 1914, when Antoine staged it. Thus, Antoine's was only the second production of the play in 200 years.[35] Consequently, even the decision to revive the work must have excited wonder and admiration. The splendor of the production seems to have swept all critics before it. The reviewer for *Comoedia* declared the production a revelation of a work usually dismissed as a hack piece, and went on to say, "It is the greatest theatrical success, the finest realization of a masterpiece that I have ever seen."[36] And another critic wrote: "Among all the productions that M. Antoine has given us, this one is assuredly the most sumptuous, gallant, and nobly evocative."[37]

Yet, despite this praise, *Psyché* is the most difficult of Antoine's productions to appraise or describe. Its enormous cost was the final step toward bankruptcy for Antoine, and his resignation from the directorship of the Odéon coincided with the opening of the play. I suspect that some of the lavish praise for *Psyché* may have been motivated by the critics' feelings of guilt about their own share in what they called "Antoine's martyrdom". In the newspapers, the wonders of *Psyché* were used as an argument against the injustice of Antoine's downfall.[38] Thus, it is difficult to sort out artistic judgments on this particular production from reverence for a great man. Possibly as a result of the chain of events, no pictures of *Psyché* have survived, with the exception of those printed in the newspaper *Comoedia*, and these are of too poor quality to reproduce.

Antoine called *Psyché* the natural extension of his earlier work.[39] In the judgment, he was correct, for in many ways it summed up everything that he had been attempting. Here he continued his respect for the text, for he presented the entire work with all of its music, songs, and dances. He employed the ballet master of the Opéra to stage the

[35] The production history is summarized in *Le Temps* (April 3, 1914), 6.
[36] April 1, 1914, 3.
[37] Robert Flers in *le Figaro* (April 2, 1914), 5.
[38] Almost every newspaper in Paris wrote of the injustice of Antoine's financial situation. *Le Théâtre Français* was particularly eloquent on this point (see the issues of April 9 and April 30, 1914). Robert Flers also pays tribute to Antoine in *le Figaro* (April 13, 1914), and calls his treatment "immoral". About the closing of the theatre and the end of Antoine's directorship, see *le Figaro* (April 29, 1914), 5.
[39] *Comoedia* (April 1, 1914), 4.

ballets, and forty musicians and thirty-two singers to perform the twenty-nine musical numbers.[40]

In its mounting, the play both resembled and differed from Antoine's earlier productions. As with *Le Cid* and *Andromaque*, Antoine conceived of *Psyché* as, above all, a work of the seventeenth century. But this time he did not represent the seventeenth century audience, nor did he try to recreate the original production. Rather, he sought to take the seventeenth century perception of the play and translate it into terms comprehensible to the twentieth century audience. Thus, he began with the idea that in *Psyché* it is Louis XIV and his court who are presented allegorically under the guise of classical mythological figures. It was the seventeenth century perception of this fusion of mythological and court figures that Antoine tried to convey.[41]

Versailles became the unifying image. In the Prologue of the original text, the setting is described as "a rustic spot, at the back a rock with an opening in the middle, through which the sea is seen in the distance". Venus is invoked and she descends in a machine. Contrary to these directions, Antoine set the Prologue on the terrace before the Palace of Versailles and Venus merely walked on stage. So far as I can tell, the palace was visible in the background of every setting. The succeeding scenes were set in different parts of the park at Versailles, but each place was chosen because of its association with an appropriate mythological figure. For example, Act IV, scene 4 of the original script is set on the desolate banks of a great river, out of which the river god appears. In Antoine's production, this scene was set before the Fountain of Neptune in the park at Versailles, and in the background "a magnificent avenue of clipped trees climbed to the horizon as far as the ever-present royal residence".[42] The use of these classically-oriented places at Versailles served to mingle the two contexts.

Likewise, the costumes were based upon seventeenth century engravings of court entertainments, especially *Les Plaisirs de l'île enchantée*. One reviewer declared: "It seemed that these heroes had stepped forth from the old engravings which portray the royal ballets. But at the same time they have been rejuvenated and given a modern stylization. The costumes have a fantasy and freedom of style tempered

---

[40] *Comoedia* (April 2, 1914).
[41] See *Le Temps* (April 6, 1914), 2.
[42] *Comoedia* (April 2, 1914). This article, with another in the same journal on April 3, gives the fullest description of the visual aspects of the production.

with documentation and care for harmony." [43] Another critic wrote: "His revival is that of the artist, not the scholar . . . M. Antoine has preferred splendid movement to doubtful accuracy. He has liberated himself from Molière's dictates." [44]

It seems to me that with this production Antoine had at last found a way of using the seventeenth century milieu to great effect. Here was greater freedom and stylization than in any of the earlier productions. Whether this would have been developed further in later productions cannot be known, for this was Antoine's last stage work.

It may be significant that *Esther* and *Psyché* were mounted after the Ballets Russes had made its great impact in Paris. In a lecture given some time after he had left the Odéon, Antoine said in reference to French scenic design: "A setting must be conceived in the character of the work and should never aspire to photographic truth. Alas, what we have done is to exaggerate our care for realism. The Ballets Russes has upset all our conceptions." [45]

There remains one question to be dealt with. If these productions by Antoine were moving toward greater freedom and stylization, why were his contemporaries not more aware of it? Why were the productions not more influential? The answers are several. First, even Antoine's most radical experiments remained closely allied to the realistic mode and none moved very far in the direction of presentationalism. There was a progression, but each experiment was a logical extension of those that had gone before. There was no radical break, such as that made by Copeau.

Second, it is probably significant that Antoine's finest experiments were made with works in which music played a significant part – Molière's farces with their interludes and ceremonies, *Esther* with its music and choruses, *Psyché* with its ballets and songs. These elements probably made stylization more acceptable both to Antoine and to his audiences. Third, the experiments tended to get lost in the sheer volume of Antoine's work. Since the Odéon under Antoine presented an average of one new production each week, the experiments failed, I think, to make a cumulative impact or to point toward any radical departure from Antoine's other productions. Fourth, it may be that Antoine was more successful than it has usually been assumed. Above all, Antoine

[43] *Comoedia* (April 2, 1914).
[44] Firmin Roy in *La Revue Bleue* (April 1914), 473-475.
[45] Lecture given by Antoine at l'Université des Annales in December 1922. Copy in Rondel Collection, Bibliothèque de l'Arsenal, Paris.

wanted to be the educator of the public, the servant of the playwright. His total program at the Odéon was built upon these aims.[46] Each season he regularly staged one series of plays devoted to the history of French drama, another devoted to the history of foreign drama, and two series devoted to previously unstaged works by new authors.[47] And each series was accompanied by lectures designed to explain the plays or productions to the public. Antoine set himself the task of being schoolmaster to his age. Thus, he wished to lead but not to alienate. I believe the record shows that he was usually one step ahead of his audiences, but not so far ahead that he lost them. It seems significant that Copeau, unlike Antoine, believed it impossible to be a true artist and to work for a mass audience.

At any rate, it seems unjustified to declare that Antoine ceased to grow after his years at the Théâtre Libre. Perhaps we would view him more justly if we perceived that to him everything paled beside his desire to render the author's text as effectively as possible and that his production techniques were always merely means toward this end and never his primary concerns.

---

[46] His balanced aims can be seen in this statement of his purpose at the Odéon: "the creation, the putting into regular operation, of a literary theatre with a very large repertory performed alternately, in which popular success will not be pursued exclusively, and which, by general agreement and individual esteem, will become an instrument of work and experience as useful to dramatists and actors as it is interesting to the theatre-going public." From a typewritten letter, dated October 24, 1911; now in the Rondel Collection.

[47] Blanchart, 93-94, argues that Antoine in his years at the Odéon is important for his work with new dramatists rather than for his *mises-en-scène*.

INDEX

DE PROPRIETATIBUS LITTERARUM

edited by

C. H. VAN SCHOONEVELD

Series Maior

1. Marcus B. Hester, *The Meaning of Poetic Metaphor: An Analysis in the Light of Wittgenstein's Claim that Meaning is Use.* 1967. 229 pp.
   f 40,—
2. Rodney Delasanta, *The Epic Voice.* 1967. 140 pp.   *f* 22,—
3. Bennison Gray, *Style: The Problem and its Solution.* 1969. 117 pp.
   f 23,—
5. Raimund Belgardt, *Romantische Poesie: Begriff und Bedeutung bei Friedrich Schlegel.* 1970. 257 pp.   *f* 45,—

Series Minor

1. Trevor Eaton, *The Semantics of Literature.* 1966. 72 pp.   *f* 12,—
2. Walter A. Koch, *Recurrence and a Three-Modal Approach to Poetry.* 1966. 57 pp.   *f* 10,—
3. Nancy Sullivan, *Perspective and the Poetic Process.* 1968. 56 pp.
   f 10,—
4. Donald LoCicero, *Novellentheorie: The Practicality of the Theoretical.* 1970. 120 pp.   *f* 16,—

Series Practica

1. Robert G. Cohn, *Mallarmé's Masterpiece: New Findings.* 1966. 114 pp.
   f 24,—
2. Constance B. Hieatt, *The Realism of Dream Vision: The Poetic Exploitation of the Dream-Experience in Chaucer and His Contemporaries.* 1967. 112 pp.   *f* 18,—
3. Joseph J. Mogan Jr., *Chaucer and the Theme of Mutability.* 1969. 190 pp.   *f* 30,—
4. Peter Nusser, *Musils Romantheorie.* 1967. 114 pp.   *f* 22,—
5. Marjorie Perloff, *Rhyme and Meaning in the Poetry of Yeats.* 1970. 249 pp.   *f* 48,—
6. Marian H. Cusac, *Narrative Structure in the Novels of Sir Walter Scott.* 1969. 128 pp.   *f* 24,—

7. W. Victor Wortley, *Tallement des Réaux: The Man through his Style.*
    1969. 99 pp.   *f* 34,—

9. Donald R. Swanson, *Three Conquerors: Character and Method in the
    Mature Works of George Meredith.* 1969. 148 pp.   *f* 24,—

10. Irwin Gopnik, *A Theory of Style and Richardson's Clarissa.* 1970.
    140 pp.   *f* 22,—

12. Sylvia D. Feldman, *The Morality-Patterned Comedy of the Renais-
    sance.* 1971. 165 pp.   *f* 18,—

13. Giles Mitchell, *The Art Theme in Joyce Cary's First Trilogy.* 1971.
    136 pp.   *f* 18,—

17. Meredith B. Raymond, *Swinburne's Poetics: Theory and Practice.* 1971.
    202 pp.   *f* 36,—

20. Edgar B. Schick, *Metaphorical Organicism in Herder's Early Works: A
    Study of the Relation of Herder's Literary Idiom to His World-view.*
    1971. 135 pp.   *f* 25,—

22. James E. Magner Jr., *John Crowe Ransom: Critical Principles and
    Pre-occupations.* 1971. 134 pp.   *f* 18,—

23. Elisabeth Th. M. van de Laar, *The Inner Structure of Wuthering
    Heights: A Study of an Imaginative Field.* 1969. 262 pp.   *f* 40,—

24. Bernard L. Einbond, *Samuel Johnson's Allegory.* 1971. 104 pp.   *f* 18,—

27. Richard Vernier, *'Poésie ininterrompue' et la poétique de Paul Eluard.*
    1971. 180 pp.   *f* 25,—

28. Hugh L. Hennedy, *Unity in Barsetshire.* 1971. 144 pp.   *f* 28,—

35. Roman Jakobson and Lawrence G. Jones, *Shakespeare's Verbal Art
    in Th'Expence of Spirit.* 1970. 32 pp.   *f* 10,—

MOUTON · PUBLISHERS · THE HAGUE